MANAGING THE TRAINING PROCESS
Second edition

Managing the training process

Putting the principles into practice

Second edition

Mike Wills

Gower

First edition published 1993 by McGraw-Hill International (UK) Limited

This edition published by
Gower Publishing Limited
Gower House
Croft Road
Aldershot
Hampshire GU11 3HR
England

Gower
Old Post Road
Brookfield
Vermont 05036
USA

British Library Cataloguing in Publication Data
Wills, Mike, 1946–
   Managing the training process: putting the principles into
   practice. – 2nd ed.
   1. Employees – Training of
   I. Title
   658.3′124′04

   ISBN 0 566 08017 6

Library of Congress Cataloging-in-Publication Data
Wills, Mike, 1946–
   Managing the training process: putting the principles into
   practice / Mike Wills – 2nd ed.
      p. cm.
   Includes bibliographical references and index.
   ISBN 0–566–08017–6 (hardcover)
HF5549. 5. T7W4934   1998   98–9618
658.3′ 124–dc21   CIP

Typeset in Great Britain by Saxon Graphics Ltd, Derby and
printed in Great Britain by MPG Books Ltd, Bodmin.

Contents

with manager; Student rehearses the
application; Student applies skills and
knowledge; Student counselled and given
feedback; Assess student's competence

List of figures

List of tables

Acknowledgements

The trouble with acknowledgements is that it is nearly impossible to list everybody who has influenced the writing of a book. Even if I were to try, I am sure I would miss out some of my most important influences.

So, rather than attempt the impossible, I would like to dedicate this book to all the people I have ever taught, and to all my colleagues who have influenced me by way of suggestions, discussion, argument or demonstration of good training practice. Thank you all.

MW

Introduction

'Training and education are now being given the prominence and priority that they deserve throughout business and industry.'

Such an optimistic statement might perhaps be a headline from a future newspaper, but when I wrote the introduction to the first edition of *Managing the Training Process* I had the impression that many companies were putting, and keeping, training on the agenda.

Today, even more companies are taking training seriously, although I am also detecting the beginnings of a polarization between companies who take a long-term view and those who concentrate on the short term. Companies taking the long-term view are investing heavily in training and other parts of their businesses. Unfortunately, the companies that take the short-term view are cutting back furiously – perhaps even to the point of organizational anorexia.

Far-sighted companies are not investing in training because of altruism but because of a deeply held value that successful companies are the ones who take the training of their people very seriously. Of course, this is not a simple cause-and-effect relationship. If good training guaranteed spectacular results we could simply sink vast amounts of money into training and immediately have highly profitable companies. It sounds too easy and it is too easy.

The relationship between training and business results is a very complex one. This is because results are affected by many differing and varying influences. Economic influences are some of the most prevalent. Identifying training's contribution to the business would involve filtering out the effects of all these other influences.

Although it is doubtful whether this calculation could ever be done with any sort of accuracy, it is something training managers often find themselves having to attempt – simply because they are asked to justify their current training curriculum.

Another approach is to assess the business needs regularly. The skills required are then identified and a training plan is developed to eliminate the skills deficiencies. In this way training becomes an essential and integral part of the business strategy and plans.

Even though training makes an essential contribution to the business, it should be remembered that training does not provide a complete solution for the development of a company's employees. I estimate that attending training courses probably accounts for about 10 per cent of people's development, with experience accounting for the remaining 90 per cent. Sometimes people are surprised at how low this estimate is – especially coming from someone in the training and development profession! However, I would maintain that this is a vital 10 per cent. Unless people have the skills, knowledge and theoretical framework to make sense of what is going on around them, how can they make the right decisions and take the right actions?

'Total quality management' is an example of a business strategy that cannot succeed without a huge investment in training. The quality principles were first put forward by Deming and Juran, taken up with shattering success by the Japanese, and are now being used by increasing numbers of Western companies.

Quality is defined as meeting customer requirements. This can only be achieved by every single person in the organization taking individual responsibility for the quality of their work. People cannot take responsibility for their own quality if they are not able to use the new quality processes and technologies. A once-off injection of training is not enough because quality means continually improving business processes. Improved processes require new skills and knowledge.

Additionally, skills can quickly go out of date because customer requirements are becoming more stringent by the day. Competition is growing fiercer and the pace of change is ever accelerating. If this isn't bad enough, the older style of organization is just not responsive enough to cope with today's changing environment because no one dares to make a move until decisions have been made and received from the people at the top of the hierarchy.

Organizations are also becoming flatter, with technology helping people to take on more work and greater spans of control. This kind of structure can be very cost effective. However, the flatter organization can only be effective, flexible and responsive if the workforce is highly motivated, trained and educated.

Another effect of flatter organizations is that responsibility for training is fragmented throughout the organization. Different processes and standards start to emerge and there is a consequent fall in quality coupled with a waste of meagre training resources. Often, exactly the same training need is met by different courses in different parts of the company. For example, one large multinational company once had 37 different courses on 'presentation skills' throughout the world. Apart from wasting resources, this approach leads to confusion and poor communication because people from different parts of the company end up using different processes and terminology.

The instinctive reaction to this situation is to centralize the training operation, but this approach can create an inflexible and unresponsive bureaucracy.

The training process described in this book arose out of a real need to standardize the quality of training delivery in a large multinational organization without the necessity for a centralized bureaucracy. In fact, writing this book helped me to refine the process further.

The first draft was a training process with elements that all our training and human resource managers recognized. Although all of the steps were familiar, very few of us had seen the entire process put together on one sheet. The power of this was that we could quickly and easily see where our current processes fell short of this benchmark.

Having a benchmark process only solved part of the problem; the process still had to be locked into the organization's business cycle and responsibilities for each step of the process had to be assigned. The development of the process and the writing of this book then proceeded together – the one feeding off the other.

The way that this book has been structured means that it can be used as:

- A checklist for training professionals.
- A guide for people, such as directors, human resource

managers and line managers, who need to understand
how the training process is managed.

- A detailed explanation for those such as training
  managers, trainers and training administrators whose
  job it is to make the process work.

The purpose of this book is to provide a guide to managing
the training process, one which meets the needs of today's
organizations. The emphasis throughout the book is one of
practicality. This does not mean to say that the theoretical
basis of training, which has been covered in detail by other
books, has been ignored. Rather, this book concentrates on
what you have to do when you are identifying the need,
bringing on new trainers, sourcing new courses and
deciding how you are going to integrate the many
demands that are cascaded down from corporate, head
office or the board.

Of course there are no easy answers to all of this, but this
book offers some practical approaches you can take to help
you through the training jungle.

The structure of the book is driven by a series of flow
charts. Chapter 1 describes the top-level process. The
subsequent chapters take one or more steps from the top-
level process and describe them in more detail. Each of
these steps has its own process and flow chart.

The second edition of the book has given me the
opportunity to develop some of the themes identified in
the first edition and to include some of the latest
developments in the ever-changing world of training and
development.

I have done this by dividing the book into two parts. Part I
retains the original flow chart structure to describe the
basics of the training process – basics which remain
constant and form the foundation of new developments.

Part II is a collection of short papers or briefings which are
designed to keep you up to date on the latest developments
in training and development. Brevity is achieved by
reference back to Part I for detailed explanations of the
basics.

Future editions of *Managing the Training Process* will include
further revisions of Part I and enlarged or changed
contributions to Part II. It is my intention to publish draft
versions of the new briefings on the Internet to judge
reaction and obtain feedback before including the most
popular briefings in a later edition of the book. You will

find them, plus other training topics, on my home page, which can be found on:

http://ourworld.compuserve.com/homepages/mikewills

Also look out for details of a proposed electronic version of *Managing the Training Process*. If you would like me to send you details when these publications become available, or if you have any comments on this book or other training-related topics, please e-mail me on:

mikewills@compuserve.com

Mike Wills

Part One

The Training Process

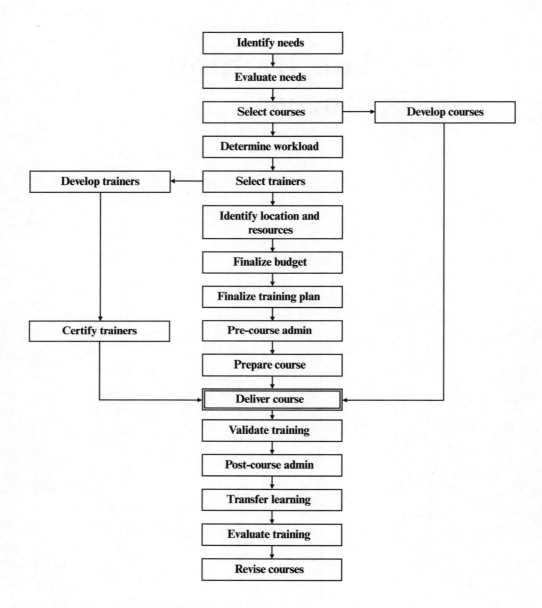

Figure 1.1 *Top-level flow chart of the training process*

1 The process of training

When people talk about the training process they usually mean the day-to-day activities that make up the annual training cycle. Concentrating on the process is the best place to start if you want a quick and significant improvement in training efficiency. Indeed, the greater part of this book is devoted to describing this basic training process.

There are, however, several dangers in considering the training process in isolation. The most obvious is that the training provided will have little or no relevance either to business requirements or to the development needs of the people. Another danger is that maintaining the process can become an end in itself. Then training becomes inflexible and insensitive to change.

It is very easy to say that effective training has to be aligned with a company's business directions and values; that the training department has to provide courses which support the company's goals; and that anyone who is involved in managing the training process has to have a clear idea of where the business is going.

All this assumes that those involved in running the business have a clear idea of where they are going. Unfortunately, this is not always the case and proactive training managers will often find themselves involved with senior management in getting the basics right. If this foundation is not firm, no training process can successfully support the business objectives.

As well as giving an overview of the training process, this chapter also describes how successful companies define their businesses and how they clarify their attitudes towards training.

Getting the basics right

Not every company uses the same method to ensure that the business is built on firm foundations, but the following is a summary of current thinking on the subject. Much of this thinking comes from Japan. If you are interested in understanding the Japanese approach in more detail, Masaaki Imai's book *Kaizen: The Key to Japan's Competitive Success* gives a detailed account.

Alignment

The key to getting the basics right is making sure that everybody has the same understanding of the current situation and that everyone is pulling in the same direction for the future.

The large arrow in Figure 1.2 represents the company's intended business direction. The small arrows are the directions of the individual departments. Each department is pursuing its own interests, and spends more time on in-fighting than on fighting the company's competitors.

Without the alignment shown in Figure 1.3 no company can make progress – and no training department could provide efficient and effective training. Training provided for one department would not be suitable for another, and little of the training would align with the company's business direction.

Philosophy

A philosophy is a statement of what the company stands for. It is a set of values and beliefs by which actions can be judged. A philosophy makes it clear which behaviours are

Figure 1.2   *Misalignment of company organizations*

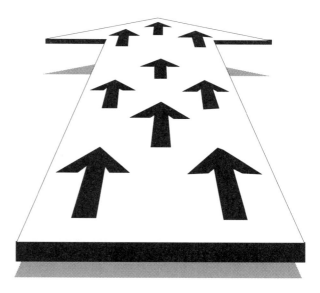

Figure 1.3   *Alignment of company organizations*

appropriate – and which are unacceptable. The following is an example of a typical philosophy. It is based on a large multinational's core values.

We succeed through satisfied customers
We value our employees
We aspire to deliver quality and excellence in all that we do
We require premium return on assets
We use technology to deliver market leadership
We are responsible members of society

Missions   A mission is a statement of what a company or organization is here to do today. It is the reason for the organization's existence. A mission should describe what is done for whom in such a way that it could not be confused with anybody else's mission. An example of a mission for a training department might be: 'To provide sales training for XYZ's UK-based sales staff'.

Communicating the mission to every employee ensures that everybody knows what business they are in. It also helps to highlight any duplication or gaps in a company's structure.

If you think a company's mission is so obvious that it hardly warrants the effort of defining it, be prepared to shock yourself. Try asking a selection of people what they think their department's mission is.

> A company had just embarked on the development of a new product. The design team was brought together to define their mission.
>
> Half of the team thought their mission was to look after the product from 'cradle to grave'. The other half of the team thought they were there to 'caretake' until the *real* design team was formed.

Assessment The mission is about maintaining today's processes, but training and surviving in today's business environment are also about encompassing and loving change. Change always has its roots in the past and has to start in the present. There is not much point in deciding where you are going if you do not know where you are starting from.

Assessment is very much about understanding where the company is today, and determining the reasons for both success and failure.

Visions A vision is a 'picture' of where the organization wants to be in the future. By describing the future in emotional rather than measurable terms, a vision can exert a strong pulling force which helps keep the organization aligned.

Examples of visions are: 'There will be a time when generations of people have lived, died and been born on Mars' and 'Every household will have their own wind-driven generator.'

Describing events in pictorial terms, and from a future viewpoint where success has already been achieved, greatly enhances the probability of a vision coming to fruition.

Like the philosophy, a vision provides a basis for deciding which actions should be taken.

Goals Goals are quantitative figures, such as sales, profit and market share, that are established by top management. Goals put the flesh on the vision. Without goals the vision will remain only a dream.

Policies A policy is a medium- to long-range course of action comprising a goal and a strategy (a 'what' and a 'how'). A strategy is the means of achieving the goal. Without the means a policy is only a slogan like 'Work Harder' or 'Think Smarter'. Imploring people to improve without providing the means cannot, and does not, work.

Be careful of how the word 'policy' is used, as it is often used interchangeably with 'philosophy' which has quite a different meaning.

Policy deployment Policy deployment is the process of ensuring that the company's policies for quality, cost and delivery (QCD) are understood from the highest to the lowest levels in the company.

The way the system works in practice is that the policy is communicated across the organization as well as being cascaded down through the line managers.

Cross-functional communication of policies is very important because it binds the functions together in pursuit of the company goals. It helps functions co-operate instead of selfishly pursuing their own objectives at the expense of others. It is this subtle but important distinction that separates policy deployment from management by objectives (MBO).

As a policy cascades down, all line managers are expected to translate the 'what' in the light of their own responsibilities, and to identify 'how' they will achieve the goals. As a result of this, the 'how' at one level becomes the 'what' at the next level down.

Policy deployment is a cyclical process. Progress against the goals should be checked, the reasons for any deviations (both positive and negative) diagnosed and the policies modified in the light of the diagnosis.

Making change happen

Change is occurring far more rapidly than ever before. Companies have to adapt to change or become extinct. Resistance to change has to be overcome.

There are two basic approaches to bringing change about deliberately. The first is through innovation and the second is through continuous improvement. Western cultures concentrate on innovation but Eastern cultures put more importance on continuous improvement. In Japan the word for continuous improvement is *kaizen*.

Innovation causes leaps in efficiency and productivity, but competitors can copy the innovation and the competitive advantage is soon whittled away. Innovation is often dramatic and causes resistance to change.

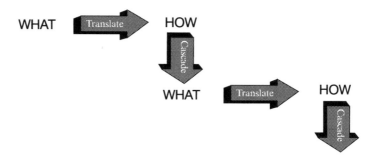

Figure 1.4   Policy deployment

Continuous improvement helps you keep ahead of the competition until your competitors introduce an unexpected innovation.

The most successful companies get the best of both worlds by both innovating and continuously improving.

The single most important factor in the successful management of change is the leadership shown by the people at the top of an organization. A company's employees rarely do what management exhorts them to do. Instead they follow the lead given by successful managers. If leaders do not model the new behaviours and attitudes, their followers cannot be expected to change.

Successful leaders provide vision and direction. They understand their people. They understand the factors that are working for them and those that are working against them.

Making change happen in an organization is like trying to light a bonfire. Although change cannot happen unless the 'logs' catch fire, you would not dream of lighting a fire by holding a match to the logs. You light the paper, add more fuel and fan the flames until the logs are consumed in the blaze.

Training plays a vital role in making change happen. Skills that once lasted for generations are now redundant. New skills have to be identified and trained.

Work processes In the end a company has to produce something, whether it be goods or services, that customers are willing to buy. No sales, no income, no company. Although much work has to be done to determine which products meet the customers' requirements, it is the work processes that ensure those requirements are met every time. So, an essential part of getting the basics right is to identify the critical work processes and constantly strive to improve them.

The company's attitude towards training So far we have talked about the company getting its own house in order. A company that has already gone to this amount of trouble is very likely to be committed to training, but it would be a mistake to take this commitment for granted. Commitment taken for granted often turns to apathy or resistance. It is not worth going any further without obtaining a high level of commitment to training. Senior management's actions and behaviours are crucial to the success of any venture.

Senior management commitment to training is not enough by itself. The training department has to get its own house in order and the organization has to be aware of the importance that is attached to training.

Getting the training function's house in order

The process for getting the basics right for any department is the same as for the whole company. This is no less true for the training function.

Training function alignment

As previously stated, training has to be aligned with the business direction of the company. If the company has got its basics sorted out, and communicated them effectively, the training function should be in no doubt as to which business directions and values should be supported.

In most companies, whether they be large or small, it is very rare for all training to be delivered by one department. This gives ample opportunity for fragmentation and misalignment of the training effort. As we have said before, it is not unknown for several different versions of the same course to exist within the same organization. One multinational corporation was said to have had 37 different 'presentation skills' courses!

Variability in the training process, as with other processes, increases the chances of poor-quality products. The answer to this is to ensure that all the key players within the training community agree on:

- the missions of the various training departments,
- a training philosophy,
- a training policy,
- training standards,
- definition of training,
- the training process,
- accountability and responsibilities.

The training forum

We tackled this problem in one organization by forming a training forum which comprised the following key players:

- total quality manager,
- human resource director,
- site human resource managers,
- group training manager,
- site training managers.

The forum first met to reach consensus on the basics. Once these had been established the forum then met twice a year to ensure continuing alignment on business direction and training needs.

Obviously the composition of a forum will depend on how the company is organized.

Training department's mission

Where there is more than one training organization within a company it becomes imperative that the 'coverage' provided by each training department is understood and well defined. This helps to avoid duplication and prevents training needs falling between the cracks. An example of a training department's mission could be:

> 'To provide sales and customer care training for all the sales representatives who work in the corporation's telecommunications division.'

Notice that this mission states what types of training are provided for which population of students. It can be inferred from the statement that this training department does not do technical training, but provides sales and customer training for telecommunications staff wherever they are located. If this is not true then the mission statement would have to be modified. For example, in a large multinational corporation the end of the statement might be modified to:

> '...who are based in France and work in the corporation's telecommunications division.'

Training philosophy

The training philosophy is a statement of a company or organization's attitude towards training. It has to define clearly the importance that is attached to training. It has to be communicated, with conviction, to every employee. If the philosophy is just a set of words without the backing of real and practical commitment, the authors of the policy will soon be 'found out' and the damage will, perhaps, be irreparable. The first paragraph of the following statement on training is a typical example of a training philosophy.

Group Education and Training Philosophy and Policies

1 We are committed to having a workforce prepared to meet current and future business objectives by providing our employees, at all levels, with appropriate education and training opportunities.

2 We are committed to defining clearly the minimum training requirements which are related to the job holder's role, responsibilities and needs, including total quality and customer satisfaction.

3 All new employees will be oriented in the philosophy, ethics, values, principles and business priorities of the company, including total quality management and induction into their own organization, within three months of their employment.

4 Our employees will only take up new job assignments when they have completed the minimum level of training specified for that job.

5 All newly hired or first-time people managers will successfully complete specified supervisory training within four months of appointment.

6 Our managers will successfully complete functional knowledge and skills training to properly coach, inspect and reinforce the work of their employees.

Training policy

In the same way that a business policy has a goal and the means to attain the goal, a training policy should also have targets and measures.

For example, having all employees oriented to the company's philosophy, ethics, values, principles and business priorities is a goal. Having new employees attend induction and quality training within three months of joining the company is the measure that will achieve the goal.

Following the principles of policy deployment, these measures now become the goals of the new employees' managers and of the training department. The managers will have to provide the means for releasing new employees for training within three months. The training department has to take measures to ensure the availability of training.

Training standards

The training policy will incorporate many of the training standards, such as:

- hours of functional training per employee,
- additional hours of training for managers,
- minimum level of training before starting a new job,
- the amount and timing of induction training.

There are many other standards that have to be agreed and met for the training process to run smoothly. The following are just a selection:

- trainer-to-student ratio,
- trainer training,
- trainer accreditation,
- face-to-face percentage,
- delivery-to-preparation ratio,
- cost per student-day,
- cost per trainer-day,
- classroom standards,
- administrative standards,
- course development standards.

These standards will be dealt with in detail in the rest of this book.

Definition of training

While it is essential to have a training philosophy, policy and standards, it is impossible to judge whether our training is in accordance with these if there is no clear definition of training.

For example, a company might have a target to give each of its employees five days of training every year. Depending on what is considered to be training, one company might say it is providing three days of training and another company might claim nine days – even though both companies' employees have received exactly the same amount of training and development!

An amazing number of activities might be considered as training. The following is just a selection:

- classroom (trainer led),
- distance learning,
- computer-based training,
- on-the-job training,
- external courses,
- large-scale workshops,
- attendance at seminars,
- attending exhibitions,
- attending conferences,
- attending communications meetings,
- evening classes,
- further education,
- assignments,
- participating in quality circles,
- reading articles and books.

Some of the above activities, such as classroom training and computer-based training, would always be considered as training. Activities such as exhibitions, conferences, assignments and reading would not usually be classified as training.

Clearly on-the-job training should be considered as training, but surely not all of the time spent under supervision should qualify for the employee's 'hours of training'. The conclusion we came to was that the time spent on producing usable output should not be included in the training time.

In Europe and the United States, participating in quality circles would probably not be considered to be training because the prime purpose of a quality circle is thought to be solving the company's problems. Any learning that comes about would be thought to be secondary. In fact, this is another indication of how Western culture misunderstood Japan's quality revolution, because one of Japan's main aims in starting quality circle activities was to enable the factory workers to study together and teach themselves quality control.

Without a definition of training, deciding whether an activity should be recognized as training becomes very subjective. The working definition of training that I use is:

> 'Training is the transfer of defined and measurable knowledge or skills.'

From this definition it can be seen that training activities should have objectives and a method for checking whether these objectives have been met.

Training, defined in this way, deals only with changes in behaviour and knowledge. Some definitions include changes of attitude as part of training. I have not included attitude change within the definition because, apart from being incredibly difficult to measure, it is the environment and culture of a business that primarily determine attitude. Training has an important part to play in this, and can help create the environment in which attitudes can change, but training alone will not change anybody's long-term attitude.

Many different attempts have been made to define what constitutes a training activity, and these all vary depending on the definition of training that is used. Having agreement on a definition of training is more important than which of the many good definitions you decide to use. This allows you to be aligned within your own company, and to make sensible comparisons with other companies.

If you have not already done so, this would probably be a good time to consider which activities in your company should be considered as training.

The French Ministry of Work, Employment and Professional Training considers that training activities are those activities which are paid for by employers and take place in accordance with a programme which:

- has pre-determined objectives,
- specifies the teaching methods,
- specifies the personnel to be used,
- has an implementation plan,
- assesses the results,
- is given in premises separate from the production area unless it includes practical training,
- can include correspondence courses, safety and security training and training outside of work hours.

The ministry specifies no set minimum duration for a training activity and any duration of course can be included in the minimum statutory time per worker (1.2 per cent) if the training agency agrees. However, in practice, the state does not often allow a training activity lasting less than a day to be included.

Training as part of the business

A useful approach for understanding the training process is to consider it as a system whose boundaries interact with the rest of the business (see Figure 1.5). Training needs are identified, training is provided to meet the needs, the output is compared to the requirements and any necessary changes are made to the system to obtain the desired output.

While this approach helps you understand how training processes operate, it does put training at the centre of the universe. The effect of this training-centred approach is that the business will see training either as a panacea for all problems or as having no direct relevance to the business. Neither of these impressions will help you manage the training process effectively.

A better approach is to extend the boundaries of the system so training is an integral part of the business (Figure 1.6).

The learning organization

Companies which have made this degree of progress have taken the first step towards being a 'learning organization'. There are many definitions of a learning organization but the one I like (based on Pedler, Burgoyne and Boydell) is:

The business

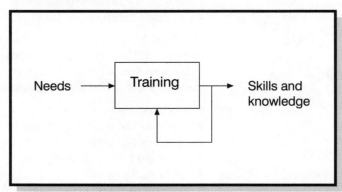

Figure 1.5 *Training as a system whose boundaries interact with the business*

'A learning organization is one which facilitates the learning of all its members and continuously transforms itself to achieve superior competitive performance.'

Figure 1.6 shows a system that is displaying 'single-loop learning'. The output of the system is compared to a set of standards and adjustments are made to counterbalance any deviations from the standards. More advanced learning organizations would have progressed to 'double-loop learning' where the standards themselves are challenged.

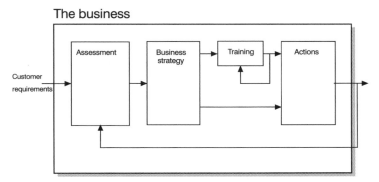

Figure 1.6   *Training as part of the business system*

The concept of the learning organization does not replace training. As you can see from Figure 1.7, training is a vital component of learning. It is important not to overlook this fact, as there have been examples of organizations which have been so intent on becoming learning organizations that they have, to their cost, overlooked the basics of training.

Figure 1.7   *Training as part of the learning organization*

The training process

Having established where training fits into the business, we can now take a look at the training process itself. The fundamental elements of any process are:

- accountability (ownership),
- identification of stakeholders,
- definition and documentation of the process,
- checkpoints,
- responsibility for the steps of the process,
- continuous improvement of the process.

Accountability and responsibility

No process will work efficiently unless somebody 'owns' or is accountable for the process. The accountable person is the person whose telephone rings when something goes wrong with any part of the process. This person is like the captain of a ship, ultimately accountable for everything that happens on board even though the crew are responsible for carrying out most of the tasks. Although the captain holds individual crew members accountable for their responsibilities, the captain's own accountability cannot be abdicated. The difference between an ordinary organization and a 'quality' organization is that in the latter people feel accountable for their own responsibilities.

The training manager is the 'owner' of the training process. This makes the training manager accountable for every step as well as the entire training process. Being accountable for every step is tough, because the responsibility for carrying out many of the individual steps lies with other people. It is the training manager who has to make sure nothing falls down the cracks between the steps of the process.

Identifying the stakeholders

A stakeholder is a person who has a vested interest in the outcome of the process. Stakeholders often have a positive or negative impact on the outcome of a process, even though they might not take a direct part in it. This is especially true if the process involves 'treading on their turf'.

This makes it vital for you to involve stakeholders during the early stages of process design. Managing directors, heads of departments, and human resource managers are all stakeholders in the training process.

Defining and documenting the training process

Definition of a process involves establishing the boundaries of the process. In theory, any process could be traced back to the 'big bang' or projected forward to 'the end of the universe'. In practice, this makes the process too large and cumbersome to handle, so you need to define the beginning and end points of your process. Although defining the boundaries is, to some extent, arbitrary, the following guidelines should help you decide:

- The beginning of your process is where you take over control from someone else.
- The end of your process is where you hand over control to another person.

The easiest way of documenting a process is to tape some sheets of flip-chart paper together and use 'Post-it' notes to represent the steps of the process. You already have the beginning and end points, so these can be stuck on to the sheets straight away. Stick additional steps on the sheets until you have a series of related steps that connect the end point to the beginning point.

Make sure you use a verb and a noun to describe each step in the process. This clarifies what is involved in each step and separates one step from another. 'Select course' is different to 'Develop course' which in turn is different to 'Deliver course'.

The flow chart shown at the beginning of this chapter (Figure 1.1) is an overview of the training process. Subsequent chapters in this book will expand on this 'level 1' process by describing a 'level 2' process for one or more of the steps. In the interests of clarity and simplicity, checkpoints, decision boxes and feedback loops have been left out at this stage.

A brief overview of the steps of the training process follows.

Identify needs

The process starts off by identifying the business needs and turning these needs into training requirements.

Evaluate needs

A check is made to ensure that the requested, or mandated, training is suitable for the people concerned. A check is also made to make sure that training can meet the identified need.

In the cases where training is not a suitable approach the need has to be analysed further so that alternatives to training can be suggested.

Select courses

Given that the business need is one where training can make a contribution, the next step is to identify suitable courses. The choice will be between:

- using an existing company course,
- buying an external course,
- developing a new course.

> **Develop courses**

If no suitable courses are available, new courses have to be developed and piloted.

> **Determine workload**

At this stage you should be able to make your first estimate of the resources you will need to meet the training need.

> **Select trainers**

Before a course can be delivered suitable trainers need to be identified. If you do not have sufficient trainers to meet the expected workload, you will need to start the process of recruiting new trainers. It often takes three months or more to recruit a new trainer so you will need to start this step as early as possible.

> **Develop trainers**

It is likely that the trainers you select to run new courses will need further development of their own skills and knowledge. It is even more likely that trainers recruited from outside will require development.

If you are developing people to be trainers, you will need to put them through a programme of training and experiences before you allow them to train unassisted. Depending on the level and frequency of the courses, this could take from three months to a year.

> **Certify trainers**

If a course is new to the trainers, they should undergo a programme of observation and practice to ensure that they reach the required standard before they are allowed to deliver the course by themselves.

> **Identify location and resources**

Before advertising the dates of the proposed courses it is best to make sure that appropriate locations and resources are available.

Finalize budget

By this stage you should have enough information to know how much it is going to cost to meet the training need. Negotiations over the actual budget are started.

Finalize training plan

After budget negotiations are complete you will need to make adjustments to the training plan.

Often there will be more demand for a course than there are places available so it will be necessary to prioritize the candidates. Prioritizing should still be done even if sufficient places are available, because the people most in need of the course will still get trained if budgets are cut later in the year.

The training plan is built up throughout the early steps of the training process and it is at this stage that the finalized plan can be put together ready for presentation to senior management.

Pre-course admin

Once the training plan has been agreed the course administrator has to ensure that the identified people get to the right course, at the right time.

Prepare course

Before the courses can be delivered the trainers need to prepare themselves, the materials and the training rooms. The trainees also need to prepare themselves for the course.

Deliver course

Although course delivery is the culmination of all the efforts that have been put into the previous steps, it should be remembered that, as far as the rest of the organization is concerned, this is only the start of the change process.

Validate training

Validation is the process of ensuring that the course meets and continues to meet its stated objectives. Tests, observations and student feedback are all data which have to be analysed to determine whether the objectives are being met.

Post-course admin

As soon as the training has been completed attendance on the course should be noted on the students' training records.

Transfer learning

The students then have to use the knowledge and practise the skills to ensure that the learning is transferred into the business.

Evaluate training

As with any process, the training process should have a method of ensuring that it has had the desired effect.

Revise courses

The courses then need to be revised to incorporate the changes identified during evaluation.

Establishing checkpoints

You need to establish checkpoints to keep the process on track, under control and producing the required outputs. Checkpoints can occur at the beginning, during and at the end of the process. Checks at the beginning answer the question of whether the correct outputs will be produced. Checks during the process answer the question of whether the correct outputs are being produced. Checks at the end answer the question of whether the correct outputs have been produced. Deviations that you detect early on in the process are easier and cheaper to correct than those found at the end of the process.

The major checkpoints of the training process shown in Figure 1.1 are:

- needs analysis and evaluation,
- pilot courses (within course development),
- trainer certification,
- finalize budget,
- finalize training plan,
- course preparation,
- validate training,
- evaluation.

The most important checkpoint is evaluating the needs. If we identify the needs incorrectly, all else that follows is built on sand. Each process step has its own checkpoints and these will be discussed in the following chapters.

Responsibility for the steps of the process

The training manager should identify, by name, the people responsible for carrying out each task or step in the process. Attaching a person's name to a responsibility is a sure way of flushing out conflicting responsibilities, gaps and potential overloading.

If more than one person is involved in a process step, one of them should be given the prime responsibility so that nobody can ever say: 'I thought that was somebody else's responsibility to make sure that the task was completed.'

Table 1.1 shows how responsibilities could be allocated for the steps in the training process. This table gives job titles in the responsibility column. In practice you would also identify the people's names.

Additional responsibility matrices should be drawn up if there is more than one training organization in the company. The additional matrices should clearly show which courses or types of course are covered by the responsibilities.

Improving the training process

We should always be looking for ways of continually improving the training process. There are two main ways of improving a process:

- reducing errors,
- reducing cycle time (the time it takes to go from the beginning to the end of a process).

To do this you should have a close look at your process by documenting what actually happens at every step.

When you design a new process it is very likely that you will have designed an ideal one. It won't show gaps, duplication, dead ends, confusing responsibilities or activities that add no value to the end product.

You can now compare your actual process with the ideal and make sure that gaps are plugged, duplication and dead ends eliminated, and responsibilities clarified. Activities that add no value to the end product are:

- correcting errors,
- waiting time,
- storage,
- transport time.

By reducing these activities to a minimum you will reduce the cost of, and the time for, providing training.

Table 1.1 *Possible responsibilities for the steps in the training process*

Step	Responsibility
Identify needs	Training manager
Evaluate needs	Training administrator Training manager
Select courses	Training manager Training administrator
Develop courses	Course developers
Determine workload	Training manager
Select trainers	Training manager
Develop trainers	Training manager
Certify trainers	Course developers
Identify location and resources	Training manager Training administrator
Finalize budget	Training manager
Finalize training plan	Training manager Development committees
Pre-course admin	Training administrator
Prepare course	Trainers
Deliver course	Trainers
Validate training	Trainers
Post-course admin	Training administrator
Transfer learning	Participants, managers Trainers
Evaluate training	Trainers Training manager
Revise courses	Course developers Trainers

Training strategies

The training process is a cycle that you need to manage continuously. You respond to needs. You ensure that the training is aligned with the business. The cycle time is short term – usually no longer than a year. Managing the training process is essentially operational or tactical.

If we always manage training at this level we are in danger of being reactive rather than proactive: starting and stopping training programmes or perhaps even failing to deliver anything.

We need to have a clear idea of how we are going to deliver training over a longer period. Training needs analysis and training policies provide the 'what' and the 'how much'. A training strategy provides the long-term orientation.

To put a training strategy together you should have a 'vision' of what training in your organization should look like in, say, five years. You should then map out the years and the key milestones along the way. When you are putting a training strategy together you should ask yourself the following questions:

- How much training will you need to do each year?
- What type of courses will you need to provide?
- What types of people will you put on what type of course?
- What resources will you need in terms of space and trainers?
- Who will you use to do your training?
- Will you use full-time, part-time or consultant trainers?
- What delivery methods will you use?
- How will changes in technology affect delivery methods?
- What business, social and environmental changes are likely to take place?

Every time you cycle through the training process you should re-examine your training strategy to see if it still holds up in the light of new training requirements and corporate policies. This is an example of 'double-loop' learning. Try to make your strategy as robust as possible, and only change strategies when there are significant business, social and environmental changes. If your strategy is really robust you will find that you can respond to many changes by adjusting your tactics rather than throwing away your strategy.

It is difficult but essential to find the right balance between constantly chopping and changing strategies, and sticking with a useless and outmoded strategy.

Communicating the importance of training

Having a training philosophy and policy is the starting point for communicating the importance of training and it is very important that everybody is aware of them.

Posters, in-house magazines, staff briefings and memos are all methods of putting the message across. But no matter how much effort is put into communicating through the usual channels, there is still no getting away from the fact that the most powerful communication always occurs through the unwritten and unspoken channels:

- the amount of training that is done,
- the budget allocated to training,
- the status of training managers and staff,
- how often a training event has to be moved to another location to make room for another business activity,
- how often training is postponed or cancelled,
- the reasons managers give for pulling their people off courses,
- the standard of the training rooms,
- whether people are allowed to start a new job before they have been trained.

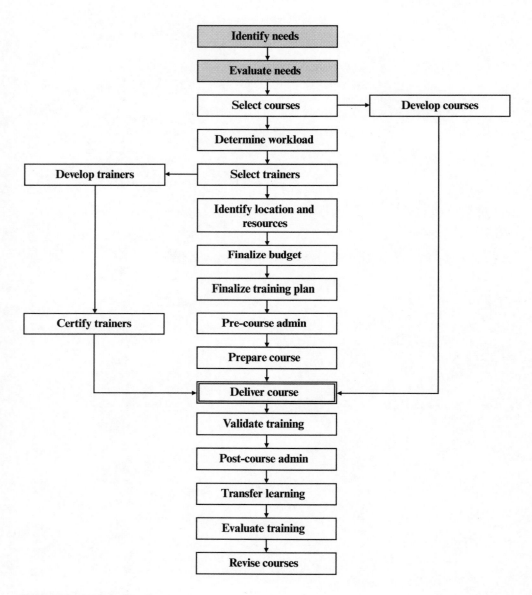

Figure 2.1   Training needs

2 Training needs

In this chapter we will be covering two steps of the training process (highlighted in Figure 2.1):

- identify needs,
- evaluate needs.

Identifying training needs is the starting point for managing the training process. Yet this is often one of the last steps to be considered seriously – probably because a proper needs analysis is both difficult and time consuming.

Initially, it might be quicker and easier to forget about analysing the needs and have your customers pick and choose from a catalogue, but this will ultimately lead to frustration and inefficiency.

Identifying training needs is not just a matter of finding the need and then simply satisfying it. There are often conflicting requirements from different interests within the company. The development needs of the individual have to be met while satisfying the skills requirements of the organization. These needs, once identified, have to be matched to appropriate training courses.

Sometimes there is a feeling that training will always be the solution for every identified development problem. However, there is no point in providing training if training is not an appropriate solution. When this is the case the training manager has to be brave enough to say that it is not appropriate – and creative enough to suggest alternative solutions.

Needs identification

Needs identification has to balance corporate demands, policies and strategies as well as individual and organizational requirements. Figure 2.2 outlines a process that balances these requirements. It shows that corporate policies and strategies should be the 'umbrella' under which individual and organizational training needs are identified. This helps to ensure alignment of training activities with the business direction.

> Collect corporate policies and strategies

Corporate policies and strategies form the boundaries within which all training and development activities should take place.

There are two ways in which corporate policies and strategies give rise to training needs. The first is directly through mandatory training. The other way is through indirect influence. When an organization puts its training plan together it should take account of both the business plan and individual development needs. This is where the process often breaks down and even the indirect influences start to disappear.

Policy deployment, which is a structured method of cascading corporate goals and strategies through the company, is a powerful method of ensuring that training needs are identified within the context of the company's business goals.

In Chapter 1 we discussed the importance of alignment and of getting the corporate basics right. If this has been done well, you will have no difficulty in collecting corporate policies and strategies. You will then be able to prepare a training plan that supports the direction of the business.

If your company is confused about its strategies, or does not communicate them effectively, you might as well miss this step out completely and be resigned to providing training that cannot completely support the business.

Figure 2.2   Needs identification

Start by reading your company's policies on training and development, reviewing the company's vision and understanding the current goals and objectives.

> Identify mandatory training

Company policy dictates which employee groups are required to undergo prescribed courses. Some courses, such as 'induction training' and 'total quality management', are an integral part of the company's culture so all new employees have to attend this training.

Company strategy may also require all personnel to go through specified forms of training in a relatively short period. Examples of this kind of training are:

- equal opportunities,
- empowerment,
- harassment,
- financial responsibility,
- new measurement systems (e.g. economic value added),
- new legal requirements.

Compulsory courses will usually be aligned with the company direction because they have been developed centrally for company-wide implementation.

> Identify business needs

Policy deployment and the training forum are two essential tools for identifying business needs. Policy deployment and the training forum's role in defining the basics of the training process are both covered in Chapter 1.

Policy deployment

Policy deployment is the process by which a company's strategies are communicated to its organizations. An organization then determines what it needs to achieve by understanding its part in the company's strategy. The 'what' should be measurable and take the form of goals or objectives.

Once an organization has determined what it has to achieve, it then has to decide how these objectives will be met. Once the 'how' has been identified it is possible to determine the skills and knowledge the organization will require.

Training forum's role

The training forum's role at this stage of the process is to:
- provide a 'forum' for identifying an organization's business needs,
- ensure that training plans are aligned with the company's direction,

- identify opportunities for sharing or exchanging resources.

The training forum comprises training managers and other interested parties who meet to discuss training plans. They also identify opportunities for sharing resources. A forum is particularly useful when there are several, dispersed training departments within a company.

The forum would normally need to meet twice a year: the first time to understand both corporate requirements and local issues; the second meeting to review draft training plans. Figure 2.3 shows typical timings for the two training forum meetings.

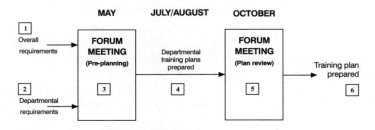

Figure 2.3   *Schedule for training forum meetings*

Timing of these forum meetings is critical and depends on which month is the start of the organization's financial year. The output of the second meeting needs to be available for inclusion in the annual business plan.

Individual development plans should be completed before the draft departmental training plans are put together. The training plans will be based on guesswork if the development plans are not available. If the development plans are available too early, the training plan could be out of time by up to six months. The following is a description of how the training forums work in practice.

1. Before the first meeting the group training manager has a meeting with the organization's general manager to understand the business direction and vision for the organization.

> Even a short statement from a general manager can have quite a profound effect on how the training plans are put together. For example, during preparation for the coming year's training plan at one company, the director said: 'If we sell a product in Europe, we will manufacture it in Europe.'
> The effect of this statement was to cause the training managers to reassess the skills that would be needed in their factories. A very different set of skills is needed to manufacture every machine that is sold rather than assemble small machines and pass the larger

machines through a warehouse. The director said he wanted everybody to make themselves thoroughly familiar with the organization's mission and objectives which could be found in the recently published 'Blue Book'.

He also highlighted the shift in technology that would be required. In the past the business had been built on optical and mechanical technology. Today's and tomorrow's emphasis would be on digital technology. Flexibility would be key: flexible people and flexible manufacturing processes. He also had a concern about the plethora of training courses being produced within the corporation and expressed a hope that they would be properly prioritized and integrated. Another concern was the transfer of learning into the workplace.

The group training manager also collects general training requirements and demands from:

- functional heads,
- human resource managers,
- corporate.

It is amazing how much information this type of digging around can unearth. In preparation for the coming year's training plan, the finance community forewarned us that functional managers were to be made more responsible for financial and other process controls. This would generate additional training for functional managers and buying staff.

2. Preparation notes for the pre-planning meeting are issued and the site training managers identify the following general training requirements and demands for their own areas:

- technical,
- induction and quality,
- business.

3. The training forum meets to understand overall requirements and issues, and to identify potential areas of co-operation. This is the pre-planning meeting. See Figure 2.4 on page 33 for the agenda of the meeting.

The first part of the meeting deals with general issues such as corporate business direction, human resources, quality issues and management training. This is to ensure that the site training managers understand the context within which they will be developing their final plans.

In preparation for the coming year's plan, the human resource director pointed out that the human resource challenges will have to be approached against a background of:

- resource constraints,
- flatter organizations,
- matrix management,
- new technical skills,
- population demographics,

- education levels,
- the European Union,
- workforce empowerment and flexibility,
- equal opportunities,
- the environment and recycling,
- the mix of permanent and contract staff,
- health, safety, security and export control.

The training plans will also have to take account of the 'total quality' initiatives – the main one being the company's application for the European Quality Award. Part of the application process will be 'self-certification' of the key business processes. It is anticipated that 'self-certification' will identify additional training needs.

During the second part of the meeting the site training managers present their draft plans. This gives an opportunity for resources to be shared and new ideas to be spread across the organization.

4. Preparation notes are issued and site training managers prepare the first drafts of their training plans, which include:

- the training needs that have been identified,
- what this would cost if the needs could be met fully,
- how many days of training per employee this would represent,
- how much of the above could realistically be provided during the coming training year,
- resources required,
- approximately when the training will be carried out,
- what this realistic estimate represents in terms of days per employee and total cost.

5. The forum meets again to review the site training plans. The meeting agenda is given in Figure 2.5. The site training managers present their draft training plans and an estimate is made of the amount of training that is planned to be delivered, as well as the cost and the resources required.

6. The site training managers finalize their training plans.

7. The group training manager prepares an overall training plan for the organization.

8. Training plans are submitted as part of the organization's business plan.

Identify individual needs

Identifying training needs via business requirements is a 'top-down' approach which satisfies the need for training to be in alignment with the business direction. If we were only to use this approach, the coverage would be too broad to pick up individual development requirements. We also

---

Pre-planning meeting agenda

Time   Topic

10.00   Review of purpose and agenda (10 min)

10.10   Business direction (20 min)

10.30   Total quality management (30 min)

11.00   Break (15 min)

11.15   Human resource management (30 min)

11.45   Management training and finance (30 min)

12.15   Lunch (45 min)

13.00   Site presentations (1 hr 30 min)

14.30   Break (15 min)

14.45   Next steps (30 min)

15.15   Next forum meeting (30 min)

15.45   Meeting review (15 min)

Figure 2.4 *Agenda for the pre-planning meeting*

need to consider 'bottom-up' training requests and to make sure that both sources of training requirements complement each other. Individual training requirements come either from direct requests or as a result of appraisal discussions.

Requests   If we were honest with ourselves, we would probably admit that the majority of training needs are identified through requests received from either the employee or the

Agenda

Time	Topic
10.00	Review of purpose and agenda (10 min)
10.10	Review action items (15 min)
10.25	Sites information sharing and processing (2 hr 55 min – including break)
13.20	Lunch (45 min)
14.05	Group (50 min)
14.55	Break (15 min)
15.10	Issues and opportunities identified (information processing 30 min)
15.40	Next steps and action items (15 min)
15.55	Meeting review (5 min)
16.00	End

Figure 2.5   *Agenda for the plan review meeting*

employee's manager. At their most basic these requests would be an informal approach to the training department with the prospective student or manager saying something like: 'Have you got a course on XYZ?'

The training administrator would then look through the training catalogues and say, 'Well, there doesn't seem to be an XYZ course, how about the PQR course in July?'

Appraisals Another route for identifying training needs is through the annual appraisal system. You know how it can go. The employee's salary is directly related to the outcome of the appraisal and the first hour and a half can be spent discussing what the person did, or did not do, seven months ago. With ten minutes left to go they happen upon a 'Training required' box at the bottom of the last page of the appraisal form.

'I've heard that the Welding for Pleasure course is pretty good,' suggests the appraisee.

'I think that Photographing Dustbins is a better course,' replies the manager.

'Well, perhaps I ought to do both courses.'

'That's a good idea,' agrees the manager, 'let's put them both down and then we can wrap this up and get some coffee.'

These sketches might seem a bit extreme but they illustrate the point that the training requests received by the training department often have more to do with perceived demand than actual need – although it has to be said it is much better to be demand led than place led.

Being place led is where the number of places on a training course has been previously fixed (usually by the size of the budget) and the training administrator has to search around to find people to fill the places.

Approaching needs analysis this way might, by chance, provide training which meets a need, but the odds of this aligning with the company's values and business directions are virtually non-existent.

The way to improve this situation is to take a developmental approach to training needs identification, and to have a broader view of where training needs originate.

A developmental approach to needs identification

The whole idea behind a developmental approach to training needs identification is that a person's current skills level is established and compared with the skills or competencies required to do today's as well as tomorrow's job.

Some companies' training request forms have a section that asks what the development need is, and how the requested course would help the candidates do their jobs better. This gives the training administrator a much better chance of suggesting an appropriate course.

A good appraisal system can produce development-related training needs. However, the waters are muddied when the next promotion, or salary increase, is linked to the results of the appraisal.

It would be better if development could be entirely divorced from salary-related assessment. This, of course, would be difficult in companies that run performance-related salary schemes, but development planning and appraisal could still be two separate discussions. Even if no separation is possible, the appraisal can be improved by having the right balance of past performance and future development.

Too many appraisals spend too much time looking backwards and not enough time discussing future development. Although it is valuable to see what lessons can be learnt, the past cannot be changed. Only the future can be changed.

Average appraisers spend only 12 per cent of the appraisal talking about the future; expert appraisers concentrate on future behaviour for 40 per cent of the time.

A developmental approach to appraisal and training would have the discussion centred around the employee's current strengths and weaknesses and would put together a developmental plan to sustain the strengths and minimize the weaknesses. Notice that it is called a 'developmental plan' rather than a 'training plan'. This is quite deliberate, because there is sometimes an immediate assumption that training is the answer to all development needs and performance problems.

Occasionally there is a confusion between personal development and career development. Personal development is all about improving a person's skill and knowledge so that they can do today's job better. Career development is about preparing the person for the next career move.

It is very important to be clear about which type of development you are talking about when you are having discussions with your staff. Most people think that all development will give rise to better prospects and increased salaries. Given the flatter, leaner nature of our organizations, these kinds of expectations are less likely to be fulfilled, and will ultimately lead to anger and frustration – especially if people think that attendance on a training course will automatically give them their next promotion.

Career development depends on opportunity, capability and luck. Opportunity is simply the availability of job at the next stage of a person's career development. Capability is the person's skill and knowledge level. Luck is being in the right place at the right time.

A person's capability can be improved through development. There is even something that can be done about luck. Determine the 'right place' and the 'right time', and position yourself accordingly.

Luck can be created but, unfortunately, the one thing that is almost impossible to influence is opportunity. The number of opportunities that are available in an organization are probably more to do with the general state of the economy and where the company is in its life cycle than anything the organization or individual can do.

Even if the discussions are centred around career development, be very careful about giving the impression that attendance at a particular training course is an automatic ticket to promotion. Careless selection of courses can also lead to false expectations. For example, sending people who are not suited to being managers on a management training course would give them the wrong impression of their prospects and abilities.

Even worse is the avoidance behaviour of sending people on courses in the hope that the course will do the 'dirty work' of revealing their unsuitability for a particular kind of job.

Development is not something that can be done to someone. People have to take the responsibility for their own development. Having said that, the company should provide development opportunities and encourage development. Opportunities which are aligned with the business needs should be given priority, but bear in mind that any development of an individual is ultimately good for the business and should be encouraged. In reality, of course, resources are limited and priorities have to be decided.

So development is a shared responsibility between a person, the manager and the company. Ideally, the individual should take prime responsibility, the manager should have the secondary responsibility, and training and personnel should be third in line. It really does have to be a combined effort.

This is all very well, but is it reasonable to expect the individual and the manager to understand the details and ramifications of all the courses that are available? Providing a training catalogue can help, but even with the best catalogue the manager does not have the background knowledge that is required to make the optimum choices.

Expert systems

What managers and individuals really need is an expert training adviser sitting beside them as the choices are made. Obviously this would not be a cost-effective prospect, so it would be worth considering the use of artificial intelligence in the form of an expert system. An expert system is a computer program that can be given a set of rules which allow it to make the same decisions as an expert. Even at its simplest level an expert system could be of great assistance to a manager.

For example, you might provide both an 'Effective Meetings' course and a more advanced 'Meeting Facilitator's Workshop'. A person who has completed the 'Meeting Facilitator's Workshop' would not need to attend 'Effective Meetings' because its content is covered by the first day of the 'Meeting Facilitator's Workshop'.

Although the two courses are mutually exclusive it can be guaranteed that you will receive requests for people to attend both. It is no use complaining that the managers should have read the details in the training catalogue. Beating up already pressurized managers doesn't help anybody. An expert system could easily and unobtrusively avoid this problem. More advanced systems could take account of the person's job, training record and career path.

Development open days

Expert systems involve a certain amount of expense and, although they can provide instant advice, it will probably be a long time before they can be as effective as discussions with professional advisers.

A way of meeting this need, which also increases the profile of training and development, is to hold a development open day. The day could be in the form of an exhibition, with training and human resource professionals on hand to discuss development needs. Any member of staff would be able to attend the event, but it would primarily be designed for managers who want to understand what development opportunities are available for their people.

Frequency and timing of appraisals

Assuming that all the problems associated with running an appraisal session have been ironed out, there are still the questions of where the output from the appraisal fits into the overall planning cycle, and whether all the needs have been identified.

One of the problems of identifying needs through appraisal is that they are identified only once, or maybe twice, a year. New training needs can surface at any time of the year and, unless the training department can react quickly to train new skills requirements in well under a year, then a company's competitive advantage could be seriously eroded.

The timing of the appraisal is also important. Most companies start submitting their plans for the next financial year about three months before the end of the current financial year. If the appraisal occurs towards the end of the year, the needs analysis will not be done in time for the training plan to be included in the business plan. If the appraisal is done too early, over half of the training would need to have been completed before the business plan was approved.

Even if there were a perfect time to complete appraisals, the chances are that other important activities would need to be done at the same time.

Development plans   The answer to these difficulties is for each individual to have a development plan. A development plan is best produced as the output of a counselling session. Instead of being 'once-off' plans, they should be kept 'evergreen' – that is, they should be revised every time an existing development need has been met or a new one identified.

Notice that the development plan shown in Figure 2.6 includes activities other than training. This shows that the manager and employee who put this plan together have a good idea of what can, and cannot, be achieved by training.

Because these development plans are always up to date, the training needs analysis can be done at any time of the year. The training administrator can request copies of the current development plan when the needs analysis has to be done.

Identify departmental needs

So far we have seen how training departments can be aligned with each other and with the corporate business direction. We have also seen how individual development requirements can be identified. We now need to see how the detailed departmental training needs are identified.

The processes already described should ensure that the department's training demands are based on corporate or company business needs and requirements. The individual requirements give us a picture of the demand within a department but not necessarily the need.

Name *J Ford*	DEVELOPMENT PLAN	Date *15th March*
Strengths	Activities to maintain	Schedule/follow-up date
1. *Project Management*	1. *Run workshop on Project Management*	1. *22nd March, 25th March*
2. *Recognizing people*	2. *Provide information on creative use of recognition and reward*	2. *3rd April, 15th April*

Identified needs	Activities to develop	Schedule/follow-up date
1. *Problem solving*	1. *Use of problem-solving process at next staff meeting*	1. *3rd May, 17th May*
2. *Team building*	2. *Hold team-building session with direct reports*	2. *2nd April, 16th April*
3. *Meeting skills*	3. *Attend Meeting Management Workshop*	3. *17th March, 3rd April*

Figure 2.6   *An example of a development plan*

In fact, the process for identifying departmental needs is very similar to the process for identifying need at the corporate level. Each department should assess where it is. The department should have a vision, a mission and a strategy for realizing the vision.

> Identify skills and training required for each job

The department's mission, and the work processes the company uses, determine the jobs the department needs to produce its products and services. Each job has an associated set of skills. New jobs require new skills.

In its simplest form, identifying the training required for each job involves:

1. Identifying the skills required to do a job.
2. Comparing the required skills to the current skills level of the people who will be doing the job.

It is training's function to bridge the gap between current and required skills.

The skills and knowledge required for every job should be documented. You should also document the courses that a representative person will need to reach the required skills level. This makes it easier to select the correct courses. A representative person is the type of person you would normally employ to do the job.

The basis of identifying and documenting the required skills is the 'job description'. A job description should include the tasks that have to be performed and the outputs that have to be produced by the job holder. Outputs are products or services that are handed on to someone else. An output should have a standard or specification attached to it so that the quality of the output can be measured.

The next step is to prepare a 'person specification' from the job description. A person specification describes the ideal person to fill the job. It is a profile of the required personal skills and characteristics. These skills and characteristics are also known as competencies.

For job descriptions which cover a large number of employees it is worth producing a 'training specification matrix'. This matrix describes the training courses that correlate to the skills described in the person specification.

You shouldn't be surprised if all this sounds rather familiar. It is exactly the same as the recruitment process – the only difference being that we are developing existing people to fit the person specification rather than recruiting the 'ideal' person.

If you are recruiting to fill a vacancy, you may not be able to find anybody who fits the person description. You might also want to give people who do not yet meet the person specification a chance to work at a higher level. In such cases you will need to provide additional training to bring these people to the required level.

Identify affected individuals

Arising out of your analysis of corporate policies, mandatory training, business needs and job skill requirements, you will be able to identify which groups of employees will need what training. For example, all new managers will need training on the basics of management, and all electronics assembly people will need training on electrostatic protection.

Effective training processes need to be managed at the level of the individual, so the next step is to identify those individuals who are part of the group which needs the training. This task is made a great deal simpler by computerized personnel and training records. If each person's job is given a job code, the computer can print out a report on the people who have a particular type of job and have yet to receive the required training.

This task is made even easier if the personnel and training records are part of the same database. If you have separate records, you will need to update the training database every time someone joins, leaves or changes jobs.

| Enter potential needs on training records |

A training record should not only list the courses a person has attended but also the training a person needs. It is easier to prepare a training plan if the record gives a range of dates for when the training is required. The potential need can be in the form of either a course or a skill.

It is important that the training record is a live reflection of current training requirements. It should be revised any time a new training requirement is identified. This can be after appraisal, when a training request form is received or after an individual has attended an assessment centre. This means that an up-to-date training plan can be pulled off the system at any time of the year.

| Produce training requirement reports |

A training record shows the training that individuals have completed and the training that they need to do. The next step is to sift through all the training requirements so you can evaluate the needs and estimate the amount of training that needs to be done. This can be done manually, but it is much quicker if you have computerized training records.

A computer can produce training requirement reports that list:

- all the people who have requested a particular course,
- all the people who need a particular skill,
- the amount and type of training requested by a particular organization.

Needs evaluation

All training requests need to be validated to ensure the training is both appropriate and necessary. The amount of effort and time required to validate the training requirements depends on the quality of the input received. The best time to evaluate training needs is when the needs are being identified. This is why it is worth spending the time to run development open days and to train managers in development needs analysis. In an ideal situation the training administrator should only need to perform a quick check when the training department receives the training requests. These checks are shown in Figure 2.7.

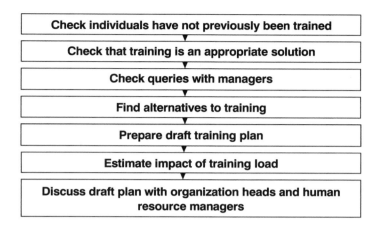

Figure 2.7   *Process for evaluating training needs*

| Check individuals have not previously been trained |

It is amazing how many requests for training involve people who have already been trained. Sometimes this is because the person has forgotten the name of the course. On other occasions it is because a nomination has been put forward without consulting the person concerned. Whatever the reason, it is highly embarrassing when people turn up to courses they have already completed.

Usually this problem can be caught when the training request is entered on the training record. This is why it is absolutely essential to have accurate training records. If you forget to amend the training record when a person has completed a required training course, you could find that the person will be automatically renominated.

Even if the training records are not as accurate as they should be, many duplications can be identified by an experienced training administrator. As a further precaution, it is worth getting the trainers to review the training requirement reports.

| Check that training is an appropriate solution |

Sometimes a business problem cannot be solved by a training solution. Where this is the case, it is the responsibility of the training department to make this known. However, if a training analyst says that a business problem cannot be solved by training, and does not suggest any alternatives, the organization will soon get the impression that the training department is being inflexible and is not interested in the rest of the business.

If training is to be an integral part of a business's change process, it has the duty and responsibility to suggest alternative approaches when a training solution is not appropriate.

Many of the individual 'training' requests the training department receives are unsuitable for the person concerned or are inappropriate performance problem solutions.

> Some time ago I was observing a report-writing course. One of the students came up to me and said that he had been on report-writing courses five times before. Being surprised by this, I asked whether he really couldn't write reports. 'Oh, I can write reports all right,' he said, 'I just refuse to write them!'

The training administrator and trainers should look through the training requirement reports to see whether any of the requirements seem to be inappropriate or unsuitable. This again underlines the value of having experienced trainers and training administrators who have extensive local knowledge.

> Check queries with managers

When it is suspected that training is not an appropriate solution, you should check this out with the individual's manager. The following are examples of questions that you can ask the manager:

- Is there an important business or strategic need for this training?
- Does the individual already have the knowledge and skills?
- Is the individual willing to use the knowledge and skills?
- Has the individual received this training before?
- Does the individual have the ability to be trained?

To demonstrate how these questions are used for determining whether training is an appropriate solution, let's take the example of the student who refused to write reports even though he had been on a report-writing course five times before.

In answer to the first question, there is a business need for training in report writing. The second question asks whether the individual has the skill and knowledge. As he admitted he could write a report, the answer to this question is 'Yes'. The answer to the third question is 'No' – the individual is not willing to use his report-writing skills. The answers to these questions tell us that training would not be a suitable solution for this person.

Contrast this with a person who is unable to write reports. She needs to write reports as part of her job, so there is a business requirement for this skill. If we were to hold a gun to her head, she still would not be able to write a report, so we know she does not have the knowledge or skill. She has not been trained before, so it is not simply a matter of her forgetting how to write reports. We would then ask whether she has the ability to be trained. It is only after making all these checks that we would say that training is a suitable solution for this person.

> Find alternatives to training

If training is not an appropriate solution, other options need to be found.

If there is no important business or strategic need for training, we should not put people on courses just for the sake of it. 'No action required' is a perfectly acceptable alternative.

If a person already has the skills and knowledge, we have to look at what is preventing them from performing. The person might be willing, but inadequate resources or poor procedures are hindering their performance. In this case, we should recognize their willingness and help them remove their barriers. A counselling session might be required if a personal problem or unhelpful attitude is the source of the difficulty.

We may have to provide refresher training if the person has already been trained, but it is more likely that on-the-job coaching and practice will be required.

If a person does not have sufficient ability for training to be economic, we would have to consider redeploying them and finding someone else to do the job. We would certainly have to re-examine our recruitment procedures and selection standards.

In the case of the person who wouldn't write reports, he had the skills and knowledge but was unwilling to make use of them. If there were no obstacles, we would be led to the conclusion that we are dealing with an attitude problem.

So, instead of sending this person on yet another report-writing course, a better answer would be for him to be counselled by his manager. This is obviously not a training solution. If any training were to be required, it would be to send the manager on a counselling course.

Counselling   Counselling is a critical skill for managers and it is especially important when training needs are being identified. The steps in the counselling process are:

1. Set climate.
2. Set expectations.
3. Seek counsellee's views of strengths and weaknesses.
4. Agree a development plan.
5. Summarize.

Chapter 4 deals with the counselling process in more detail. Although the process there describes a training manager counselling a trainer, the techniques are just as applicable to appraisal and development discussions.

> Prepare a draft training plan

When you have validated the training requirements you are in a position to put a draft training plan together. This should include estimates of:

- the number of trainer-days you think you will have to provide,
- the spread of the training load over the year,
- the cost of the training,
- the number of days of training per employee.

We cover how to put a detailed training plan together in Chapter 6.

> Estimate impact of training load

Take the draft training plan and consider its impact from two perspectives:

1. the impact on the training department,
2. the impact on the organization.

The impact on the training department is really a question of whether it has the capability, space, budget and resources to meet the demand. If it does not have the capability to deliver the demand, now is the time to signal that you may need more resources.

The impact on the organization is a little more subtle. Try asking yourself the following questions to help you understand the impact:

- What do the estimated hours of training per person mean in terms of people being away from the workplace?

- What are the expected short-term penalties, in increased production times and costs, compared with the long-term benefits?
- How many people can you afford to have absent from one department at the same time?
- What other claims are there on the budget you need to deliver the training plan?

> Discuss draft plan with organization heads and human resource managers

Considering the impact of the training puts you in a good position for discussing the draft plan with senior management, departmental managers and human resource managers. The purpose of this step is to get 'buy-in' from the stakeholders before you go public with the final plan. It is far better to deal with 'fatal flaws' and objections at this stage than later on in the training cycle.

You can discuss what the demand and training load mean to avoid 'nasty surprises' later in the year. You can get agreement to the proposed budget. You can discuss issues. You can discuss whether all the requested training is appropriate.

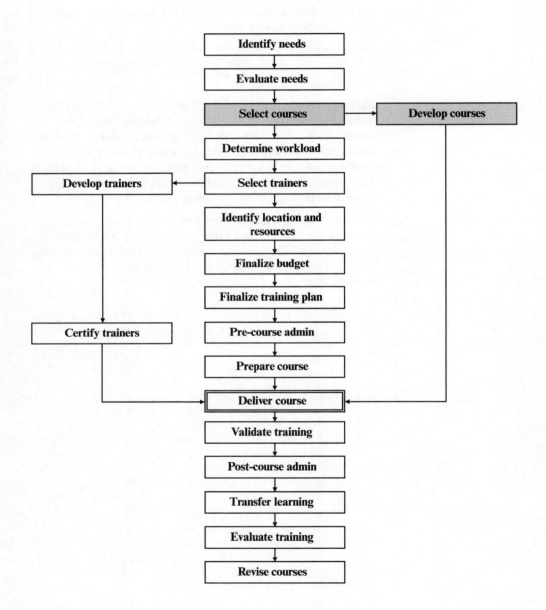

Figure 3.1   Training courses

3 Training courses

In this chapter we will be covering two more steps of the training process:

- select courses,
- develop courses.

Having established that training is appropriate for the identified development needs, the next step is to find courses that meet the needs. We have to make choices about whether we buy or develop our courses. Developing a course from scratch can be both expensive and time consuming. Even purchasing a course that exactly matches all the requirements is not as easy as it sounds.

Course selection

When it comes to selecting courses you have the following options:

- using an existing course,
- modifying an existing course,
- buying or licensing an external course,
- developing your own course,
- using an 'in-house' course,
- using a public course.

Whichever of these options you choose, you need to consider the availability of existing material and the urgency of and demand for the course. Figure 3.2 is an algorithm that will help you make this decision.

```
Consider using company course
```

First, check whether a suitable course already exists within your own training department. If you're fortunate, and you have a good system for storing your materials, you will be able to find a course on the shelf that exactly fits the bill. If you are managing a new training department, the chances of your finding a suitable course on the shelf are considerably reduced.

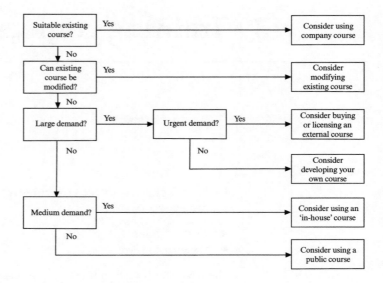

Figure 3.2   *An algorithm for selecting courses*

If you work for a small company, your search may have to end there. However, don't give up too quickly if your first searches draw a blank. You'll be surprised how many courses are developed and run over the years. Tracking these courses down can be a bit like finding a needle in a haystack.

First try the personnel department – personnel often get called on to run training courses. Also try asking supervisors and section managers – sometimes managers independently arrange training courses for their own people.

Did your company disband its training department some years ago? This can be a cyclical process. In good times training departments expand, and in difficult times training is often one of the first activities to be hit. If you are fortunate, the trainers may still be in the company but working in other departments. In these circumstances you will have to use all your powers of tact, persuasion and diplomacy. Nurture these ex-trainers. Their cupboards, shelves and filing cabinets are often gold-mines of training material.

If you work in a large or multinational company, you will have a much larger search area with which to contend. Spend some time on the telephone to the other training departments within your company. Ask for copies of their training catalogues. Follow up items that you read in the house magazines. Check out rumours you hear on the grapevine. It can take some time and persistence to get to the right person and the right training course, but it can be very rewarding.

Another approach is to form links with training managers in other companies in your area. This is always a good idea because it is very useful to exchange notes and compare methods of working. You may also find that it will be mutually beneficial to exchange training material – provided that no proprietary information is involved.

Despite all your efforts you may still not be able to find an existing course that will meet your needs. Even more frustrating will be the times when you are faced with the classic response of: 'I only threw that out last week – I didn't think that it would ever be needed again!'

> Consider modifying an existing course

Having exhausted all the possibilities for finding a suitable existing course, the next step is to see whether any other course could be modified to meet the need.

How easy this is depends on how the course was originally developed. Some courses are so tightly structured that it is impossible to remove parts of the course without destroying the structure of the whole, or losing the meaning of the individual parts. Any change in one part of this type of course will have a ripple effect through the entire course. You will find yourself entering into a major rewrite.

If the course has a modular structure, the tasks of modification and adaptation become much easier. Parts can be added, removed and rearranged until you have the course you require.

When you come to develop your own courses you should consider using modular structures which are easy to adapt for future requirements. In some areas of training, such as management training, the content will remain constant over many years. Yes, the emphasis may change and some topics may be added or subtracted, but the basics will still be the same. Good management is still good management whatever you like to call it. Good managers have been exhibiting the same skills over the centuries.

An introduction to management will nearly always have modules on:

- communication,
- motivation,

- leadership,
- the role of the manager,
- coaching and counselling,
- decision making,
- planning and organizing,
- meetings,
- delegating,
- interviewing.

You also might want to throw in modules on time and stress management. To do all these topics justice would probably take about 60 hours.

A menu of these modules, showing what is involved for each subject, will help you or your client prioritize and make decisions about the content. See Figure 3.3 for an excerpt from a typical menu.

There is a great deal of argument among trainers about the use of 'training menus' or 'training catalogues'. Many trainers feel uneasy about giving clients a menu because they feel the customers will just choose what they 'fancy'. You can avoid this danger by being present to provide advice when the customer is making a selection.

One of the main advantages of a menu is that you can quickly draw up a specification for a course which is based on your interpretation of the customer's requirements. Any misunderstanding is soon flushed out by presenting the specification to the customer.

> Consider buying or licensing an external course

If you have a large and urgent demand, you will need to buy or license an external course.

Buying suitable courses

Even if you have a large budget, which few of us do, finding a suitable course can still be very difficult. Looking through magazines and putting yourself on mailing lists can be helpful, but be warned that you will have to spend some time wading through all the mail you will receive. You will also need a very good filing system to recover the relevant brochure when you need it. A small database on a computer will help you retrieve the information, although you will have to be very disciplined about inputting the data as you receive it.

Some courses come as a complete package with transparencies, lesson plans, student materials and a video. Look very carefully at packages that come with a video as standard. Sometimes I feel that a video has been included

```
BASICS OF MANAGEMENT

A. Role of the manager (3 hr)

            1. Challenges of management (0.4 hr)
            a) Video: 'Role of the Supervisor'                          0.2 hr
            b) Discussion: Challenges facing participants               0.2 hr

            2. Functions of management (2.6 hr)
            a) Exercise: 'Operation Land Deal'                          1.3 hr
            b) Case Study: 'Computer Systems Inc'                       1.3 hr

B. Decision making and problem solving (4.5 hr)

            1. Decision making (2.5 hr)
            a) Lecturette: What is decision making?                     0.3 hr
            b) Lecturette: Decisions & problem solving                  0.2 hr
            c) Lecturette: The steps of decision making                 0.5 hr
            d) Example: 'Replacement Windows' case study               0.5 hr
            e) Exercise: 'The New Cars' case study                      1.0 hr

            2. Problem solving (2.0 hr)
            a) Discussion: Review of problem solving                    0.3 hr
            b) Exercise: 'Carry the Torch' case study                   1.7 hr

C. Communication (2 hr)

            1. Communication principles
            a) Lecturette: Communications model                         0.4 hr

            2. Communication barriers
            a) Exercise: 'Silencers Ltd'                                0.4 hr
            b) Exercise: 'Chinese Whispers'                             0.4 hr

            3. Communication helps
            a) Exercise: Feedback                                       0.5 hr
            b) Lecturette: Effective communication                      0.3 hr

D. Understanding finance (2.5 hr)

            1. Budgetary control (2.5 hr)
            a) Lecturette: Budgeting process                            0.3 hr
            b) Lecturette: Cash forecasting                             0.3 hr
            c) Lecturette: The profit and loss account                  0.6 hr
            d) Lecturette: The balance sheet                            0.3 hr
            e) Exercise: 'XYZ plc' budgetary planning                   1.0 hr
```

Figure 3.3 *Excerpt from a training menu*

because it is the 'thing to do' rather than being an essential part of the training.

Also look out for whether you have been given the copyright to make photocopies of the student materials. Otherwise, you might find yourself with the unexpected cost of purchasing more student materials every time you run the course. Some of these materials are very well produced and you may want to use them instead of photocopies. This is fine if you do this knowingly when you buy the package.

You also might like to look at the support you get with these packages. For example, there may be no 'trainer training'. This is all right if you have very experienced trainers, who have an in-depth understanding of the subject. Otherwise you might find that you are leaving your trainers very exposed – especially with the 'livelier' classes.

Licensing courses   There is another approach you can take if you do not have enough time to develop your own course. You can have your own trainers licensed to run a commercial course. You will have to pay to have your own trainers trained. Additionally, you may have to pay a fee to give you the rights to run the course, plus a licence fee every time the course is run. Licensing has a large initial cost, but the more people you put through the course the more cost effective it becomes. Another reason for needing a reasonable demand to make this approach viable is that it can take up to four courses to bring a trainer up to speed. (See the section on trainer certification in Chapter 4.)

Licensing is not commonly advertised, but you may notice one or two advertisements in the training magazines. Even though a training company may not advertise the licensing option, a surprising number will be willing to negotiate the licensing of their courses if you are likely to put some more business their way.

> Consider developing your own course

Even assuming that you have all the expertise and time, it is only economic to develop your own course if you have a large demand. You can either use the expertise of your own trainers or you can hire consultants to develop the course for you. This will prove more expensive than using your own staff to develop the course, so only follow this approach if the course is specific to your company, and there is a large and urgent demand for the course.

Developing your own courses is covered later in this chapter.

> Consider using an 'in-house' course

An 'in-house' course is one where a training company runs one of their courses on your premises. This keeps your travel costs low and training providers usually charge less. An 'in-house' course is a good solution when there is medium demand for a course that is not in your own repertoire.

Using consultants continually over a long period is considerably more expensive than having your own staff.

If you have to use consultants over a long period, it is worthwhile negotiating the fees. Most consultants do not expect to have paid work every day of the year. They factor the time they spend selling into their daily fees. This means they might be willing to give you a discount in return for a guaranteed medium- to long-term commission.

You are more likely to get a discount from one-person bands and small groups of consultants. Surprisingly, the big institutions stick to their standard rates even in times of recession. Don't let this put you off. Make sure that you negotiate with the head of the institution. If you still meet resistance over discounts, try talking in terms of free places.

Some companies charge by the trainer-day and this can be very expensive when a course needs two trainers. If the course requires a lead trainer and a co-trainer, you can save some money by offering to supply your own trainer as the co-trainer. This is particularly appropriate when the co-trainer's role is to observe and give feedback.

> Consider using a public course

Where there is a small or individual demand, the most cost-effective approach is to send people on an externally run public course. Judging the quality of external courses is difficult without going on all the courses yourself – which is perhaps not the best use of your time. This is especially true if you are only going to send one or two people on each course.

The reputation of the company running the course and the experiences of other training managers can help here. Don't be afraid of asking for the names of companies that have used the course. When you telephone these companies you nearly always get an honest appraisal of the course.

Talk to the providers of the training and to the potential delegates. This also will help you form an opinion of the course's suitability. Some training companies hold open days where they present extracts from their courses. This will help you gain a feeling for the style, content and professionalism.

Developing your own courses

In many ways developing your own courses can be very satisfying, even though it can be expensive and time consuming.

Course development is an extremely large subject. It is very important that you understand what it involves because it is a vital and intrinsic part of the training process. Being such a large subject, the development process really requires its own dedicated book. However, the following description should give you a very good idea of what it is all about.

The process I use has evolved over the years. Like all the processes described in this book, developing your own training courses is much messier than the neat, linear diagram shown in Figure 3.4. Real life is usually a great deal more circular and iterative.

You don't have to follow this process slavishly. By all means explore some other methods of course development and – if you do get lost – you can use this process as a guide for getting you back on track. The process given here will help you produce excellent training materials but it is no substitute for your own creativity. You could follow the process to the letter and still produce a deadly dull course.

> Define subject

The training needs analysis should have clearly defined the subject matter of the course. Do make sure that the training you think you have been asked to develop is what is really required.

Lack of clarity is one of the most common pitfalls. For example, you might have been requested to develop a course on planning and control. This seems simple – but is it 'project management' or 'personal organization' that is required? 'Project management' would cover subjects like critical path analysis and Gantt charts, whereas 'personal organization' would include topics such as time management and coping with paperwork.

Another example of this is the common request for 'finance for non-financial managers'. Typically this course would cover balance sheets, profit and loss statements, and the common financial ratios. However, in large companies most managers would never have to deal with these. Although these subjects might be interesting, they would only be useful if the managers were to leave the company and set up their own businesses. What is really required is an explanation of how their departments' budgets are formed and controlled.

> Describe aims

The aims of a course should be closely related to the business requirements that first generated the need for a new course. It is here you describe what you want the people to know, or do, when they have left the course. You will also want to describe the effect the training will have on the business results or the business environment.

If you have carried out a good needs analysis, you will already know what you are trying to change or improve. If

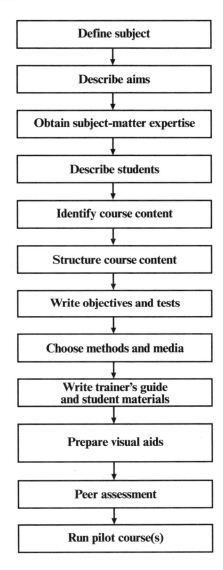

Figure 3.4 Process for developing training courses

so, this step of the process should be comparatively easy. Also think of this step as a checkpoint. After you have written down what you believe to be the aims of the course, you should go back to your clients and check whether you have interpreted their requirements correctly.

Do not fall into the trap of thinking that training is the complete solution. A course is usually only a solution to part of a much larger problem. Therefore, you should be very careful that the aims of the course describe which part of the problem the course will solve.

Identifying the aims of your training is essential for evaluating training effectiveness as well as developing the course. Aims are the indicators of what you are trying to achieve and allow you to 'complete the loop' as far as the training process is concerned. Chapter 12 covers evaluation in detail.

> Obtain subject-matter expertise

Having described the subject and aims, a source of subject-matter expertise is next required. In many cases you will have been chosen to develop a course because you are already an expert in the relevant subject. If you are not an expert then you could do the research required but this can take a great deal of time – often more time than you have available to develop the course. If there is not enough time to become an expert, you will need to call on other people to give you the benefit of their knowledge.

> Describe students

As you might expect, a description of the students should include their current level of skill and knowledge. More surprisingly, it also should describe the types of people you will be training, along with their attitudes, physical characteristics, what they enjoy and what they dislike. The reason for going into all this detail is that it can make a tremendous difference to how you approach the development of the course.

> One technical training course required service engineers to read vast amounts of written material. If the course's authors had written a student description, they would have realized that service engineers are very practical people who spend little of their leisure time reading. The course developers would also have realized that the engineers would find a text-based course boring and frustrating.

Physical characteristics should include hearing ability, sight and strength. All these will influence the training methods, practical exercises, and the colour and size of the visual aids.

> I was once running a train-the-trainer course in Singapore and one of the trainees was having difficulty in choosing a suitable training project. As he was an engineer I suggested he teach the resistor colour code. (The resistor colour code is a numbering system where numbers are represented by coloured rings.)
> When I was coaching him on 'Describe the students' I emphasized how important it is to describe the physical characteristics of the students – including colour blindness.
> I then heard laughter and chattering in Chinese from the rest of the class. When I asked what was causing the laughter, I was told that the

student himself was colour blind. I had made the incorrect assumption that engineers would not be colour blind – there is nothing like being hoisted by your own petard.

If the students come to training with a negative attitude about the course, you know you will have to allow extra time to diffuse these feelings. Learning cannot occur while grievances are being aired.

Above all, build up a mental picture of your students which will allow you to develop the course specifically for them. Novelists often use this technique: when they are writing a novel they imagine that they are telling the story to a typical reader who is sitting in front of them.

> Identify course content

The content bridges the gap between the students' current level and the level they should have after the learning experience. The use of the term 'learning experience' rather than 'course' is deliberate. Only part of the required behavioural change can develop during the short duration of a course. It is unrealistic to expect a course to do any more than develop an awareness of the required changes. A course also provides supervised practice of the new skills.

In very simple terms, you should take the desired knowledge and skills (as described by the course aims) and subtract the students' current knowledge and skills (as given in the student description).

A useful technique for doing this is called 'mind mapping'. Mind mapping is a creative technique that is described in Tony Buzan's book *Use Your Head*. 'Mind maps' are also known as 'spidergrams' or 'bubble diagrams'.

To apply this technique you first draw a bubble shape in the middle of a sheet of paper. You then write the subject of the course in this shape. The main categories of topics that make up the course are written in 'bubbles' that are attached to branches radiating from the central bubble shape. You can then have the detailed topics radiating from the main category bubbles (see Figure 3.5).

> Structure course content

This is where you determine the structure and timing of the course. It helps if you have an overall framework to work within. A good framework for the structure of a course comes from the 'Army School of Training':

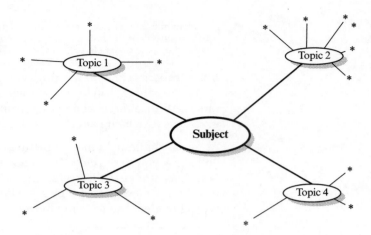

* = detailed topics

Figure 3.5   *Using a mind map to determine course content*

- Tell 'em what you're goin' to tell 'em.
- Tell 'em.
- Tell 'em what you told 'em.

Or put another way:

- overview,
- body and
- summary.

The main course modules are to be found in the body of the course. The body needs to be sequenced so that there is a logical flow from one topic to another. A logical flow goes from:

- the simple to the complex,
- the general to the specific and
- the known to the unknown.

Although the detailed topics shown on the mind map form the content of the course, the larger bubbles will not necessarily be the course modules. You created the mind map while you were coming to understand the relationships between the detailed topics. This means that the structure that develops may not be the most efficient one for learning the subject. Some people can write down the correct order straight away, but I find it easier to use 'Post-it' notes.

Start by writing one of the course components (it doesn't matter which one) on a 'Post-it'. Then stick this on a sheet of flip-chart paper and ask the following questions to help decide which components should come before or after:

- What has to be taught before this component can be taught?
- What can be taught now that this component has been taught?
- What can be taught at the same time?

The answers to these questions will suggest which components should be stuck on to the chart next. Keep asking these questions as each new 'Post-it' is added. Draw lines to connect the components and a network will be built up showing a logical sequence for the course.

There are two basic methods for determining the length of the course. The first is to estimate the duration of each component and simply add them up. The second is to start with a fixed time and see what you can fit in.

Obviously the second method is the less satisfactory, but there is always something that can usefully be taught – no matter how little time you have. It's just a matter of you, and the person who requested the course, being aware of the resulting limitations and consequences.

The effectiveness of a limited amount of training depends very much on the students' current state of knowledge. If there is no existing knowledge, any amount of training will make an improvement. Where knowledge is very limited, simply communicating 'three things you need to know to get you through the day' can have a large and significant effect.

When there is a limited amount of time, or when you have to shorten a course to reduce costs, there are only two viable ways of doing this. The first is to look at the training methodology to see if there are more efficient ways of meeting the same objectives. For example, you might use the same exercise to give practice for both coaching and counselling rather than having two separate exercises.

The other method is to take content out of the course. In this case the decisions you have to make are all about what you put in and what you leave out.

We shouldn't make the mistake of thinking that we can shorten a course by simply running faster or exerting very high pressure on the students. The effectiveness of the course will suffer. A training menu described earlier in this chapter is one method of helping the client prioritize what should be done in the available time.

> One of my clients once asked for all the content shown in the training menu to be taught in four days. A quick addition of the times soon revealed that it would take more than 60 hours to complete the training. Further discussions about the client's requirements and priorities resulted in 50 hours of training, spread over five days. To keep disruption to a minimum the course was split into two parts. The first part was to run for two working days and the second, three-day module was to run three weeks later from Thursday to Saturday.

When you have to make complex decisions it is better to analyse the content of the course very carefully against certain criteria. Agree the criteria with your client, because you will be using them for including or rejecting course content. The actual criteria you use depend very much on your client's requirements, so it is very important that these criteria are determined very early on in the process. An example of how you can use criteria to determine the content of a course is given in Appendix 6.

The output of structuring the course content should be a course agenda or programme. If the course is short and uncomplicated the agenda will be like a meeting agenda (see Figure 3.6). You would use the type of course programme shown in Figure 3.7 when the course is longer and more complex.

> Write objectives and tests

An objective is a statement of what the students should be able to do once they have completed a section of the course. It is an indicator of what learning has taken place. Notice that I said indicator rather than measure. Learning is what goes on inside a student's head and therefore cannot be directly measured. So while it is perfectly possible to have an objective of 'understanding interpersonal skills', this is not very useful for measuring the effectiveness of the training. The students could be asked whether they understand interpersonal skills, or the trainer could gain a 'feeling' for how much has been understood by general questioning or observing body language.

Another approach is to use indirect indicators such as something the students should be able to do if learning has taken place. The skill in this approach is deciding what these indicators should be.

For example, a student who really understands interpersonal skills should be able to recognize and use all the different categories of verbal behaviour. Although a trainer can hear the trainees using the verbal behaviours, checking whether somebody has recognized something is a

```
┌─────────────────────────────────────────────────────────┐
│  AGENDA                                                   │
│                                                           │
│  Introduction                                      9:00   │
│  – Introductions                                          │
│  – Expectations                                           │
│  – Agenda                                                 │
│                                                           │
│  Why total quality management?                     9:20   │
│  – The need                                               │
│  – Initial steps                                          │
│  – Quality gurus                                          │
│  – Birth of a strategy                                    │
│  – Key elements of the strategy                           │
│                                                           │
│  What is quality?                                  9:40   │
│  – Definition                                             │
│  – Standard                                               │
│  – System                                                 │
│  – Measurement                                            │
│                                                           │
│  Quality is free?                                 11:00   │
│  – Cost of quality                                        │
│  – Conformance                                            │
│  – Non-conformance                                        │
│  – Lost opportunities                                     │
│                                                           │
│  Who's the customer?                              11:20   │
│  – Suppliers                                              │
│  – Internal customers                                     │
│  – External customers                                     │
│                                                           │
│  Tools of the trade                               12:00   │
│  – Problem-solving process                                │
│  – Quality improvement process                            │
│  – Process capability                                     │
│  – Fishbone diagram                                       │
│  – Pareto analysis                                        │
│  – Forcefield analysis                                    │
│  – Interactive skills                                     │
│                                                           │
│  Where do we go from here?                        16:00   │
│                                                           │
│  Review                                           16:30   │
└─────────────────────────────────────────────────────────┘
```

Figure 3.6   *Course agenda*

little more difficult. One way round this would be to show a videotape of a number of different behaviours and have the student state the name of each behaviour.

The next question is how many of the responses would have to be correct to satisfy the trainer that the student had really understood interpersonal skills. Would it be 5 per cent, 20 per cent, 80 per cent or 100 per cent?

Taking all this into account, the objectives for 'understanding' interpersonal skills would look like this:

- Given a videotape showing 20 examples of verbal behaviour, the student will be able to name correctly at least 18 of the behaviours.

	DAY 1	DAY 2	DAY 3	DAY 4	DAY 5
8.00	Introduction	Motivation	Financial		Project
9.00	Role of the	and	planning		management
10.00	manager	leadership		Staff	(2)
11.00				selection	
Lunch			Effective		
13.00	Communication		meetings		
14.00		Managing			Stress
15.00	Decision	time	Coaching	Project	management
16.00	making		and	management	
17.00		Wrap-up	counselling	(1)	Wrap-up
Evening	*Desert Survival exercise*		*The Numbers Game*	Plan project	

Figure 3.7   *An example of a course programme*

- Given a list of 11 verbal behaviours, the student should be able to give correct examples for a minimum of 10 of those behaviours.

A good objective has three components:

1. Behaviour – what the student will be expected to do.
2. Conditions – the conditions under which the behaviour has to occur.
3. Standard – the acceptable level of performance.

In the interpersonal skills example the behaviours are:

- naming behaviours,
- giving examples of behaviours.

The conditions are:

- 'Given a videotape showing 20 examples of verbal behaviour...'
- 'Given a list of 11 verbal behaviours...'

and the standards are:

- '...at least 18 out of 20 behaviours correctly named.'
- '...a minimum of 10 correct examples of behaviours.'

Writing objectives is hard work, but if they are done to the above standard writing the tests becomes very easy. As a good objective gives the standards and conditions under which the behaviour should occur, it also gives the conditions and standards for the test.

A test does not have to be an 'examination'. The minimum condition is that the trainer should be able to observe the desired behaviour so the standards can be checked to see whether the training has been effective.

Objectives are an essential tool for course developers, course presenters and students. Course developers use objectives to determine the content of the course; course presenters use them to measure what has been learnt; and students use objectives as an overview of what they are going to learn. Be careful of giving students the same detail on the objectives that you would use for presenting or developing a course. Although detailed objectives are required for presenters and developers, students would be confused if they were presented with the following objective at the beginning of the course:

> 'By the end of the module you will be able to identify the central processing unit, the random access memory, the read-only memory, the visual display unit and the input/output interfaces.'

After all, if they already knew what these terms meant they would not have to attend the course.

A better objective to give a student at the start of a course would be:

> 'By the end of the module you will be able to identify all the main components of a microcomputer.'

Some objectives describe behaviours or conditions that can only exist in the classroom, such as 'will have participated in three simulations'.

It is much better to have objectives that describe behaviour and conditions that can be measured both inside and outside the classroom. This allows you to monitor learning inside the classroom and monitor the transfer of learning to the business.

Written question-and-answer tests should only be used when it is not possible to use a practical example of a task that has to be done in the workplace.

As a final check, make sure that every objective has a corresponding test and that every test item is related to an objective.

Choose methods and media

There are many different points of view about what are the 'best' training methods. The following is a summary of the most frequent arguments:

- Should courses be 'trainer led' or 'self-directed'?
- Should students be told the facts or be encouraged to go on a 'voyage of discovery'?

- Should you use a case study or should you use a real-life example?
- Should you start with a 'big-picture' overview and then work down to the details, or should you start with the basic 'building blocks' and develop the learning upwards from there?

Some trainers insist that trainees be given freedom of choice. One method of doing this is to have a course map that has alternative routes through the course (see Figure 3.8).

The students are allowed to take any of the routes through the course as long as they have completed the prerequisites. The prerequisite modules are the ones that are above, and on the same path as, the module the student wants to take.

But does this approach mean that the trainees have a real choice? Do they have enough information to come to sensible conclusions? It could be argued that if the students did have enough information to make rational rather than random choices, they wouldn't need to take the course in any case!

Proponents of any training method can be very persuasive with the arguments they bring forward to support their favourite approach. Training managers, personnel managers and directors should be very careful of being seduced into spending huge amounts of money on new training technologies that are the 'only way to train'.

There are two other warnings when it comes to training technology. The first is that the vision of what people want from the technology is often years in advance of what the technology is able to deliver today. The second, counterbalancing warning is not to look at technology with

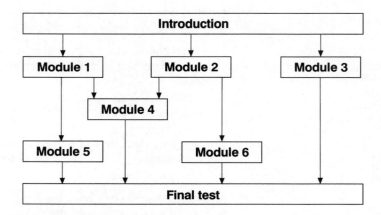

Figure 3.8　An example of a course map

a jaundiced eye, even though the last 20 demonstrations you attended were little more than gimmicks. One day you will miss that significant innovation you really need.

The truth is that there never will be one 'best' method or one 'best' medium for training people. Every student is different and every person learns in a different way. Some people have to know the detail first. Others couldn't possibly understand the detail until they have a mental framework to pin it on. Some people like facts and figures, others like a more inspirational approach to training.

There are many personality theories and questionnaires that claim to classify people into different types. Many of these are based on the work of Jung, who identified four basic classifications:

- thinker,
- feeler,
- sensor,
- intuitor.

Each approach has its own names for the four types, but usually the types fall into the following categories:

- logical people,
- people people,
- task-oriented people,
- intuitive/entrepreneurial people.

Given an understanding of how people are different, we can make better choices of which methods and media to use on our courses. Table 3.1 indicates how different types of people learn. It also shows the types of learning activities to which they respond.

Table 3.1 *Learning methods and media for different types of people*

	Suitable methods and media
Logical people	Lecture, reading, case studies, underlying theory, debate, programmed instruction
People people	Case studies, discussion, role play, games coaching, simulation
Task-oriented people	Practice, experimenting, simulation, demonstration, coaching, self-directed learning
Intuitive/ entrepreneurial people	Video, multimedia, discovery, OHPs, experimenting, simulation

This again emphasizes the importance of having a good description of the students who will be attending your course.

If you have a homogeneous group of students, you will have a good idea of which types of methods and media you should be using. If you have a varied group of people to teach, the chances are that there will be a fairly even spread of the four different types. In this case it would probably be advisable to have a wide range of differing methods and media so that you can reach as many different types of people as possible.

However, considering the learning preferences of the group is not all the story. Consideration should also be given to which methods and media are the most suitable for each part of the course. The best courses have a wide range of media and learning experiences.

Table 3.2 shows the range of media that are available, along with their advantages and disadvantages.

> Write trainer's guide and student materials

In one of his *Lettres Provinciales*, Blaise Pascal wrote: 'I have written a long letter because I did not have time to write it shorter.' In the same way, it is much easier and quicker to write a long course than a short one. It takes time to analyse what is essential and what could be left out. The virtue of writing at length is that you will probably include everything you need. The problem is that you will never know what you could have left out. Writing the materials as lean as possible has the advantage of producing succinct training and it will become obvious if anything has been left out.

Make sure that the manuscripts are given a really good proofread. Although it seems unfair, you have to come to terms with the fact that some students judge the overall quality of the materials on their first impressions. Spelling and grammatical errors interfere with their learning. If the materials have been written on a word processor, you will be able to put them through a spellchecker.

Some words of caution here. Only the very sophisticated spellcheckers, those which dabble in artificial intelligence, can do anything more than to tell you whether a particular word exists. Generally, spellcheckers don't take any account of the grammar, context or meaning of the words. So, a sentence such as: 'Thee employees took there complained too their manger' would hardly cause a spellchecker to stutter.

Table 3.2 *Advantages and disadvantages of different media*

Step	Advantages	Disadvantages
Presenter	Relatively quick and inexpensive, flexible response	Quality depends on the individual presenter
Flip chart	Inexpensive, flexible	Good handwriting required
Whiteboard	Clean, easy to alter	Difficult to clean if wrong pens used
Blackboard	Easy to alter	Dusty, reminiscent of school
Overhead transparencies	Easy and economic to produce, equipment widely available	Tendency to be over-used
35 mm slides	High quality, standard format, equipment widely available	Equipment unreliable, slides prone to jamming
35 mm slide/tape	Moderately easy and economic to produce	Unreliable synchronization of audiotape to slide projector
Videos	Wide range of videos available, reliable	Expensive, difficult to make, varying standards around the world
16 mm film	Good quality	Expensive and difficult to produce, unreliable, equipment obsolescent
Text	Fairly easy and economic to produce and revise	Not suitable for all students
Audiocassette	Fairly easy and economic to produce, equipment widely available, easily used outside classroom	Limited by lack of visual content
Text/tape	Economic and easy to produce, good combination of sound and visuals	Student has to keep pace with audiotape
Computer-based training	Paced to student, wide range of programs available	Expensive and time consuming to produce. Becoming very accessible as more homes and offices have access to multimedia computers
Interactive video	Paced to student, high-quality graphics	Expensive and time consuming to produce, very expensive equipment

There are also some grammar checkers on the market. The following shows what one of these made of the above example:

ARCHAIC: Thee
SHOULD 'too their' BE 'two' OR 'to their'?

The grammar checker caught some of the problems, but it didn't catch 'complained' instead of 'complaints' or 'manger' instead of 'manager'.

Also be very careful that you do not 'teach' the spellchecker to be a bad speller. When the spellchecker does not recognize a word it gives you the choice of skipping the word, correcting the word or adding the word to its dictionary. When you are working through a long document pressing the 'add' button almost becomes a reflex reaction and, before you know it, another misspelt word is added to the computer's dictionary. Another way of adding errors to a spellchecker's dictionary is when you are convinced a misspelt word is correct. After all, you have been spelling the word this way for nearly all your life! For some unknown reason it is nearly always much easier to add than to remove a word from electronic dictionaries.

Although there is no substitute for a thorough proofread, a spellchecker is a very useful tool. It can spot many errors that we overlook. A computer, unlike the human brain, does not 'see' what it thinks should be there.

Trainer's guide   A good trainer's guide includes:

1. Course objectives.
2. Course programme.
3. Course prerequisites.
4. Course pre-work.
5. Number of training and break-out rooms required.
6. List of student materials.
7. List of equipment required.
8. List of audiovisual materials (transparencies, posters, prepared flip charts, audiotapes and videotapes).
9. Room layout.
10. Preparation notes for each session.
11. Lesson plans for each session.
12. Masters for the overhead transparencies.

Items 1 to 7, taken together, form the course specification which provides essential information for the course administrator. The order shown above reflects the structure of a trainer's guide – not necessarily the order you would write it in.

If you have been following the process for developing training materials, you will find that you have already prepared some of the components of the trainer's guide. You would have already written the objectives (1) and you would also have determined the course programme (2).

The course prerequisites (3) are determined by comparing the course content with the student description. A prerequisite is a level of competence that a student should have before attending a course. It could be attendance at another course, a certain level of education or a particular skill.

You would normally identify the other components of the trainer's guide as you write the lesson plan. In fact, it is a good idea to have sheets of paper headed 'Student materials', 'Videotapes' etc. so that you can note the requirements as you identify them.

Lesson plans   Writing a course is writing the lesson plan. It is a 'script' that not only provides you with your 'lines' but also describes detailed timings, structure and activities.

There are many formats that you can use for a lesson plan. My preference is for a three-column format. The first column is for timings and type of activity, such as State, Ask, Stress, Action and Exercise. The middle column is reserved for the actual statements, questions and directions, and the third column lists the media. Figure 3.9 shows an example of this type of lesson plan. Notice that the timings are clock times. You have more than enough to do when you are running a course without adding up the times of the individual modules to see whether you are running to time.

> Prepare visual aids

Preparing the visual aids is something that can be done at any time during the development of the student materials and lesson plan. My preference is to do it as I am writing the lesson plan. As you develop the course, you should be

NEW COURSE		First module
08:30	**FIRST MODULE** (1 hr 20 min)	
	Introduction	
State:	Welcome to the new course.	OHP 1
Ask:	How many people have been on a similar course to this?	
Action:	Count the number of people and write this on a flip chart.	FLIP CHART
Stress:	That this course builds on similar courses.	
Show:	'Attending Courses'.	VIDEO

Figure 3.9   Example of a lesson plan format

constantly thinking whether a learning point could be better illustrated with a visual aid.

During this step of the process you should review the visual aids you have prepared so far, and create any additional visual aids that are required.

The most popular form of visual aid is the overhead projector transparency (OHP). Keep the OHP uncluttered and simple. Resist the temptation to put too much on it. A copy of an existing document rarely makes a good overhead. The following guidelines will help you produce OHPs:

- Don't make the lettering too small
  Rule of thumb: 18 point (approximately equivalent to 6 mm for capital letters) is about as small as you want to go; 44 point (15 mm) is good for titles and 28 point (10 mm) is good for the main text.
- Don't put too much on one OHP
  Rule of thumb: Six words per line and six lines per slide is a good guideline.
- Restrict the number of fonts that you use
  Rule of thumb: Restricting yourself to two proportionally spaced fonts plus careful use of bold and italics will cover most of your needs. Underlining is rarely necessary and OHPs usually look better without it. A good combination is a sans serif font (e.g. **Arial, Univers**) for the titles and a serif font (e.g. Times New Roman, Century Schoolbook) for the text.
- Restrict the number of colours that you use
  Rule of thumb: Two colours will cover most of your needs.

If you follow these guidelines you shouldn't go far wrong, but don't feel that you have to follow them slavishly. There will be times when you will have to bend these rules to get the effect that you want. The final test is what it looks like on the screen.

Computer programs such as Microsoft PowerPoint and Lotus Freelance will help you create professional transparencies quickly. You can also use PowerPoint and Freelance to produce the student notes. The 'Slide Sorter' views of these programs can be of great assistance in getting the structure of the course right. You can use the mouse to drag the slides to different positions (see Figure 3.10).

| Peer assessment |

Before you unleash your course on a group of unsuspecting students, it is a very good idea to have your colleagues

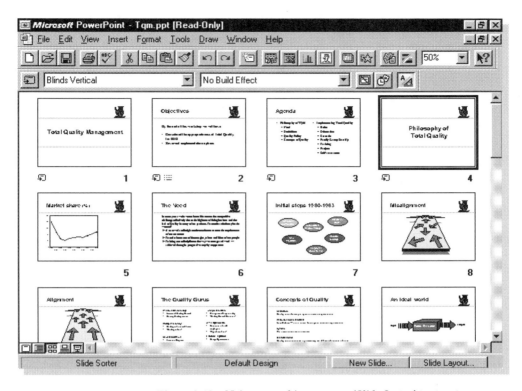

Figure 3.10 *Using a graphics program 'Slide Sorter' to structure a course*

review the materials. It is an even better idea to teach the course to your peers.

After all this time you will be too close to the course to notice even the more obvious mistakes. An experienced colleague will be able to spot the fatal flaws, annoying inconsistencies and irritating errors.

> Run pilot course(s)

Pilot courses are the 'test flights' for your newly developed course. With a brand new course you will normally need to run two pilot courses. The first, sometimes called a developmental test, is run to get all the bugs and gremlins out of the course. It is not essential to have representative students on the developmental course, but it is risky to have stakeholders present. A stakeholder is a person who has a vested interest in the course and could damage its reputation.

The reason for this is that the errors and the pauses will only serve to distort an observer's perception of the course.

Reports of the 'disaster' will still be heard long after the course has established itself as a great success.

The second pilot course should have students who are representative of the target student population. This second course is a good time to invite some stakeholders along to observe and give some feedback. The course will be sufficiently developed to prevent annoying errors from getting in the way, but not so set in concrete that you would not be able to make changes based on the observers' feedback.

If the course is self-taught, you can take on the role of passive observer – only intervening if things start to go seriously wrong. It is much more difficult to be a passive observer when the course is trainer led and you are the only person who can run it. You will be too involved to notice all the subtle, and not so subtle, reactions to the course. In this case you need to enlist the services of a colleague. Provide a copy of the lesson plan and student materials and ask your colleague to do the observations for you.

If the course is large, and you are leading a team of training developers, you can either do all the observations yourself or take turns in making the observations.

When you are running a pilot course you must be extremely careful to avoid rationalizing away any negative reactions the students might have. It is all too easy to think that a problem was a chance occurrence. You might be persuaded that 'real' students wouldn't have the same difficulty. Always assume that minor difficulties, encountered on the pilot course, will become major problems if they are left uncorrected for the final version of the course.

Be a fly on the wall. Record any difficulty, hesitancy or problem. Avoid coming up with solutions or rewriting the material at this stage because you might miss some of the other problems. Try not to interfere with the training.

Immediately after the training get the students to fill in a written feedback form. Then have general discussions about what went well and what could have gone better. Again, don't try to solve any of the problems at this stage. Don't try to explain why you wrote in a particular way. Above all, don't argue if you think their comments are wrong. Just record, without editing, all their comments on a flip chart. Some students will make suggestions for changing the course. These should also be recorded. This does not commit you to making those changes if, after reflection, you do not agree with them.

Always try to understand why the student wanted to have that change. Even if the suggested change is not a good idea, there is nearly always an underlying problem that needs to be addressed. Other students might just feel uncomfortable about something or feel that something is 'not quite right'. By all means ask some questions to help you understand what the problem might be, but don't pressurize them to come up with explanations or solutions. After all, solving training problems is your job, not theirs.

When you have finished collecting information from the students, have a meeting with the trainers to get their feedback. Now you can work with the trainers to develop proposals on how the course should be changed, amended or revised.

Appendix 5 gives an example of how this process was used to develop a real course.

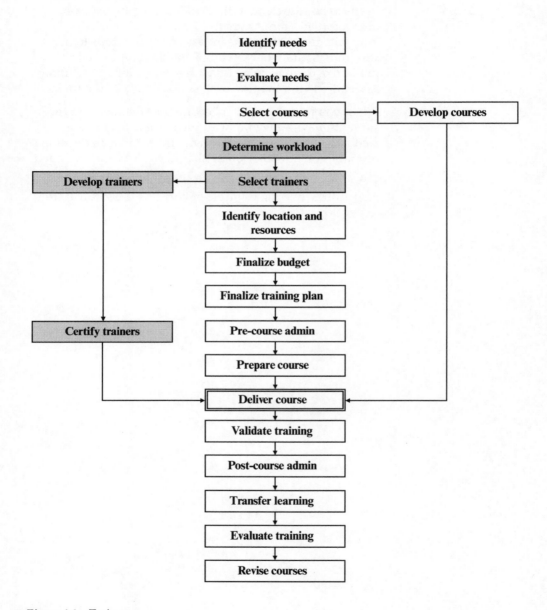

Figure 4.1 *Trainers*

4 Trainers

In this chapter we will be covering four more steps of the training process:

- determine workload,
- select trainers,
- develop trainers,
- certify trainers.

The first step is to determine the workload. If you have sufficient staff or contractors to meet the training needs, you can then select the most appropriate trainer(s) to run each of the identified courses. You also need to consider whether these trainers will need any further development.

If you cannot cover the load with your existing resources, you will need to recruit additional trainers or find more contractors. This will involve you in writing job descriptions and vacancy notices as well as interviewing prospective trainers. If you are unable to find experienced trainers you will need to consider which people would make good trainers and what training these new trainers should receive.

Even if you recruit experienced trainers, they may not have had experience of the type of training you will be asking them to provide. They will also need to undertake a programme of development. To do this you need to understand what skills and knowledge your trainers should have for these courses.

Once the trainers have the basic skills and competencies needed to run the courses, you still have to plan how they will learn to train the new courses that you will be running. This is the process of certification.

Determining the workload

When you decide how many trainers will be required, you have to make an estimate of the workload each trainer can handle. The factors you have to take into account are:

- the number of courses,
- the duration of the courses,
- face-to-face ratio (the amount of time a trainer spends in front of a class),
- the number of trainers needed to run each course,
- how much time is spent in preparing courses,
- how much time is spent in developing courses,
- how much time is spent in other activities such as planning, supervising and evaluating,
- the learning curve of new trainers.

Number and duration of courses

The number of courses you need to run depends on:

- the number of people you need to train,
- the number of people you can train per course.

The number of people you need to train comes from the needs analysis. The course specification will tell you the maximum number of people each course can accommodate, but don't base your estimates on this figure. It is unlikely you will be able to run with the maximum number on every course. The availability of people as well as sickness and cancellations will erode this figure. Always try to book the maximum number of people on to the course and you will probably find that you will be running the course with the optimum number of students.

Rule of thumb: Assume you will put people through the course at the rate of two-thirds of the maximum number.

If you find you can train people at a faster rate than this, nobody will complain if you finish a training programme ahead of time.

The course specification will give you the duration of the course.

Face-to-face ratio

The amount of time a trainer can spend in front of a class depends on many factors, such as the difficulty of the course and the number of different courses that the trainer has to train.

It is possible for trainers to spend 100 per cent of their time in the classroom if they have full administrative support and the courses always fill a complete week (it is difficult to schedule courses without any gaps between them).

Eventually fatigue will set in, with a corresponding decline in standards. If you have to support a massive training effort, and your trainers are committed to the programme, it is possible to sustain a face-to-face ratio of 80 per cent.

More realistically, you would expect trainers to spend some of their time on preparation, administration, revision of existing materials and development of new materials. The proportion of time spent on these activities will vary depending where the trainers are in their career development. We will consider what these proportions might be when we look at developing trainers.

Rule of thumb: You would normally expect trainers to have a face-to-face ratio of 50 per cent.

This is supported by data from several benchmarking exercises that I carried out with other companies.

Number of trainers per course

The number of trainers you need to run a course depends on the complexity of the course and the number of students on the course. These are the factors you take into account when you plan the number of trainers required for a new course. The course specification should tell you how many trainers you need for existing courses.

The complexity of a course is driven by:

- the course logistics (the amount of preparation and 'scene shifting' that has to be done before each session);
- the amount of observation, facilitation and coaching required;
- the amount of data processing that is required (e.g. running computer simulations or producing graphs and ratios from observation data).

It seems sensible to say that the more students you have, the more trainers you will need; and the more students each trainer has to deal with, the less effective the training becomes.

This would seem to be borne out by the argument about the size of classes in our schools. The problem of having a simple measure of effectiveness makes it difficult to put this hypothesis to the test. However, we had the opportunity to test it out when we introduced Trainee Centred Learning (TCL).

The idea behind Trainee Centred Learning is the same as that for self-paced learning:

- Students learn better at a pace which matches their own abilities.
- They do not move on to the next stage of learning until they have demonstrated competence at the previous stage.
- All the students have their own learning station and a set of training materials.
- Trainers are on hand to answer questions, demonstrate techniques and check that the course objectives are being met.

Using this approach it is intended that everybody leaves the course having reached a common standard, even though people may have taken different times to reach that standard.

Individually the time taken to go through the course depends on the person's own learning pace and starting ability, but the average duration can be used as a measure of training effectiveness.

When the course durations were correlated to the 'student-to-trainer' ratio we found, as expected, that the course duration increased as the ratio went up from 6:1 to 10:1. Imagine our surprise when the course duration also increased as the ratio fell below 6:1 (see Figure 4.2). While it is easy to explain the increase in duration with greater numbers of students in terms of longer waiting times, it is much harder to explain why the length of the course should increase when there are more trainers on hand.

We came to the conclusion that there must be an optimum level of trainer intervention. Too little contact from the trainer and the student starts to flounder. Too much contact and the trainer starts to interrupt the learning process, or worse still takes over the learning tasks from the student!

Another interesting result that came out of this exercise was that a ratio of 20:2 is not the same as a ratio of 10:1. What this means is that two trainers spread over 20 students is not as effective as making each trainer primarily responsible for a sub-group of ten students. With this approach the trainer only has to remember and monitor the progress of ten trainees in detail, rather than remembering the details of all 20 students.

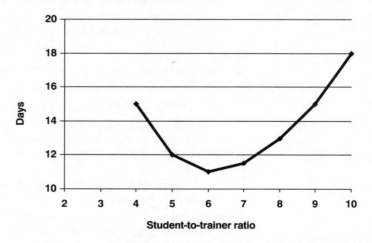

Figure 4.2 *The effect of student-to-trainer ratio on course effectiveness*

So we concluded that the best student-to-trainer ratio for this type of training was in the region of 6:1. Of course this optimum is different for different types of training; in some cases such as tutoring or coaching 1:1 will be the optimum ratio. You should always consider the effect that this ratio will have on your training and not always assume 'the more, the better'.

Each course should have a course specification which specifies the number of trainers, observers and so on who are needed to run the course. The 'student-to-trainer' ratio should be expressed as two ranges: an optimum range, and a minimum to maximum range.

For example, an optimum range might be from 10:1 to 16:1. This means that the course works best when there are between 10 and 16 students for every trainer. The 'minimum to maximum' range for the same course might be from 8:1 to 18:1. This means that the course is either unworkable outside this range, or its effectiveness is seriously eroded above 18:1, or it is uneconomic to run the course with fewer than eight students.

Rule of thumb: Generally speaking, courses will work well up to the following student-to-trainer ratios:

Simple courses: 18:1
Complex courses: 12:1
Individual feedback: 6:1

Preparation time The amount of time it takes to prepare for a course depends on the complexity of the course and the trainer's familiarity with the course. If a trainer is unfamiliar with the material, it can take as much as a day of preparation for every hour of presentation time.

A great deal of time and effort may be required to calculate the preparation times for courses of different complexity. Often the results are no more accurate than taking a 'broad-brush' approach. A useful guide for determining preparation time is given below.

Rule of thumb: On average, it takes one day of preparation for every three days of training.

This means that trainers would normally spend a maximum of 75 per cent of their time in front of the class. This figure also takes interruptions into account (it is impossible to do a day's preparation without other business issues intervening).

Course development time The time required to develop a new course is about as long as the proverbial piece of string. It depends on:

- the complexity of the course;
- how much material has to be produced;
- the standard of the materials;
- what is already available.

What is clear is that most people have no idea how long it takes to develop a course; and when they find out they are very shocked.

Rule of thumb: Table 4.1 gives estimated development times for different types of course.

If you need to make a significant revision to an existing, complex, five-day course, then you would need to plan 85 person-days to do the job. At first sight 85 days is a very long time, so let's see where the time goes.

The first thing to note is that the figure is a planning assumption – it assumes that very few days will pass without interruption and it is unlikely that development will take place in one, uninterrupted block. The figure also assumes that the trainers are producing their own materials. Using a secretarial service will reduce the time by about 25 per cent, but it will also increase the costs.

A significant revision is one where every page of the lesson plan and the student materials needs to be changed and substantially retyped. A five-day course could have 400 page-equivalents of lesson plans, student materials, handouts, posters and slides. This means that the trainer will have to research, revise and restructure the course at the rate of five pages per day.

The same considerations apply when you are writing a new course, but you also have to add in a substantial amount of time for researching, learning and condensing the subject matter.

Table 4.1   *Development times for different courses*

Type of course	Development time
Computer-based training	100:1
Complex/technical courses	40:1
Extensive restructuring/revision of an existing course	17:1
Moderate restructuring/revision of an existing course	11:1
Constructing a modular course from existing modules	6:1

Time spent on other activities

In addition to standing up in front of a class, trainers also need to spend time on planning, supervising and benchmarking. The proportion of time spent on these activities varies depending on the individual. Generally, these activities will increase as a trainer progresses from instructor to training manager. We look at these issues in greater detail in the section on developing trainers.

Rule of thumb: The proportions of time spent on activities, other than preparing and training courses, are as follows:

Instructors: 30 per cent
Trainers: 40 per cent

Learning curve time

A trainer who is 'learning the ropes' will be less productive than an experienced trainer. You also have to allow time for experienced trainers to learn new courses. You can calculate the length of time based on the experience of the trainer and the number of new courses that have to be taught. The section on trainer development looks at this in more detail.

Rule of thumb: A new trainer will take about three months to become partially productive, and a year to become fully productive.

Rule of thumb: It will take an experienced trainer two courses to become familiar with a short, simple course, and four courses for a long, complex course.

Selecting trainers

In this step you are selecting trainers to match the type and number of courses you need to run.

Using existing trainers

There are only two factors to consider:

- experience;
- availability.

Does the trainer have, or can the trainer acquire, the experience to run the course? Will the trainer be available to run the course when the client needs it?

When I discuss training needs with my clients I ask them whether it is possible for them to give me a 'window', or range of dates, for when they want a specified number of people trained. Matching trainers to a range of dates is much easier than matching them to fixed dates.

Full-time trainers or consultants?

Whether you use full-time trainers or external consultants depends on the criteria (such as cost and flexibility) you use for making your decision.

Rule of thumb: If the decision is on the basis of cost, consultants start to become more expensive than full-time employees when you employ the same consultants for more than 50 per cent of their time.

Some training organizations prefer to use only external consultants for training. They like the flexibility and the cross-fertilization from other companies. External consultants also specialize, which means that they are able to be experts in their field. Full-time trainers can only specialize if there is enough demand for their speciality to keep them fully utilized. Otherwise, the trainers will have to spread themselves thinly over a larger number of subject areas.

If you choose external consultants at random you will have the problem of ensuring consistency and quality. The answer is to have a core of consultants, or associates, to whom you have given your organization's seal of approval. External trainers and courses should be certified in the same way you certify your own trainers and courses.

Using external consultants for delivery is expensive but the cost is generally well understood. However, the cost of using external consultants for development of materials can give you a shock.

If you assume that an average development time for a five-day course is 10 days of development for every day of training, and take a consultant day rate of £500, the cost for developing this course would be £25 000. It would be far more cost effective to buy an off-the-shelf course or to use one of your full-time employees to develop the course.

The problem arises when the consultant's day rate is applied to the development of the course. As far as you are concerned you are not interested in how much time the consultant spends developing the course as long as it is ready by the time you need it. What is important is how much you think the finished product is worth to you.

If your application is a very specialized one, you may be prepared to pay a lot of money to have the course developed. If the course has wide applicability, you may feel you should not pay anything for the development – because the consultant can defray the development costs over a number of different customers. The situation is similar to buying a new car. If you were the first customer for a new model you would not expect to pay millions of pounds to cover the manufacturer's research and development costs. It is important to remember that the negotiating issue is not time but price.

External consultants will obviously not want to make a loss over the deal so, before taking on the contract, they will carefully consider:

- whether they have existing materials which can be modified rather than developing the course from scratch;
- whether they could charge less because of the prospect of having two months of continuous work (day rates are calculated on the basis of not being able to get work every day, a certain amount of personal preparation that is required before every course, and a certain amount of product development);
- how much they would expect to earn in a year, and what proportion of that expectation would be met by a fixed-price contract;
- whether there are any costs or time associated with being away from base which would not be incurred during the development of the course;
- as it is not possible to work continually on course development (it is often more productive to give it a rest and work on something else for a while), whether there are any other money-making activities that could be worked on in parallel;
- what additional work this project could lead to;
- whether there is a guaranteed minimum number of courses the consultant will be asked to run;
- whether the client will be tied to the consultant for running future courses;
- whether the consultant will be able to run the course for other clients and thus be able to defray the development costs over a larger number of courses.

Recruiting trainers

If you cannot cover the workload with your existing trainers or consultants you will need to recruit additional trainers.

Ideally you would want somebody who is currently very successful at doing the same kind of job. This unfortunately poses the questions: 'Where do "new starters" get their experience?' and 'If someone is already doing this job, why would they want to come and work for our company?'

Internal or external recruitment?

First see if there are experienced trainers in other parts of the company. Resist the temptation of always bringing in 'new blood' from outside. New ideas and different experiences will add richness to a training department, but don't underestimate the importance of company knowledge and experience. Avoid the 'grass is greener' trap.

Internal candidates bring with them a record of achievements, failures, strengths and weaknesses. Unless you probe very thoroughly external candidates will only tell you their strengths and achievements. The first time you get to find out about external candidates' failures and weaknesses may be after you have employed them!

If you have time you can develop somebody who does not have training experience but has the desire and potential to be a trainer. Recruiting internally for someone who has no experience is a risk. Recruiting inexperienced people externally is an even greater risk. But how do you tell whether somebody has the potential and the desire?

Training is an activity you have really got to want to do, so it is very likely that people with the desire to train will approach you. If a person has always wanted to do something, it is also very likely that they have always done it. This would not necessarily be formal training, but they would have a history of successful presentations, or of coaching their colleagues.

As with all things it is a matter of getting the balance right. You need both experience and 'new blood'.

Rule of thumb: If you need a team of six trainers, you would probably want four existing trainers with company experience, one externally recruited trainer and one 'apprentice' trainer.

As far as I am concerned there is no difference between recruiting a permanent member of staff and finding a new consultant, except that you probably would not want to use an inexperienced consultant. The criteria for deciding whether you would recruit a new employee or find a new consultant are exactly the same as we discussed in the section on selecting trainers.

The recruitment process

Recruitment is the process of finding and attracting a person who matches the requirements of the job.

Recruiting trainers is much the same as recruiting for any other profession. Employers have to identify potential candidates and satisfy themselves as to which candidate is best able, and most willing, to do the job. Many interviewers concentrate on ability to the exclusion of willingness.

This matching process cannot start unless we understand what the job involves, and the type of person best suited to the job.

Job descriptions The job description tells you what the job entails. It is the basis on which you can decide the kind of person you need for the job.

The way to do this is to identify which tasks have to be completed to meet the requirements of the job. 'Developing a lesson plan' and 'Analysing training needs' are examples of tasks. Note that both a verb and a noun are required to define the task.

Person specifications The person specification describes the ideal person to fill the job. It is a profile of the personal skills and characteristics you will look for in the recruitment and selection process. The best way of writing a person specification is to take the job description and analyse the knowledge, skills and behaviours that are needed to perform the tasks.

The interview The selection method in which most companies put their trust is the interview. The purpose of selection interviewing is 'to determine whether an applicant fulfils the requirements of the job'. A good interviewer does this by investigating past experience for evidence of the candidate's strengths, weaknesses and attitudes.

Don't be misled by your perceptions, but don't ignore them either – they often serve as warning bells, indicating areas where you will need to dig up some more facts.

Being an interviewer is like being a detective. While intuition is useful, the final conclusion must be firmly based on facts and data.

Most jobs are filled through interviews, but the widespread reliance on this method is often based on assumptions which do not bear close examination. It cannot be automatically assumed that all experienced managers are good judges of an applicant's character and skills who are able to sum up an individual in an interview that often lasts for no more than an hour.

Even when the job lends itself to practical selection tests, or when companies are able to use extensive psychometric testing, the interview almost invariably forms the final selection process.

Given these limitations, it is important that the interview is used effectively, and that those likely to be involved in interviewing are given training.

In any interview, the interviewer's task is to determine whether the candidate is both willing and able to do the job. As we have already said, sometimes we concentrate on one of these to the exclusion of the other.

Checking a
trainer's ability

Checking a candidate's ability is easier for training than for many other professions. It is relatively easy to simulate a training environment where you can observe a trainer's performance. A training session is the culmination of all the work and preparation the trainer has done. Most of the candidate's strengths and weaknesses will become apparent in a 45-minute session. The more accurately you can simulate the training environment, the better data you will get. Many companies ask the candidates to make a presentation when they come for a second interview.

Unfortunately, the trainer will often try to do something 'special'. This, combined with performing in front of an interview panel, can give a distorted and misleading impression of the trainer's true abilities. Try to provide a natural environment for the presentation. Presenting to a single interviewer is very different to making a presentation to a large group.

Ideally, it would be better to observe trainers in their 'natural' environment such as a course they had already planned to run. Of course, this is very difficult if the person is currently working for another company. It is unlikely that a trainer's present employers would allow you to 'poach' on their own premises unless it was part of an 'outplacement' programme.

During the interview you will have established which courses the trainer is already able to train. If there is a good match between the candidate and the job, it is more than likely that one of these courses will meet one of your training requirements. In this case you could invite the trainer to run a training session for a group of your own students.

If the prospective trainers are consultants who want to take up full-time employment, it is relatively easy to get permission to observe them. You could even offer a fixed-term contract and observe the trainer in the environment in which they would be working.

The observation form shown in Figure 4.4 (page 98) can be used as a checklist of points to look out for. Don't just observe the trainer, also look at the students to gauge their reaction.

Another good indicator of a trainer's abilities are the lesson plans they have prepared. Ask prospective trainers to bring examples of lesson plans they have developed and use them as a basis for discussion. Examples of handouts and other student materials also give a lot of information about a trainer's ability.

One of the best predictors of future performance is past and present performance. During the interview get the candidate to talk about how they have handled past situations. It is not a good idea to ask them how they would handle a hypothetical situation, because they will either be stuck for words or they will describe how they feel the situation should be handled – not how they would actually perform.

Don't reject people just because they have been made redundant – many excellent, dedicated people only come on to the job market in times of redundancy. The fact that a person is redundant is not as important as the reason for the redundancy.

In any case, you should always take up references and talk to people the candidates have worked for and to the students they have trained.

Experience may be related to age, but this can be a trap. Someone may claim to have fifteen years' experience, but this may turn out to be one year's experience fifteen times over. Some companies have age blocks which are difficult to justify. An age block is even more difficult to justify for trainers, because many trainers continue to work as consultants long after they have taken 'early retirement'.

You can easily check whether the person's education and training meet the requirements of the job, but be careful not to use education and qualifications as predictors for all job requirements.

Physical qualities such as stamina are important for a trainer. Good hearing, vision (including colour vision where necessary) and clarity of voice are essential for communicating with students. Boxes of training materials are surprisingly heavy, so a trainer needs to be physically fit. Don't make assumptions on the basis of physical stature or disability. Small people can have immense strength, and the physically disabled learn to be enormously resourceful. The only way you can be sure the person is physically able to do the job is to observe them prepare and run a training session.

Appearance can be a trap for the unwary. It is unreliable to assess a person on the basis of appearance, but it is important that a trainer's mode of dress does not distract or intimidate the students.

Intelligence is difficult to assess without testing. Obviously trainers have to be intelligent enough to understand the concepts they are teaching, and not to look foolish in front of the class. A secondary indicator of intelligence is knowledge and it is relatively easy to check this out during an interview.

Maturity and emotional stability are essential to gain respect and credibility. Again, achievement in the past can help. Pure gut feelings will probably mislead.

Checking a trainer's willingness

A trainer's attitude to work answers the important question of whether the candidate will do the job as well as being able to do it. Probe the candidates' reasons for applying for the job as well as their aims, intentions and ambitions.

Make sure they understand what the job means in terms of carrying boxes, unsocial hours, travelling and nights away from home. Watch for any hesitancy in their reactions as you describe the job. Don't fudge the issue of describing the demands of the job for fear of discouraging a 'good candidate'. It is far better for applicants to be put off at this stage rather than after they have been employed.

Training is the kind of job that can be hell if you don't thoroughly enjoy it and get some kind of buzz out of teaching people. In some ways this characteristic of training makes it easier for an interviewer to judge a candidate's willingness. If enthusiasm for training and the subject matter does not shine through at the interview, it is unlikely that the applicant will be able to survive as a trainer.

Selection and the law

Every interviewer should be aware of how the law applies to recruitment. The following are not law in every country, but you will find that they encapsulate the policies and values of most multinational companies.

- It is unlawful, unless the job is covered by an exception, to discriminate on the grounds of a candidate's belonging to a particular category (i.e. gender, marital status, race, religion etc.).
- It is advisable to keep records of interviews, showing why applicants were rejected, for at least six months.
- Questions at interviews should relate to the requirements of the job. Questions about marriage plans or family intentions should not be asked, as they could be construed as showing a bias against women. Information for personnel records can be collected after a job offer has been made.
- Each individual job applicant should be assessed according to their personal capacity to meet the requirements of a given job. Applications from men and women, married and single, of whatever race or

religion should be treated in the same way. Where it is necessary to assess whether personal circumstances will affect the performance of the job (e.g. unsocial hours) this should be discussed objectively without detailed questions based on assumptions about marital status, children and domestic obligations. Interview questions should probe the experience and skills necessary to carry out the job.

- Employers should give careful consideration to the selection criteria that they use (including age bars, mobility and hours of work) and whether this would discriminate disproportionately against a particular category. Criteria which cannot be shown objectively to be necessary should be withdrawn.
- Selection criteria (job description and person specification) should be determined before the recruitment process starts.
- There are very few exceptions where it is legal to select a person of a particular category while excluding people of other categories (e.g. gender or race). These are called genuine occupational qualifications (GOQs). Basically these are authenticity, privacy, decency, and laws regulating the employment of women. Be very cautious about using a GOQ as a reason for not employing a person. You need to be very sure of your ground, and you will need to have demonstrated that you were unable to make suitable alternative arrangements for the person concerned.

You should not assume that:

- women are less ambitious or committed than men;
- women put their family commitments before their careers;
- men put their careers before their families;
- women work for 'pin money';
- a man will not work for a woman;
- women with children cannot work long or unsociable hours or attend residential training courses;
- women are not prepared to relocate to follow their careers;
- women are unsuited to certain kinds of work (e.g. scientific, technical, heavy manual or senior management).

Allowing your treatment of employees to be influenced by any of these assumptions may result in unlawful discrimination.

Developing trainers

Developing your trainers is a very important part of managing the training process. There are three areas of development:

- developing the skills required to run courses, identify needs and develop new courses (trainer training);
- continuous development (assessing trainer performance);
- finding career paths either within or through the training department (career development).

Training trainers

The exact process for training new trainers depends on the trainer's experience and the type of training to be done. The process given in Figure 4.3 is for a management trainer. It certifies trainers at two levels: instructor and training officer. An instructor is a person who has the professional skills to deliver courses. Training officers also carry out needs analyses and develop courses.

Induction into training department

This step is used to introduce both new and experienced trainers to the department. It assumes that the person has

Figure 4.3   *Train-the-trainer process*

attended the company's induction course and it includes:

- the mission of the training department (see Chapter 1 for an explanation of what a mission is);
- where the training department fits into the organization;
- roles and responsibilities of the training department's personnel;
- meeting members of the training department, clients and suppliers;
- location of offices, training rooms, storage areas, photocopying and other facilities;
- current issues;
- future direction of the department.

> Use of technical equipment

There are very few courses that are run without any technical equipment. An overhead projector seems to be the absolute minimum – even though it is perfectly possible to run a course without one. In addition a trainer can be expected to deal with audiocassette recorders, video recorders, video cameras, camcorders, computers, multimedia, interactive video, satellite links, 35 mm slide projectors and 16 mm film projectors.

Film and 35 mm slide projectors are becoming less common, which is just as well as they are notoriously unreliable. I would always try to avoid these 'technology traps' by having the films transferred on to video.

Although all trainers cannot be expected to be technical experts and to fix every fault, they should at least have a minimum level of expertise. This will keep delays due to embarrassing equipment failures down to a minimum.

Table 4.2 shows the minimum technical knowledge that a trainer should have for each type of equipment.

> Interpersonal skills observers course

The ability to observe and give feedback on students' interpersonal behaviour is an important tool for management trainers but, while this would be a useful course for many trainers, it would not be essential training for all trainers. Technical trainers, for example, could miss out this step.

> Techniques of instruction course

Many organizations provide techniques of instruction courses and choosing one is the same process as for

Table 4.2　*Minimum knowledge of technical equipment*

Equipment	Minimum technical knowledge
Overhead projector	Changing the lamp Cleaning the optics Adjusting colour fringes Keystone effect (how to adjust for)
Audiocassette recorders	Head cleaning Azimuth adjustment
Video recorders	Formats and standards (VHS, Super-VHS, 8 mm, Hi8, Betamax, Betacomm, U-matic, PAL, NTSC, SECAM) Colour, hue, brightness, sharpness, contrast, tracking and skew adjustments Cuing Head cleaning Leads and connectors Counter/time relationship
Video cameras Camcorders	Manual/auto iris, focusing, panning, tilting, zooming, tracking Sound and lighting Leads and connectors
Computers Interactive video	Operating systems Booting up Random access memory Copying and deleting files Disk formats (5¼", 3½", single-sided, single-density, double-density, hard disk, CD-ROM) Word processing Databases Graphics Desktop publishing
35 mm projectors	Loading Lamp changing Optics cleaning
Film projectors	Film threading Lamp changing Leaders and lead-in Sound leads and connectors Splicing broken film Rewinding

choosing any other course (see Chapter 3, Training Courses). I would recommend selecting a supplier who issues a recognized certificate or award as this sets the standard. A professional qualification is good for trainers' morale and the credibility of the training department.

```
┌─────────────────────────────────────┐
│  Trainer goes through at least one course │
│         certification process          │
└─────────────────────────────────────┘
```

The course certification process is the means by which an instructor or trainer becomes proficient to train a course without assistance. This process is described later in this chapter.

```
┌─────────────────────────────────────┐
│   Training manager certifies instructor   │
└─────────────────────────────────────┘
```

At this point the training manager reviews the new instructor's progress. This should be no more than a formality if the process described here has been followed up to this point. If your trainers are following the path of vocational qualifications, you may want to delegate this step to an external assessor.

```
┌─────────────────────────────────────┐
│        Train-the-trainer course         │
└─────────────────────────────────────┘
```

Once an instructor has become proficient in delivering courses, a development discussion may reveal a desire on their part to become a training officer. The first step is to attend a train-the-trainer course, followed by gaining a recognized qualification or award.

```
┌─────────────────────────────────────┐
│  Training officer develops new course   │
└─────────────────────────────────────┘
```

New training officers will now demonstrate what they have learnt on the train-the-trainer course by developing a new course. This should be done under supervision and using the process described in Chapter 3.

```
┌─────────────────────────────────────┐
│  Training manager certifies training officer │
└─────────────────────────────────────┘
```

The training manager reviews the training officer's progress and provides formal certification. Again, you may want to delegate this to an external assessor.

Assessing trainer performance

Assessing trainer performance is a very important skill. Good assessment ensures that suitable trainers are employed as well as maintaining and improving the quality of existing trainers. To be effective, an assessment must:

- provide the training manager with relevant data which enable appropriate development activities to be recommended;
- provide an opportunity for trainers to explore their performance strengths and weaknesses;
- motivate trainers to investigate new developments in instructional techniques.

How often should trainers be assessed?

There are no 'hard and fast' rules on how often a trainer should be assessed but intervals of three to six months usually give the maximum benefit. New trainers should be observed more often than experienced trainers. The final decision on how often assessment should be conducted also depends on the workload of the trainer and the availability of the observer.

How long should assessment take?

The time an assessment takes also depends on many factors, but it is unlikely that sufficient data would be collected in under 45 minutes of observation. It is also unlikely that any meaningful feedback could take place in under 20 minutes.

How objective is assessment?

Although observation is more reliable than selection interviewing it is not entirely objective. If all students were influenced by trainer performance in the same way, to the same degree and at the same time, then it might be possible to have objective assessments.

But it isn't that simple. Every trainee is an individual and each will respond differently to the trainer. An action which may have the desired effect on one trainee may not have the same effect on another. What makes objectivity even more difficult is that it sometimes takes many hours to see the effects of that action. Sometimes it is impossible to assess the effects of a trainer's actions.

Similarly, observers' evaluations are influenced by their own subjective reactions. Sometimes observers confuse style with substance and will give a low rating simply because the trainer has a different style and feels more comfortable with different jokes and anecdotes. While assessment should be designed to be as objective as possible, it is important to understand the influence of subjective factors.

Even though assessment may be influenced by subjective factors, it is still vital for maintaining and improving the standard of training. Training managers must have a basis for evaluating what their trainers do and how well they do it. All trainers are entitled to an evaluation of their performance, and most trainers will actively request it.

Trainers will also have their own opinions of how well or how poorly they are performing their tasks. These opinions are extremely important to the trainer – and to the training manager. Yet the fullest benefit cannot be obtained from both the trainer's and the training manager's opinion unless comparison and discussion take place.

This means that training managers must base their opinions on what they actually see. They must observe trainers in the classroom and then set up a meeting where both the manager and the trainer can share their opinions and agree on appropriate follow-up activities.

What is assessed? Trainers are sometimes regarded primarily as subject-matter experts. Whatever other qualities they bring to the classroom they are, by definition, subject-matter experts. Trainers tell, show, test and then decide when a topic has been adequately covered.

There is, however, much more to training than the mechanics of presenting information. Trainers work with individuals. They must be able to deal with student motivation. They should try to remove the obstacles that prevent learning.

Trainers also need to pay attention to the fact that they are role models for the trainees. Their enthusiasm for a subject or their adherence to policies affect student behaviour. Although being a role model will not necessarily cause students to follow suit, its absence will almost certainly be copied by students – 'If the trainer doesn't care, why should I?'

How should assessment be handled? Although there are many different views on how an assessment should be done, all workable systems have four elements in common:

- preparation;
- observation;
- feedback;
- follow-up.

As each of these elements involves both the trainer and the observer, planning the availability of suitable observers is essential.

Preparation (45 minutes) Before any assessment takes place, training managers should discuss the process with the trainers. When everybody involved understands what is involved, individual observations can be scheduled. At least one week's notice should be given.

Observation   The observer should be seated as unobtrusively as possible.
(45 minutes)   The best position is off to one side and behind the students.
                  Try not to sit in the middle at the back of the classroom as
                  trainers will feel that they are being stared at all of the time.
                  The trainer should not be interrupted at any stage of the
                  observation period.

                  During the observation the training manager should record
                  the observations. If a new trainer is being observed an
                  observation checklist (see Figure 4.4) should be completed.
                  If an experienced trainer is being certified on a new course,
                  notes can be made on a copy of the lesson plan.

Feedback   Feedback should be given immediately, or as soon as
(20 minutes)   possible after the evaluation. Only the trainer and the
                  observer should be present. It is recommended that a
                  counselling approach be taken. Counselling, in this

Trainer:	Date:
Session:	Observer:

(1) = Not acceptable   (2) = Poor   (3) = OK   (4) = Master performer

Behaviours	Assessment and comments
<u>Preparation</u> — Rehearsed lesson — Administration — Classroom layout — Materials and equipment prepared — Arranged to be free from interruptions	(1) (2) (3) (4) (5)
<u>Presentation</u> — Introduced subject — Communicated objectives — Communicated agenda — Followed logical sequence — Summarized — Checked students' understanding — Kept to time — Kept to subject	(1) (2) (3) (4) (5)
<u>Manner</u> — Showed commitment — Showed enthusiasm — Created interest — Sensitive to group — Credible — Knowledgeable	(1) (2) (3) (4) (5)
<u>Technique</u> — Voice — Questioning — Pace — Movement — Eye contact — Mannerisms — Use of audiovisual aids	(1) (2) (3) (4) (5)

Figure 4.4   Observation checklist

situation, is an attempt by the observer to help the trainer explore strengths and weaknesses so that the strengths are reinforced and suitable actions are taken to improve performance. Figure 4.5 gives the elements of counselling.

The observer should start off by *setting the climate*. This is to make sure that the trainer is relaxed. If the observer knows the trainer well, setting the climate will only take a few minutes. Always be sincere. Do not delay getting down to business any longer than necessary or tension will be needlessly increased.

The observer must take the time to *set expectations*. This means that the trainer understands the purpose and process of the session.

The next step is to *seek trainer's views of strengths and weaknesses*. Here the observer invites the trainer to express opinions on the trainer's own performance strengths and weaknesses. Questioning techniques should be used appropriately to ensure that the trainer fully explores all of the observed strengths and weaknesses. Where opinions differ, evidence should be provided by the observer.

It is much better if trainers are able to identify their own strengths and weaknesses. They are more likely to want to do something about improving their performance. However, they can be unaware of some of their performance strengths and weaknesses, so the observer should not be afraid of prompting and giving direct feedback. There are guidelines for giving constructive feedback in Figure 4.6.

Towards the end of the feedback session the observer should help the trainer *develop an action plan*. List the strengths and weaknesses on a development plan (see

1. Set climate

2. Set expectations

3. Seek trainer's views of strengths and weaknesses

4. Develop an action plan

Figure 4.5   *Elements of counselling*

1.   IT IS NOT JUDGEMENTAL

Making judgemental statements such as 'You really are a bad listener' is not very useful and they can cause the receiver to react defensively.

2.   IT IS SPECIFIC

A far better approach is to describe a specific incident, e.g. 'At the end of the lesson you interrupted Hazel before she could finish explaining her problem.'

3.   ITS PURPOSE IS TO HELP THE RECEIVER

Sometimes we give feedback to make ourselves feel better. It helps us to get things off our chests. This might be good for the giver but it does nothing for the receiver. Ensure that the only reason for giving feedback is to help the receiver improve performance.

4.   IT IS ABOUT BEHAVIOUR THAT CAN BE CHANGED

Frustration is only increased when a person is reminded of some shortcoming that cannot be controlled.

5.   IT IS CLEAR

One way of making sure that the feedback is clear is to have the receiver paraphrase the feedback.

6.   IT IS TIMELY

Generally, feedback is most effective immediately after the behaviour. The exception to this is when the receivers are not ready to hear the feedback, such as when they are feeling depressed or are 'on a high'.

Figure 4.6   Guidelines for giving constructive feedback

Figure 2.6 in Chapter 2) and then invite the trainer to suggest appropriate activities that will maintain the strengths and minimize the weaknesses. Figure 4.7 gives guidelines for improving performance.

Follow-up (unspecified time)
After the session the observer should assess how well the feedback session went and what would be done differently during another feedback session.

The trainer's performance should be monitored and, if necessary, additional observations and feedback sessions planned.

Career development
There are two ways in which training can be part of a person's career development:

- training as a profession;
- training as part of a development plan.

Training as a profession
Many trainers consider themselves to be career trainers. They would like to develop their careers within the training profession. Although they enjoy training, they don't want to spend the rest of their working lives doing wall-to-wall training. It is important to have a career path within the training department if these trainers are not to lose their motivation.

- Do not try to change too much at once. It is better to improve one or two aspects of performance than to make no progress on twenty.

- Always agree a completion date for each of the activities.

- It is easier, and probably healthier, to do more of a new behaviour than suppress an existing behaviour. For example, if the trainer talks for too long it is better and more helpful for them to use more visual aids and ask more questions than to simply suggest that they talk less.

- Always summarize what is going to be done, by whom and by when.

Figure 4.7   *Guidelines for improving performance*

Figure 4.8 shows part of a career path within a management training department. The right-hand side shows the skills and education that are needed to perform at each level. The left-hand side of the diagram shows the activities that each job involves.

Notice that even the most senior trainers are still expected to do the basic activities. What does change is the proportion of time spent on these activities at each level. Figure 4.9 shows how this varies for the management training jobs.

If you do this kind of analysis for your own training jobs, your compensation and benefits manager will be able to assess the jobs and fit them into your company's existing grading structure.

Somebody with no training experience could 'learn the trade' by starting as a training administrator, progressing to a training assistant and then on to a management skills trainer. If they had managerial experience, they could also progress to higher levels.

If trainers have insufficient experience, skills or knowledge to progress from one level to the next, actions would be identified for their personal development plans. This might include leaving the training department for a year or two to gain managerial experience.

Training as part of a development plan   The career path shown in Figure 4.8 is essentially a longitudinal progression with each step serving as an entry point. Training can also be used for the development of

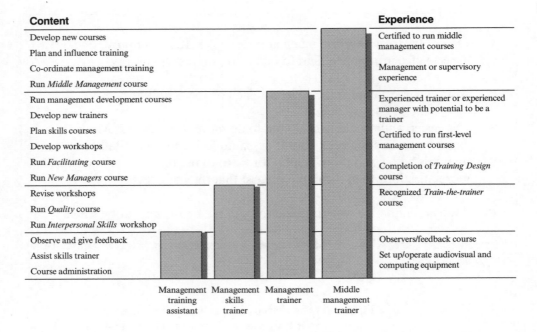

Figure 4.8　*Part of a career path in a management training department*

people from other parts of the company. There is nothing like teaching for learning and forming contacts!

A secondment to the training department is particularly useful for managers and 'high fliers'. It also broadens the experience of people whose career paths have been within one department.

The benefit works both ways because secondment brings new ideas into training and helps keep training in touch with reality.

Certifying trainers

Certification or accreditation is the process of ensuring that a trainer is ready to train a new course. The exact process that is used to accredit or certify trainers depends on the complexity of the course and the trainers' experience. The trainers' experience also affects the time it takes to go through the certification process:

- Are the trainers experienced trainers?
- Have they trained this type of course before?
- Do they already understand the underlying concepts?
- Have they practised the skills in the workplace?

Figure 4.10 shows a process that is used for a complex five-day course.

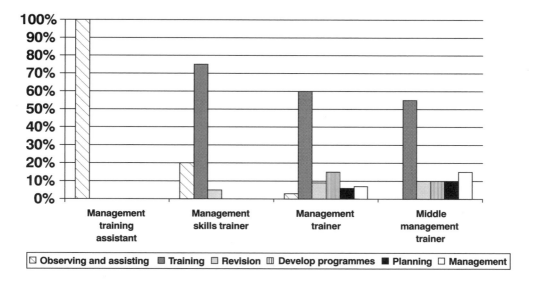

Figure 4.9   *Activity profiles for different levels of trainer*

Trainer attends course

The first step is to have the trainer take the course as a student. This is very important for two reasons. The first reason is the obvious one: to have any credibility trainers need to possess the knowledge and skills that they will be teaching. The second reason, although not so obvious, is just as important. Trainers who take a course under the same conditions and pressures as the students will be better

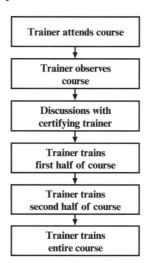

Figure 4.10   *Certification process for a complex five-day course*

able to appreciate their students' learning difficulties. This makes for greater empathy and a better student–trainer relationship.

> Trainer observes course

After taking the course as a student the trainer is then given a lesson plan so that the next course can be observed and followed. The trainer is encouraged to make copious notes during this observation and to start considering which parts of the course should be tackled first.

> Discussions with certifying trainer

Soon after the completion of this observation the trainer has a discussion with the certifying trainer. The certifying trainer should ideally be the course originator or a trainer who has extensive knowledge and experience of the course. The discussion should include any questions the trainer has and the final decision as to which modules should be practised first.

> Trainer trains first half of course

On the third course the trainer co-trains with the experienced trainer. Usually half of the course is trained, but it may be advisable to train only a third of a very complex course.

The experienced trainer should observe and give feedback to the trainer throughout the course. For maximum effect it is important that this feedback is given as soon as practically possible. Trainers vary in the formality of the feedback they require. For some a few words at the end of the session is all that is required; others may want a full-blown counselling session at the end of the day. It will all depend on their experience, confidence and ability to teach this type of course.

> Trainer trains second half of course

The other sessions should be practised on the fourth course. Again, this should be done under observation and with feedback.

> Trainer trains entire course

With the feedback that has been received so far, the trainer should be able to teach the fifth course alone. So you can see that for a complex course, which is run only once a quarter, it can take over a year for a trainer to be brought up to speed.

At the other end of the scale it should be possible for a trainer to take a simple one-day course as a student and then, given a comprehensive lesson plan, be able to teach the next course alone.

Although it is possible for an experienced trainer to train straight from a lesson plan without having seen the course before, you should really try to avoid this as even the best lesson plans cannot capture all the details that are required to make the course a success.

Certifying the certifiers

Of course, all this begs the question of who certifies the certifiers. Ideally accreditation should be done by the people who originally developed the course. However, this is not always possible because of time, distance and cost. These problems are further compounded in large multinational organizations because of language and cultural difficulties. Foreign subsidiaries of these multinational corporations do not always appreciate having to pay for the cost of flying somebody in from abroad every time they need to have a new trainer accredited. In any case, not all trainers have sufficient expertise in the corporation's primary language that would enable them to train and be observed in that language. In fact, it could be argued that a trainer's certification would not really be valid unless their performance is observed under the conditions in which it would be taught.

The answer to this is to have some trainers developed to the point at which they would be able to certify their own trainers in their areas. Where language is an issue the local certifiers would have to be bilingual and would probably have to run a course at the corporation's own training centre. A certain amount of trust would have to be in place for this scheme to work, but the advantage is that the quality of the training is maintained at a level which meets the corporation's standards while at the same time giving flexibility to the local organizations.

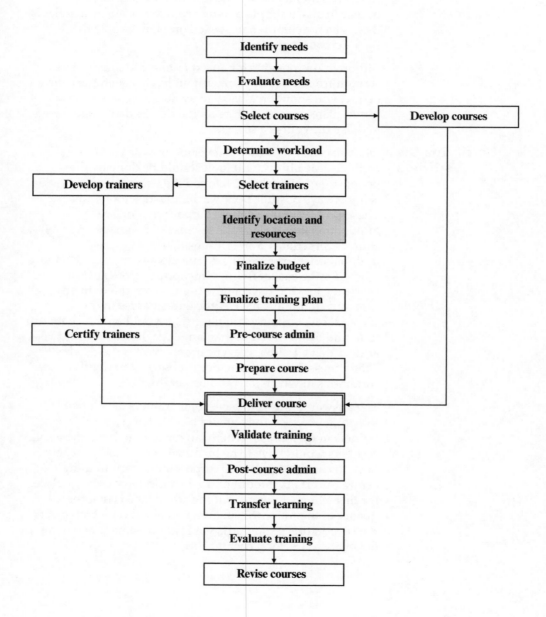

Figure 5.1   *Training locations and resources*

5 Training locations and resources

This chapter covers another step in the training process:

● identify location and resources.

By this stage you will have selected the courses and trainers. The next decision you have to make is where you are going to run the courses, what the best learning situation will be, and where you are going to obtain the equipment and materials.

If you run residential courses the accommodation costs can be the single biggest item in your training budget. Running courses on your own premises will allow you to keep travel and accommodation costs low.

Identifying training locations and resources

Figure 5.2 illustrates the process I will be describing for identifying training locations and resources.

> Obtain course specification

The course specification details the facilities, materials and equipment that are needed to run the course. This information is essential for deciding the type of learning environment required for the course. It allows you to check whether a location meets your specification. The specification is also an excellent method for communicating your exact requirements to a training centre.

> Determine type of learning environment

The factors that affect your choice of learning environment are the cost, the facilities you need, the type of instruction and whether the students need to be separated from home and work pressures.

Don't assume that all training has to take place in the classroom. 'Open learning' and 'distance learning' widen

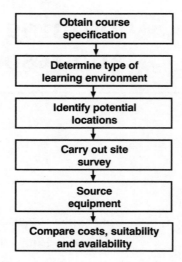

Figure 5.2   *Process for identifying training locations and resources*

the choice of learning environments. (See Chapter 9, Delivering the Course, for a discussion of open and distance learning.) Choices of learning environment can cover:

- at home,
- the workplace,
- open learning centres,
- meeting rooms,
- dedicated training rooms,
- hotels,
- sports centres and social clubs,
- residential training centres.

Home   Home learning is suitable for programmed instruction, it is inexpensive and many people would welcome the opportunity to learn at home.

The disadvantages are:

- possible distraction by home pressures,
- isolation from tutors,
- lack of specialized equipment.

When we think of home learning we often think it is limited to text-based training. Home learning can be more creative if ways are found to overcome the disadvantages of isolation and lack of access to equipment.

Isolation can be overcome by using the telephone or computer links. Messages can be sent between tutor and students by e-mail. Access to learning materials all over the world can be obtained via the Internet. Videos can be broadcast from existing television stations, either during the day for large audiences or as a scrambled signal during the night for small specialist audiences. The night-time programmes can be automatically recorded by anyone who has a suitable decoder.

The Open University sends laboratory kits to its science and technology students by road. It is also possible for service engineers to learn how to repair small photocopiers on their kitchen tables!

In the workplace People do most of their learning outside the classroom, but much of it is random and unstructured. To make the most of experiential learning the student needs to have an experienced coach and a planned series of structured experiences.

Open learning centres Open learning centres are purpose-built rooms fitted with all the equipment and materials needed for private study. They provide flexibility in terms of time and students can learn at their own pace. Open learning centres are particularly useful in manufacturing areas because breaks in production are difficult to predict.

Meeting rooms Purpose-built meeting rooms are suitable for short training courses, but they are usually too small and the wrong shape for larger classes.

Dedicated training rooms Dedicated training rooms may well be ideal if you were involved in the design and paid attention to the following:

- size and shape of training room,
- capacity of training room,
- heating and ventilation,
- lighting,
- light switches,
- acoustics,
- equipment.

Further details of these aspects are given in the section on carrying out a site survey.

Distraction by work-related problems is the main disadvantage of an on-site training room. Some companies have dedicated training rooms at their head offices which means that most people have to travel to their courses. This helps to minimize disruptions. They also block-book bedrooms at a local hotel. This is cheaper than running courses at a commercial residential training centre, and avoids the problems and cost of running your own residential centre.

Hotels Many hotels are properly equipped to function as conference centres, but too many others see conferences and training courses only as a means of filling empty rooms. They often have to hire-in all the training equipment. Function rooms double as meeting rooms, and bedrooms have the beds removed to provide syndicate rooms. I have even seen instances of syndicate rooms not being ready until 11 o'clock because the hotel had rented them to guests the night before!

Sports centres and social clubs

Much of what has been said about hotels also applies to sports centres and social clubs, except that the standard is even more variable. Don't automatically disregard these venues, however, because some of them provide excellent service and facilities at competitive prices. Always make sure that you carry out a thorough site survey nevertheless.

Residential training centres

Residential training centres are in the business of providing excellent training facilities in suitable surroundings. They are also very expensive. You would only use a residential training centre for longer, more complex courses.

> Identify potential locations

Once you have decided on the type of training location, the next step is to identify a number of potential alternative locations. You may already have a number in mind from past experience, but if you are new to the job or have just relocated to a new area you will need to look further afield. Training magazines and *Yellow Pages* are useful sources of advertising.

Many of the country's largest companies run their own training centres and, although they do not always advertise, they are often willing to hire rooms to other companies to improve their own utilization rates.

Finally, don't forget to ask your own colleagues – they may have attended training centres with other companies.

> Carry out site survey

If you have never used a particular training centre before, it is imperative that you carry out a site survey to make sure the training location is suitable for your needs. It is worth taking a couple of hours really getting the feel of the place. The centre's management will be only too pleased to show you around – after all, it could lead to a great deal of business.

Talk to the staff, trainers and students. Explore the buildings and the grounds. Use a checklist like the one shown in Figure 5.3.

Date:	Location:

Checkpoint	Comments
Location	
Parking	
Reception	
Contacts	
Delivery arrangements	
Staff	
Access to training room	
Size/shape of training room	
Capacity of training room	
Heating and ventilation	
Lighting	
Power sockets	
Light switches	
Acoustics	
Equipment	
Wall space and fixings	
Syndicate rooms	
Toilets	
Access for preparation	
Food	
Meal and break arrangements	
Bedrooms	
Leisure facilities	
Security	
Emergency procedures	

Figure 5.3 *Checklist for doing a site survey*

Location Most training centres are situated in remote areas. This is not usually a problem for residential courses but you will need to check whether:

- the centre is accessible by public transport with, perhaps, just a short taxi journey at the end (you would normally expect very remote training centres to provide a minibus service to and from the nearest train station, bus terminus or airport),
- there is a reasonable connection to the motorway (expressway) network,
- foreign students have enough time to get to the airport after the course has finished,
- students who arrive by car have no more than a five-hour drive.

If the course is not residential, the training centre needs to be far more accessible.

Parking It is another of those universal laws that the number of cars expands to fill the available parking space. When you arrive to carry out the site survey you will soon see how easy it is to park your car. When you leave, check to see if anybody is blocked in and whether cars are parked on the road outside.

Reception The first impression you get of a training centre is of the reception area. It is at the reception where frustrations and inefficiencies surface. The receptionist should be expecting you and you should not have to wait too long to be seen. This will give you an indication of how well the place is being run. For a better indication you should try to be in the reception area when students are booking in and booking out.

Contacts It is best to get the names of the staff you will need to contact if you decide to use the training centre. As well as making your life easier, it will also give you an indication of whether people have specific roles and responsibilities.

Delivery arrangements If you need to have materials delivered to the training centre, check out the process for receiving the deliveries and getting them to the classroom. Again, get the name of a contact for this purpose.

Staff The relationship you have with the training centre's staff can make all the difference between a smoothly run course and a course that is a series of irritations. Make sure you talk to the staff to get a feeling for their attitude towards you and the training centre.

Access to training room If your trainers intend to bring their own materials, see how close they can park their cars to the classroom, how many steps have to be climbed and check the width of the passageways. Also see what help is available – either in the form of trolleys or willing hands.

Size and shape of training room Generally speaking, training rooms tend to be rectangular and too narrow. This is especially true if you have a preference for a horseshoe layout of tables and chairs.

With a class of fifteen then you would probably have five people down each of the sides and five people along the back.

Rule of thumb: Allow 80 cm of desk space per person.

Allowing 80 cm per person you would need a horseshoe of tables five metres long and four metres across. The width of the room would need to be increased to about seven metres to allow space for the chairs and a passageway down the sides. To allow room at the front for the trainer and equipment, plus space for movement round the back, would require a room that is eight metres long.

Obviously you can use a narrower room if you have a longer horseshoe (with three or four people along the back) and less room for movement along the sides. This squeezes everyone in, but the people along the sides will have difficulty in seeing all the audiovisual equipment. This can be overcome, but you will probably find that you will have to indulge in a bit of 'scene shifting' by moving the television monitor and flip-chart stands. Building training rooms back-to-back permits a small room for audiovisual equipment to be built between them.

Rule of thumb: An ideal shape for a training room is a square. Try to keep the ratio of length to width at less than 4:3.

This might give the impression that the larger the training room, the better. However, there is a limit to the size of the room and this is determined by whether the students can read the visual aids. A person with good eyesight can usually read a flip chart up to nine metres away.

Rule of thumb: Try to limit the distance between the flip-chart stand and the furthest student to eight metres.

Capacity of training room
Taking all the above into account, you should be able to see whether the room is large enough for your course. The horseshoe layout takes more room than theatre style or a traditional classroom layout.

The training centre brochure should give an indication of the capacity of the room in these configurations. These estimates are usually on the optimistic side.

Heating and ventilation
Check that the training room has adequate heating and ventilation. Students who are too hot, too cold or too stuffy do not learn as well as those who are comfortable – but not too comfortable! In fact, students seem to be unable to concentrate if the temperature is more than 5°C above or below their comfort zone. For optimum learning it is probably better to have a slightly cool rather than a slightly warm temperature. Don't underestimate the value of having an air-conditioned training room – even in temperate countries.

Rule of thumb: Try setting the thermostat to 18°C.

Lighting
Many rooms have far too low a level of lighting. This is especially true if you use hotel function rooms. Here the lighting has been designed to provide a certain ambience.

It is also possible to have too much light. This makes it difficult to view videos and overhead transparencies. Check the efficiency and ease of use of blinds and curtains.

Some training rooms have no natural light and air. When the question is asked why the training room does not have any windows, the rationale is nearly always that a view would be distracting. Perhaps the students might occasionally look out of the window, but if they are constantly looking out of the window then I would question the effectiveness of the course and the trainer. On balance, the motivational benefits to be gained from having a pleasant environment and undisturbed body clocks far outweigh any potential distraction.

Power sockets Check the positioning of the power sockets and that the room has sufficient sockets for the equipment. It is surprising how many you need: one for the OHP, two for the video, three for the computer set-up...

Rule of thumb: Have a minimum of four power sockets available at the front of the room.

Light switches Make sure that the light switches are conveniently placed. You don't want to rush from one side of the room to the other every time you start or stop a videotape. Dimmer switches are useful for getting the optimum light level and for getting people's eyes used to the light after showing a videotape.

Acoustics Acoustics are not usually a problem unless you are using a very large room. Make sure you test the acoustics when people are in the room, as an empty room sounds very different.

Check the sound insulation from the outside and from neighbouring classrooms. A raucous class or a lawn mower can be very distracting.

Equipment You would normally expect a training or conference centre to supply flip-chart stands, an overhead projector and a screen. Some centres have their own video equipment, others have to hire it in. Check the positioning, ease of use and the operation of the equipment.

Wall space and fixings Many courses need to have posters and flip-chart sheets fixed to the walls, so it is surprising how little attention is given to the space and fixings required. Many training centres, especially the converted manor houses, abhor the use of Blu-tack or masking tape but don't provide sufficient alternatives such as pin-boards or rails.

Syndicate rooms Check that the syndicate rooms are conveniently situated and are large enough to accommodate the number of people in each sub-group plus any observers. Look out for other areas that can be used for paired, or triad, activities.

Toilets Check the number, position and cleanliness of the toilets.

Access for preparation Depending on the complexity of the course, you may spend anything from 30 minutes to three hours preparing the training room. Ideally, you would like to do this the night or the Friday before the course. You will need to check whether the training rooms are used during the evenings or over the weekends. Even if the rooms are not being used, you will need to check whether you can gain access at the time you need to prepare.

Food There can be considerable variation in menus from one training centre to another. Some provide meals to gourmet standards! You will need to decide whether the standard of the food and service is compatible with the type of course you are running. When you are doing a site survey you would normally expect to be provided with a meal so that you can judge the standard for yourself.

Meal and break arrangements Check the times and the flexibility of the meal and coffee arrangements. Also check to see how long it takes to serve a complete meal, as this can be critical if you are running evening sessions.

Bedrooms With the increase in the standard of living and holidays abroad most people expect a high standard of accommodation. Most training centres now provide:

- desk, chair and reading light,
- bed,
- wardrobe (but never enough coat hangers!),
- separate bath/shower/toilet/wash basin,
- television,
- clock/radio/alarm,
- coffee/tea-making facilities.

Look at the variation in standard and size between bedrooms. People do compare notes and it is inconsistency of standards rather than the absolute standard that causes people to complain.

Leisure facilities If the course is more than a couple of days long, the training centre should provide sport and leisure facilities. This is especially important if the centre is in a remote area.

Security Check that the training and accommodation blocks are secure and that the car park is supervised. Is it possible to open the windows in the bedrooms without providing access for an intruder? If the accommodation is separate from the training block, are the paths well lit and supervised?

Emergency procedures   Ask what the procedures are in the case of a fire or bomb alert. Gathering locations should be identified and, in the case of a bomb alert, these should be over 800 metres away and out of direct sight of the training centre.

> Source equipment

If you are running courses in a commercial training centre, all you need to do is to hand over a precise specification of your requirements and the equipment will be provided as and when you need it. If you do a lot of training on your own premises it is worthwhile buying the equipment you need. This is especially true of overhead projectors and video players which are also needed for meetings.

Unless you make frequent use of the more expensive and specialist equipment such as computers and projection televisions, you will find it more economic to hire rather than buy.

> Compare costs, suitability and availability

The results of the site survey will allow you to compare the suitability of alternative training venues. Comparing costs will prove to be a little more difficult. Most residential training centres will give you a day rate and a 24-hour rate, but these rates are not always directly comparable.

It is very important that you understand what the rate includes. Some rates include everything, others provide a minimum and make additional charges for anything else. The golden rule is to ask for a written summary of what is included in the price. The following is a list of items which may, or may not, be included in a 24-hour rate:

- main classroom,
- syndicate rooms,
- pencils,
- paper,
- flip-chart stands,
- flip-chart pads,
- flip-chart pens,
- food,
- coffee,
- audiovisual equipment,
- computers,
- special table arrangements in restaurant,
- making use of empty rooms for short exercises.

The costs of telephone calls (often priced at hotel levels), photocopying and faxes (sending and receiving) vary widely from centre to centre.

The other method of comparing prices is to have training centres quote against a pre-determined specification. The following is the specification that I use when I am getting quotes for non-residential training:

- 1 main classroom for 12 people with OHP, screen, flip-chart stand, flip-chart pad and flip-chart pens.
- 1 VHS player and monitor.
- 1 syndicate room with flip-chart stand, pad and pens.
- Coffee/tea and biscuits in morning.
- Cooked lunch (two courses).
- Tea/coffee in afternoon.

Running your own training centre

As the amount of training you do increases, one question that will come up is whether it is worthwhile to have your own training centre. Your own training centre can vary from a dedicated room to a separate building or a residential centre.

The disadvantage of having your own residential centre is that you have to worry about making sure it is full. If you cannot fill the centre yourself you will have to hire it out to external customers – and then you might find yourself in the hotel business rather than the training business.

Many companies do not want to be in the hotel business, and they do not like to have their cash tied up in a training centre, so they get a specialist company to buy and run the establishment for them. These companies make an annual charge for running the centre. If this charge is independent of the number of students, you will again be faced with the problem of filling the place. Unless you have nearly 100 per cent utilization rates this option will be just as expensive as hiring a commercial training centre only when you need it.

Designing a new training centre is a skilled activity. Architects are not trainers and do not always come up with the most practical layout. If you follow the advice given in this book you should be able to work with the architect and design the rooms you need.

Another possibility is to go to one of the suppliers of audiovisual equipment who will design the training rooms and will also provide a project manager to oversee the installation. Of course, there will always be a suspicion that the design will be more biased to the sale of equipment rather than what is exactly required. The most common problem people have when training rooms are designed for them is over-specification.

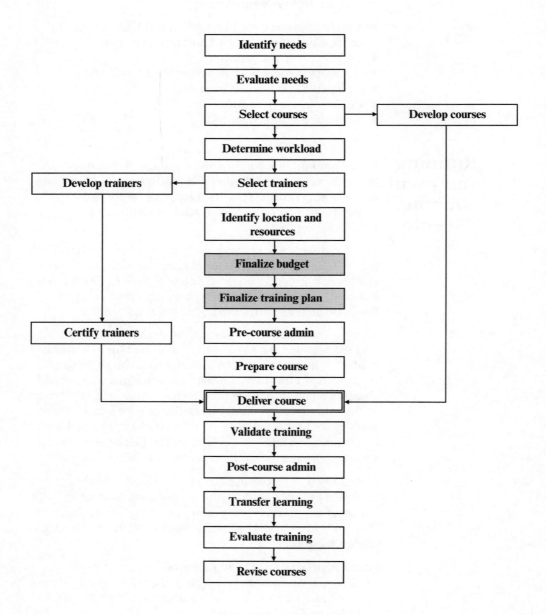

Figure 6.1 *Training plans and budgets*

6 Training plans and budgets

This chapter covers the content of a training plan and the preparation of a training budget, both of which are required to complete the next two steps of the training process:

- finalize training budget,
- finalize training plan.

In previous steps of the process we have covered the need, identified the courses to meet the need and estimated the resource required to deliver the workload. Now we have to prepare a budget, match the desired level of training to the available resource and prepare the final training plan.

Finalize training budget

One of the questions that has to be answered when a training plan is being put together is: 'How much will the training cost?' It is interesting to note that we are nearly always asked how much training will cost rather than what is the size of our training investment. A better question might be: 'How much would it cost us if we don't do this training?'

Whatever question is asked, and no matter what we call it, working out the figures may not be quite as simple as it first appears. This is because of the difficulty of deciding what should be included in the costs. For example, should you include the trainers' salaries, the students' salaries and the loss of production during training? You may end up doing a very detailed cost analysis or you may decide only to count what is normally deducted from your budget.

You may also have to decide whether your training department should be run as a profit centre. A profit centre means that you will sell your courses and training expertise in order to defray the expense of running your own training operation. This will involve you in preparing estimates and working agreements.

Whatever you include or exclude from your budget, the golden rule is to be consistent and to make your assumptions very clear. With all these parameters sorted out you will then be in a position to prepare a training budget.

The size of the budget is one of the main limiting factors when it comes to determining how much of the training demand will be delivered. There are many ways of preparing a budget and the way you choose will depend on your company's accounting systems. What you include or exclude from the budget depends on these practices. The steps for finalizing the budget are shown in Figure 6.2.

Determine whether to be a profit centre

This step will not be necessary for many training organizations – you are there to provide training only for your own organization or company. However, in a large company you could be asked to run your training organization as a profit centre. In this case you will need to consider this step very carefully and include an estimate of your income in the budget.

Being a profit centre can mean many different things so you will need to clarify the rules of the game. For example, it may simply mean you have to contribute to the budget by selling any excess training capacity. At the other end of the scale the intention might be for the training department to have a 'zero-based' budget. This means that it has to justify and completely maintain its existence by selling all its 'products' to other departments and perhaps to customers outside the company as well.

You will also need to understand the reasons for making the training department a profit centre. It might be to put a value on the training so that managers can make a business

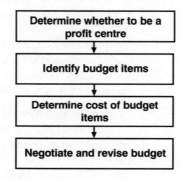

Figure 6.2   *Process for finalizing the training budget*

decision as to which training they buy. It might be to keep internal training competitive with external suppliers, or maybe a profit centre was the only way to justify the cost of a brand new, purpose-built training centre.

Strictly speaking, it might be impossible to have a true profit centre without making the training department a separate company. The reason for this is that it is extremely unlikely that any company would let the training department make its own decisions with regard to staffing levels, salaries, benefits and capital investments. Even if the training organization were given this free hand, you could imagine the amount of aggravation that would occur if you were busy recruiting trainers while the rest of the company was making people redundant.

The decision to form a separate company would be a very brave one but it also has its advantages. One curious example of this is a measure called the 'direct to indirect ratio'. This ratio, of how many direct staff you have compared to the number of indirect staff, is one of the more popular measures of a company's efficiency. By direct staff we mean the people who touch the product or its design. That is, they are directly involved with the design, manufacture or sale of a product. People who provide a service to an external, paying customer would also be considered to be direct staff.

Indirect staff are the people, such as managers and administrators, who support the direct staff. It is said that in the UK it takes one manager to supervise ten production workers, whereas in Japan it takes only one manager to ensure that 200 workers go home on time. So you can see that in the interests of efficiency, pressure will always be on to reduce the numbers of indirect staff.

All the staff in a training department would, without a moment's hesitation, be classified as indirect staff. Yet if that department were made a separate company, the trainers would then be classified as direct staff even if they were doing exactly the same work for the same people.

There is another important consideration that must be taken into account before launching yourself into a profit centre mode of operation. This is the question of who the customer is.

In a large company the training department was probably formed to meet the training needs of one organization. This organization would probably expect to have first call on the services of its own trainers – not an unreasonable request, you might think. Now the paradox of the situation is that the more successful you are as a profit centre, the less likely you are to be able to meet the needs of your own organization, because you will be too busy training other departments' staff. (You might even be asked which department you are working for.) This need not be a problem if your organization's needs analysis and planning have been done really well. In this case you will know how much spare capacity you have and you will be able to start taking bookings from other departments.

If you have spare capacity you might be asked why the training department needs to be as large as it is. On the other hand, if you do not have the capability to provide additional training you cannot expect your potential customers to wait a year to get their training. They will simply go elsewhere. That lost business will be very hard to regain.

The real problem arises when circumstances change, such as an urgent need to train every manager on financial control. You are asked to provide additional training for your own organization at the same time as you have contracted to train other departments. Obviously the first thing you will do will be to try to re-negotiate the contracts with your paying customers. You might be lucky and find that their circumstances have changed as well. If this doesn't work then you are faced with the question of who your customer is. Is it your own organization? After all, supporting them is the very reason for your training department's existence. Or is it the paying customers? If you cancel the contracts you will not get any business from them again. Your reputation will be destroyed and it is unlikely that anyone else would use such an unreliable supplier. Perhaps the only way around this, if you are really serious about running the training department as a profit centre, is to take a loss on these contracts and bring in consultant trainers to take on some of the workload.

Identify budget items

The following is a list of items that can find their way into a training budget:

- cost of external courses,
- purchase and hire of equipment, books and videos,
- production of training materials,
- training staff wages/salaries,
- training staff overheads,
- hire of training venues,

- student accommodation costs,
- student travel costs,
- student wages/salaries/overheads.

Rule of thumb: Include everything that will be charged to the training department's budget during the financial year.

The aim of the exercise is to determine whether the cost of the training plan exceeds, falls below or meets your allocated budget. Most budgets also show the expected spend by month so that you will be able to monitor the budget during the year.

If you are selling training to other departments you will also need to show the expected income for each month.

Be sure to find out what your company's financial year is. Some start in April, some start in November, while others are the same as the calendar year. Confusion can arise over financial years, especially if your suppliers or customers have a different financial year to your own, so be very careful about what should be in this year's budget and what should be in the following year.

> Determine cost of budget items

The cost of some of the budget items is fairly easy to determine. Others, like the cost of a trainer or the cost of a day of training, can become quite involved.

How much does a trainer cost?

The cost of employing anybody is not just the cost of their wages. There are other employment costs and overheads that have to be taken into account. Table 6.1 gives a fictitious example of the real cost of employing a trainer whose current salary is £22 000. I have assumed that the job involves a great deal of travel so that a car will have to be provided.

After taking away holidays a trainer is available for work for about 220 days a year. This means that this trainer costs

Table 6.1 Example annual employment cost of a trainer

Item	Cost (£)
Trainer's salary	22 000
National Insurance	1 600
Benefits	340
Car	5 500
Accommodation and facilities	2 700
Computer and information systems	1 000
Total	33 140

about £150 a day to employ. If the trainer is working at a face-to-face ratio of 50 per cent, the trainer will cost about £300 per training day.

How much does a training course cost?

This is a reasonably easy question to answer for a commercial course. It is simply the advertised price plus anything else such as travel, accommodation and wages that would normally be charged to the training budget.

To answer the same question for an internal course is more difficult. It all depends on:

- the type of training,
- the number of delegates per course,
- whether you train off-site or on your own premises,
- whether you use your own or external trainers,
- whether the course is residential or non-residential.

Not that you should let the difficulty daunt you. Your training plan should give you a good idea of the type and number of courses you need.

While I cannot give you any definitive answers to how much a training course costs, I can give you some examples of cost estimates for a number of different training courses. At least that will give you an approximate idea of how much training courses cost and it will certainly allow you to calculate your own costs.

In the following examples I have made the following assumptions:

- Neither the trainees' wages nor any costs due to lost production have been included.
- When training on your own premises I have not shown a direct cost for the training rooms but have assumed that this is covered by the general overhead which has been included in the cost of the trainer. (This would only reflect part of the cost of the training rooms because every employee's overhead contributes to this cost.)
- When using your own trainers the costs shown are the trainers' wages plus the general overhead plus an allowance to cover the trainers' salaries when they are not training. The same figure is used when the trainers work off-site because the overheads still have to be paid.
- Tax is not included.
- Travelling expenses are not included.

The cheapest classroom training that you can do is to use your own trainer on your own premises. Table 6.2 (Decision Making) is a one-day, on-site workshop and is non-residential. The calculation has been made on the basis of

Table 6.2 *Example of the cost of a Decision Making course*

Decision Making Course

Type of training	Non-residential
Duration (days)	1
Number of students	10
Number of trainers	1
Type of trainer	Own
Location	Off-site
Additional rooms	1
Trainer cost/day	£300
Materials/student	£15
Main room hire/day	£0
Seminar room hire	£0
Accommodation/student	£5
Equipment hire/day	£0
Simulation costs	£0
TOTAL COST	£505
COST/STUDENT	£51
COST/STUDENT/DAY	£51

ten students. This is a fairly typical number for skills courses that are run to meet individual development needs.

- I have used the figure of £300 per day for the trainer cost. This was the figure that we estimated in the section on 'How much does a trainer cost?'
- The sum of £15 for 'Materials/student' is to cover things like copies of the training materials, binders, pens, pencils and flip-chart pads.
- No charges are shown for room hire as the cost of the room is covered by the general overhead.
- The £5 shown under 'Accommodation/student' only needs to cover coffee for breaks and sandwiches for lunch.
- Because it is a very straightforward course no equipment needs to be hired, and no expensive simulations are required. The cost per student turns out to be just over £50, but naturally this would change if the number of students is different.

This example, and the others that follow, were worked out using a spreadsheet on a small computer. The advantage of doing this is that once you have set up the parameters you can quickly work out the costs for a wide range of different courses.

A spreadsheet is also useful because you can 'experiment' with different numbers of trainers and students (but keeping the student-to-trainer ratio the same) to see which combination would be the most cost effective. The formulae used for this spreadsheet are given in Appendix 1.

Table 6.3 is very similar to the previous example with the exception that a consultant trainer was used to run the course.

Costs for consultant trainers can vary wildly depending on the type of training and whether the trainers are part of a large consultancy organization or just running their own show. These fees can range from £300 to over £1000 a day! The fee of £500 shown in this example is below the commercial average of £700 a day for management training, but you can still get some really excellent training for around £350.

With this, as in all things, a higher price does not necessarily mean better training. You have to make your own decisions on what you can afford, the type of training, the fees that the type of training normally commands and your own assessment of the consultant.

The quality training shown in Table 6.4 was part of the company's introduction of total quality management. The decision was taken to use the company's own trainers where possible, and it was also decided to use an off-site training facility to avoid monopolizing the company's

Table 6.3   *Example of costs for an Assertiveness at Work course*

Assertiveness at Work Course

Type of training	Non-residential
Duration (days)	1
Number of students	10
Number of trainers	1
Type of trainer	Consultant
Location	On-site
Additional rooms	1
Trainer cost/day	£500
Materials/student	£15
Main room hire/day	£0
Seminar room hire	£0
Accommodation/student	£5
Equipment hire/day	£0
Simulation costs	£0
TOTAL COST	£705
COST/STUDENT	£71
COST/STUDENT/DAY	£71

Table 6.4 *Example of costs for a Quality course*

Quality Training Course

Type of training	Non-residential
Duration (days)	3
Number of students	12
Number of trainers	1
Type of trainer	Own
Location	Off-site
Additional rooms	1
Trainer cost/day	£300
Materials/student	£40
Main room hire/day	£0
Seminar room hire	£50
Accommodation/student	£49
Equipment hire/day	£50
Simulation costs	£0
TOTAL COST	£3 591
COST/STUDENT	£299
COST/STUDENT/DAY	£100

meeting rooms for the two years it would take to train every employee.

- The training centre did not make a direct charge for the main training room but included it in the day charge of £49 per delegate.
- The trainer was counted as a delegate for the purposes of meals etc.

Table 6.5 is a five-day residential course for first-time managers.

- The course runs with 15 to 20 students.
- Two trainers are needed to run the course.
- Four seminar rooms were required because of the number of sub-group exercises.
- The accommodation charge of £120 per student included the main lecture room and audiovisual equipment.
- A computer was hired for £50 per day to analyse the observation data collected during the day.

The final example, Table 6.6, is for a middle managers' course which involves a computer simulation and extensive behavioural observations of the participants. The simulation was specially commissioned by the American parent company to ensure that, as well as giving middle managers practice in running a large organization in

Table 6.5   *Example of costs for a Basics of Management course*

Basics of Management Course

Type of training	Residential
Duration (days)	5
Number of students	20
Number of trainers	2
Type of trainer	Own
Location	Off-site
Additional rooms	4
Trainer cost/day	£300
Materials/student	£50
Main room hire/day	£0
Seminar room hire	£50
Accommodation/student	£120
Equipment hire/day	£50
Simulation costs	£0
TOTAL COST	£18 450
COST/STUDENT	£923
COST/STUDENT/DAY	£185

coalition with other middle managers, the corporation's vision and values were clearly communicated to the participants.

- The simulation costs include licence fees for the simulation, air fares and accommodation costs for the computer simulation consultant.
- The three trainers are the company's own middle management trainer and two facilitators who observe the teams and give feedback throughout the course.
- The equipment costs include the hire of five computers that are needed to run the simulation.

So, the cost of one day's training can vary from £50 to over £300 even when you are arranging the courses yourself. Although this sounds like a great deal of money, it is still cheaper than sending everybody to public courses.

If you only have one or two people to train on a particular topic, then sending people on public courses would be more cost effective. Again, the cost of a day's training varies tremendously.

For example, sending someone to a course, similar to the Decision Making workshop in Table 6.2, at a local management training centre would probably cost something in the region of £150. A one-day non-residential

Table 6.6 *Example of costs for a middle manager's training course*

Middle Manager's Course

Type of training	Residential
Duration (days)	5
Number of students	20
Number of trainers	3
Type of trainer	Own
Location	Off-site
Additional rooms	4
Trainer cost/day	£300
Materials/student	£50
Main room hire/day	£0
Seminar room hire	£50
Accommodation/student	£120
Equipment hire/day	£250
Simulation costs	£9 000
TOTAL COST	£30 550
COST/STUDENT	£1 528
COST/STUDENT/DAY	£306

course with one of the large London-based training organizations would work out at about £250 a day. Residential courses would add at least another £50 to the daily costs.

If a famous business 'guru' has come to town, you could easily sit in a room with a thousand other people and be entertained for the day for the princely sum of £300. Whether these seminars could be considered to be training as defined in this book is debatable. In any case, you might well consider whether you would get a better deal by buying the book or the video!

Rule of thumb: If you want to get a 'wet-finger' estimate of the size of your training budget, work on an average of £150 per student-day of training. This includes the trainer's employment costs but excludes the trainee's employment costs.

> Negotiate and revise budget

You now know how much it will cost to deliver the training demand. I am willing to bet that this figure is larger than your allocated budget. In this case you will need to negotiate a larger budget or agree what training should be left out. Understanding what a reasonable training budget is can help enormously during these negotiations.

How big should a training budget be?

The size of the training budget is one of those perennial questions which will always be difficult to answer. A way of approaching this is to use 'benchmarking'. Benchmarking is a process by which you compare yourself to the best of your competitors with the aim of exceeding or surpassing their performance in all aspects. So, if a company in your sector is doing better than you are, it would be reasonable to assume that its level of training contributed to its business success. Therefore it would be valid to compare its training investment to your own.

Getting to the figures can be difficult. This is not because of any reluctance to disclose the figures (many training managers are only too willing to share ideas and information) but because of a lack of systems to retrieve the information. It will also take time to arrange and make these visits.

You may also find that the figures have been calculated on a different basis to your own. Differences occur over the inclusion or exclusion of items such as employment costs, overheads and loss of production. You will find that most training managers exclude as many items from the cost of training as they can get away with. The most common difference is the inclusion or exclusion of trainees' wages. This is not an insuperable problem because it is possible to make an estimate.

Rule of thumb: Inclusion of wages doubles the cost of training.

To give you an idea of a 'benchmark' for training budgets, successful multinational corporations recommend that each employee should receive five days of training per year. Managers should receive a further five days of management training.

Another guideline given by these companies is that the training budget, exclusive of wages and other employment costs, should be about 2 per cent of the total labour cost.

Most companies fall far short of these recommendations. Typical figures range from half-a-day to three days' training for each employee per year, with annual expenditure on training per employee varying from 0.4 per cent of total labour costs to 1.0 per cent. These figures are averages and the actual figures vary according to region, industry and size of company. Textile, footwear, clothing, construction and distribution industries are to be found at the lower end, and banking, finance, insurance and high-technology industries are to be found at the higher end of the range.

Training costs as low as 20p (excluding wages) a year per employee can be found in textile, footwear and clothing firms with fewer than 50 employees. Other typical spending levels are £4.80 a year in the food, drink and tobacco industry, £3.66 in the timber and wooden furniture sector and £31 in electrical and electronic engineering.

There is a direct relationship between the numbers of employees and level of training expenditure. Large employers have a consistently better record of training and have shown the greatest improvement over time.

The conclusion from this is that a training budget (excluding wages) of 1 per cent of labour costs is a reasonable figure, but this would need to be increased to nearer 2 per cent for 'benchmark' performance.

Finalize training plan

The kinds of information that you need on a training plan are:

- Who is to be trained?
- Why are they to be trained?
- When are they to be trained?
- What course has been identified to meet the training requirement?
- What is/are the occupation(s) of the people who need to be trained?
- How long is the course?
- How much will the training cost?

An example of a training plan is given in Figure 6.3.

Figure 6.4 shows the overall process for finalizing the training plan.

> Assess capability to deliver

In some ways this step is just a summary of what you have done before. From 'Determining the workload' you will know how many courses you will need to run, and you will have had the opportunity to 'lobby' for additional resources. You will also know what training locations are available and when they are available. From this information you can tell how much of the training demand you can deliver with your existing resources.

WHEN	COURSE	WHO	NUM	WHY	HOW	WHERE	TRAINER/S	COST
13 December – 15 December	Total Quality	Managers, supervisors, engineers, clerical staff	9	Company-wide programme to support introduction of total quality	Classroom	Studley	PH	465
8 December	Equal Development Opportunities	2nd/3rd level managers, supervisors	11	Awareness training to comply with company policy	Classroom	Marlow	IPD	1036
10 January – 12 January	Total Quality	Line operators	15	Company-wide programme to support introduction of total quality	Classroom	Studley	PH	465
12 January	Noise seminar	Designers and engineers	17	Future skills requirement	Classroom	Engineering Centre of Learning	JD	N/A
17 January	Understanding Personnel	L Fage	1	New appointment	Open learning	Open Learning Centre	RBP	50

Figure 6.3   An example training plan format

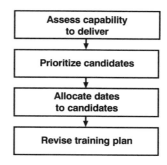

Figure 6.4 *Process for finalizing the training plan*

Prioritize candidates

As a result of capability or budget restrictions you may find that you are unable to meet the training demand. In this case, before you can finalize the training plan you need to prioritize the list of candidates. Another reason for prioritizing candidates is to determine who should attend the early courses on the basis of the urgency and importance of the training. Prioritizing also minimizes the damage that would be done by a budget cut towards the end of the financial year.

These priorities could be decided by the training department, but I feel that the organization should be responsible for its own priorities. One mechanism for doing this is the human resource development committee (HRDC).

Human resource development committees

An HRDC is a committee of peer managers who meet to make, review, validate or approve decisions which are related to the organization or development of people in their own areas.

The training department brings a list of people who have been nominated for the courses which are within the committee's responsibility. As the training department has already validated the demand there should not be many people on the list who obviously should not receive the training. The committee makes a final check on the validity of the list and then concentrates on prioritizing people for the limited number of training places.

Allocate dates to candidates

The timing of a course depends on when skills are required and the availability of training rooms, trainers and trainees.

Public holidays are another complication. Some are easy to avoid because they have a fixed date or because they are the first Monday after a fixed date. Other public holidays are just too 'moveable'. There has been a recent tendency for calendars and diaries not to show public holidays and, if they do, they only give the dates for the current year. This is not very useful if you are trying to put a training plan together six months in advance.

Easter is one of the trickiest holidays. It can catch out even the most wary. Originally Easter was associated by the early Church with the Jewish Passover, but the exact date has been a matter of controversy for centuries. In AD 325 a method of determining the date was agreed at the Council of Nicaea. This definition, which is still used today, is (wait for it):

> 'The first Sunday after the first full moon after or on the vernal equinox.'

This means that Easter can fall on any Sunday between 22 March and 25 April. No wonder moves are being made to have Easter on a fixed date. In fact, on 15 June 1928, a Bill was passed by the House of Commons which would 'fix' Easter to be the Sunday after the second Saturday in April. This would have the effect of restricting Easter to between 9 April and 15 April. However, this Bill can only take effect after it has been agreed by the World Council of Churches. Assuming that this agreement may be some time in coming, Appendix 2 gives the expected dates for Easter Sunday well into the twenty-first century.

If you train abroad or if you have students coming from abroad, then things are further complicated because of all the different holidays observed in various countries. Don't be too surprised if there are only three weeks in the year when you can avoid a public holiday. To reduce these complications for planning purposes I usually only recognize the public holidays of the country hosting the training course. This may mean that people miss their public holidays when they are travelling, but this is usually far more acceptable than training when the rest of the country is having a day off.

Revise training plan

Now that the budget has been agreed and the priorities have been decided, the final touches can be made to the plan in readiness to take its part in the company's business plan. The next phase of the training process is to implement the plan.

Respon-sibilities

It is very important that one person has overall responsibility for the training plan. This does not mean to say that all the training has to be delivered or arranged by this person. It means that somebody should be responsible for the quality, timely delivery and cost of the training.

Will your plan be successful?

To a large extent the question of whether your training plan is successful will depend on how over- or under-optimistic you have been about your training department's capability for delivering the plan. Over-optimism leads to rushed preparation, fire-fighting and a general reduction in the quality of the training. Under-optimism means that your trainers will be under-utilized and the cost effectiveness of the training will be diminished. If the under-utilization is extreme, low motivation and lethargy will set in. This also will lead to a reduction in quality.

In most planning there is usually a tendency to err on the side of over-optimism. This syndrome is sometimes known as 'planning for success'. What it really means is that absolutely everything in the plan will go right, there will be no setbacks and it is assumed that all tasks will be completed in the shortest possible time. This, of course, is a recipe for failure. So, rather than 'planning for success', I prefer to 'plan to succeed'. This means that you take a realistic view of your department's capability, have contingency plans and put the emphasis on preventing things from going wrong.

Having a realistic view of the capability of your training process will depend on your experience, but you should also collect data from previous years. This will give you the most accurate estimate of the department's capability. If you are new to managing the training department then the guidelines given in this chapter on student-to-trainer ratios and trainer workload will give you a pretty good starting point.

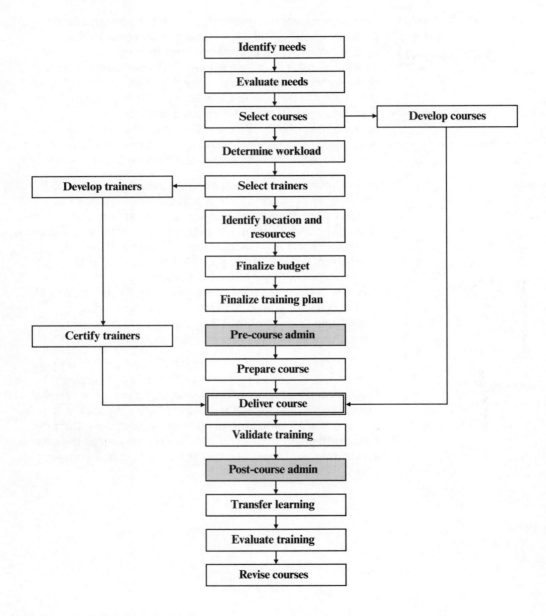

Figure 7.1 *Training administration*

7 Training administration

Training administration – the 'glue' of the training process – is covered by two steps of the training process:

- pre-course administration,
- post-course administration.

Although training and development needs are becoming more complex, you still have to get the right people to the right courses at the right time. This, as anyone who is involved in training administration will know, is much easier said than done. Just filling the course places and keeping the drop-out rates low are major challenges in themselves – let alone meeting the development needs of the individual and the business requirements of the organization.

In addition to all the work that was done in completing the training needs analysis and training plan, there are still myriad details to be seen to:

- booking the trainers,
- booking the rooms,
- booking courses,
- booking accommodation,
- ordering materials, food and coffee,
- notifying delegates of their course places,
- keeping cancelled places to a minimum,
- ensuring delegates are fully prepared,
- getting them to the right course, on the right day and at the right time,
- keeping training records up to date,
- paying the bills.

Pre-course administration

Figure 7.2 shows the pre-course administration process.

> Book location, accommodation, food, refreshments, equipment and trainers

Once you have finalized the training plan you need to book specific dates at your selected training locations. You need

137

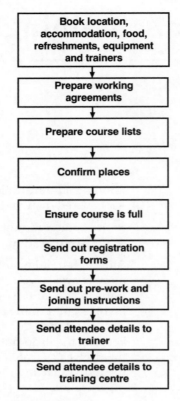

Figure 7.2   *Pre-course administration process*

to do this as early as you can. On-site meeting rooms need to be booked between two and three months ahead. Residential training centres often have their most popular dates booked a year ahead.

When you make the booking, make sure that you have your preferred dates, plus several alternative dates, to hand. You should previously have made sure that the trainers are available on these dates. Confirm the booking in writing and be very specific about your requirements (you should already have the requirements listed on your course specification). Finally, confirm the dates with your trainers.

Prepare working agreements

If you decide to set up as a profit centre it will be necessary to increase the administrative part of the process to keep track of what is being re-charged to other departments.

● The trainers (or sales staff) let the training administrator know of any future re-chargeable work.

WORKING AGREEMENT

Supplier doing the work	Customer paying for the work
Division: Manufacturing Department: Training	Division: Manufacturing Department: Training

Description of work being undertaken

Course: Coaching	Dates: 15–19 June
Number of trainers: 2	Sets of materials: 24

Re-charge

Amount: £1760.00	
Cost centre: 631270	Payment: Within 30 days

Supplier approval	Customer approval
Name: Signature: Date:	Name: Signature: Date:

Figure 7.3   *An example of a working agreement*

- The training administrator draws up a numbered working agreement (see Figure 7.3).
- Signatures to authorize the payment are obtained. A copy of the working agreement is given to the customer and the original is kept on file.

A working agreement is simply a contract between yourself and your paying customer. It should cover what work is going to be done, when it will be done, how much it is going to cost, when the charge is going to be made and who will be paying for the work.

> Prepare course lists

The heart of an administration system is the course list. On receipt of the course dates and numbers, the administrator prepares a set of blank course lists. There should be a list for every course. When it is complete it should show:

- the title, date and location of the course,
- the maximum number of places,
- the names and locations of the delegates,
- unfilled places,
- reserve and 'wait-listed' delegates.

Reserves are people who:

- did not get a place on the prioritized list,
- are on a later course but are on standby for an earlier one.

If there are no 'wait-listed' people you can nominate students who are on later courses to be reserves. This also makes it easier for a student to change from one course to another.

There should be only one list for each course and only one person responsible for its maintenance. The list can be a sheet of paper in a book or it can be part of a computerized administration system. Although only one person should own the list, its information should be available to anyone who has a need to know.

I believe in 'charts on walls' or, in this case, 'lists on walls'. Managers of the training process need to know the status of course bookings at any time. They need to do this quickly and without disturbing the course administrator. A wall display showing all the course bookings allows them to do this. The display could be hand-written charts, a computer printout or a whiteboard.

A method that we have found very useful is the 'T-card system'. It is made up from a set of metal frames that have slots cut into them. 'T-shaped' cards fit into the slots. The 'ears' of the 'T' prevent the cards falling through the slots. The trunk of the 'T' is hidden when the card is in the frame. Each card has a space for the name and location of one

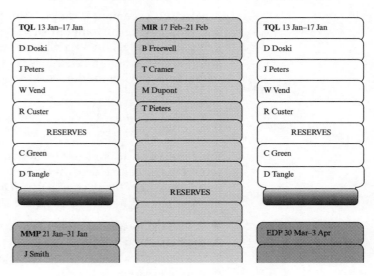

Figure 7.4　*'T-Card system' for displaying course places*

student. Other less frequently used information is shown on the hidden part of the card. Different colours represent the different courses. Details of the system are shown in Figure 7.4.

When the blank course lists have been drawn up the training administrator has to assign candidates to each course. This is most easily done from a priority list or on a first come, first served basis.

The system is more complicated than this in larger companies because the individual organizations will want to decide who goes on which course. In this case the training administrator allocates blocks of places to each organization.

The administrator determines the size of the block from the demand forecast. Figure 7.5 shows how the blocks would be reserved using the 'T-card system'. The allocations for the different organizations or locations are identified by an abbreviation, e.g. LON.

Getting the names right   A customer's perception of quality depends on the care the supplier takes to get the details right. The details that matter are those which many suppliers would consider to be trivial.

Misspelling a student's name is a good example of this. Although it might be as trivial as spelling a name with 'tt' instead of 't', the student will form an immediate and unshakeable perception of the course's quality.

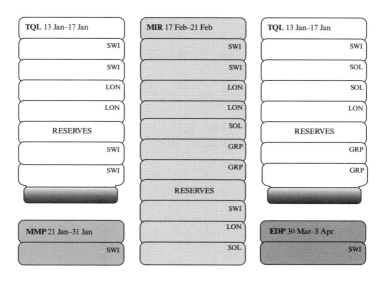

Figure 7.5   *Allocating training places to other parts of the organization*

Getting the names right is not simple. Often we rely on the original training request for the correct spelling of the names. This is the first mistake. Training requests can pass through many hands before they reach the training department. It is also surprising how many managers do not know the correct spelling of their people's names.

A good source of information is the internal telephone directory. Although not infallible, people do complain if their names are not correct in the directory. Often these directories will only have the initials of the forenames and this will make it difficult to discriminate between similarly spelt surnames. It is also difficult if the course is to be run on a first name basis.

Personnel, pensions and payroll records are the most accurate sources. As these records deal with formal names, they are less useful when people prefer to use their middle names or nicknames.

The only foolproof way of getting a name right is to ask the people themselves. This need not be arduous if the administration process makes use of a registration form.

| Confirm places |

The next step is to inform the candidates, and their managers, of the course dates. Also inform the local training representatives.

Inform candidates of their places as early as possible so that they can book the dates in their diaries. The reserves should also block out the dates in their diaries.

| Ensure course is full |

The training administrator should keep a constant eye on how the course places are being taken up. If anybody drops out, the administrator informs one of the reserves that a place is now available.

Keeping cancellations to a minimum

The main cause of cancelled places is 'pressure of work'. A cancellation fee can help keep cancellations to a minimum. Some people think this is punitive, but this is not the idea behind the fee.

One of the reasons for charging a cancellation fee is that an unfilled place is a wasted opportunity. It reduces the amount of training that can be done because an empty place costs nearly as much as a filled place. At least a cancellation fee will pay for an additional place on another course.

Sometimes you have to cancel a course because there have been too many cancellations. Always consider a cancelled course as a failure because it is a total loss of learning and resource. It might be worth re-charging the entire cost of the cancelled course to the organizations that pulled their people off the course.

Another reason for introducing a cancellation fee is to allow managers to make a business decision on whether they should withdraw their people from a course. For example, a manager might withdraw someone to write an important report. If there is no consequence, many managers would put the report before the course. However, if the cost of cancelling a place is £1500 then managers can make a business decision. Is getting the report written in the next five days worth an expenditure of £1500? If it is, then the right business decision is to withdraw the person from the course.

Having a good reserve system and letting people know the dates well ahead of the course may also help avoid cancellations.

Then there is the question of double booking. The airlines favour this to make sure that there are no empty seats. I am against this practice because we should never promise a customer something we cannot deliver. When I am told that the seat that I have booked and paid for has been taken by somebody else, I am a very unhappy customer. I am not the slightest bit interested in the airline's problems or its utilization rates.

Double booking sets an expectation that cancellations will occur and that we condone cancellations. We should set the expectation that the only reason for a cancellation is a personal emergency.

Always try to book the maximum number of students allowed by the course specification. If there are last-minute cancellations, you should still have the minimum number of students required to run the course successfully.

All the above suggestions for keeping cancellations to a minimum are no substitute for people, and their managers, really wanting the training to happen. People and organizations do what they believe to be important. This underlines the importance of getting the basics right and delivering the training that meets both the individual's and organization's requirements.

Send out registration forms

The registration form reminds students of their attendance. It also flushes out the people who are unable to attend. Send out the registration forms six weeks before the course is due to start. If you send the forms much earlier there is a chance that the course will be forgotten. Sending the forms much later will not leave enough time to find a replacement if somebody drops out. An example of a registration form is given in Figure 7.6.

The form should have the name of the course as well as its start and end dates. It is always a good idea to put both the date and the day. This helps to identify mistakes and avoid misunderstandings.

Clearly show charges and cancellation fees on the registration form. This will keep future arguments to a

---

COURSE REGISTRATION FORM

PLEASE COMPLETE IN **BLOCK CAPITALS** AND RETURN TO:
The Training Administrator, Group Personnel

COURSE TITLE:

COURSE DATES:

COURSE FEE:

COURSE LOCATION:

NAME:
(As you would like it to appear on a certificate, e.g. Bertram J Bloggs)

NAME:
(As you would like to be called during the course, e.g. Bert Bloggs)

STAFF NUMBER:

JOB TITLE:

GRADE:

ORGANIZATION:

DEPARTMENT:

LOCATION:

ELECTRONIC MAIL ADDRESS:

INTERNAL TELEPHONE NUMBER:

MANAGER'S NAME:

MANAGER'S LOCATION ADDRESS:

MANAGER'S ELECTRONIC MAIL ADDRESS:

MANAGER'S INTERNAL TELEPHONE NUMBER:

COST CENTRE:
(For course cancellation charge – does not apply in a personal emergency)

MANAGER'S SIGNATURE: _____

Figure 7.6   An example of a course registration form

minimum. Also identify the person, or organization, responsible for paying the fee. A budget or cost centre number does this unambiguously.

Advising students of the course venue at this stage allows them to plan their travel arrangements.

It is a good idea to ask for the students' full names as well as the names they would like to use during the course. It is surprising how different these can be. Don't forget to amend the course list if you discover any spelling differences here.

If certificates are awarded it is also a good idea to check how candidates would like their names spelt on the certificates.

It is better not to use the term 'Christian name' as this may cause irritation, if not offence, in multicultural societies. A better term would be 'first name' or 'given name'.

A staff number uniquely identifies a person's personnel or training record. This is the only way to ensure that the right person is coming on the course. Having the staff number also makes it easier to update the training records. It also makes it more likely that changes to the training record will be made after the course.

The job title, grade and organization provide a final opportunity to make a check on the course's suitability for the delegate. This information also allows the trainer to make better decisions about sub-group composition. Many courses work better with diverse sub-groups, other courses require homogeneous sub-groups. Chapter 8 deals with the composition of sub-groups in more detail.

The registration form should also ask whether the delegate has any special dietary, access or other requirements.

> Send out pre-work and joining instructions

Send out the pre-work and joining instructions no later than two weeks before the course. Increase this time if the students have to gather information, if there is a lot of reading or if there is a holiday period before the course.

Keep pre-work to a minimum. Never issue pre-work that is not a prerequisite for the course. Similarly, do not go over the pre-work in class. This irritates the students and it also discourages them from completing the evening work.

Joining instructions should cover the following at a minimum:

Internal Memo

From: **A Traynor**	Location: **Newark** Extension: **2542**	Division: **Human Resources**
To: **Attendees**	Location:	Date: **25 May**

Facilitation Workshop

Date:	Wednesday 16 June–Thursday 17 June
Location:	Conference Room 1, Newark
Start:	8.30 am
Finish:	6.00 pm (both days)
Trainer:	Andy Traynor

I am writing to confirm your place on the above workshop and to provide you with information on the following:

• The purpose, desired outcomes and agenda of the workshop

• Your pre-workshop assignment

Please find enclosed the above attachments and a copy of *Facilitating for Gold.*

Notes on the pre-work:

• Please read *Facilitating for Gold*

• Summarize the main learning points from the first three chapters

My experience of this workshop is that completion of the pre-work is essential.

The time we have available for useful practical work is limited, so we will need to make the best use of our time between 8.30 and 6.00.

A thorough understanding of the contents of *Facilitating for Gold* will enable us to make best use of this time. I estimate that the pre-work will take you at least three hours.

I look forward to seeing you on 16 June. Please contact me if you have any questions or concerns.

Regards

Andy Traynor

Figure 7.7   An example of a joining instruction letter

- the course title,
- the start and finish dates of the course (use the day as well as the date),
- the location,
- starting and finishing times,
- directions to the venue,
- accommodation arrangements,
- dress code,
- what they have to pay for (e.g. drinks in the bar).

An example of a joining instructions letter is given in Figure 7.7.

Delegates also find it useful to have a booklet which gives additional details about the training centre. These details include:

- meal arrangements,

- message arrangements,
- sport and recreational facilities,
- smoking policy,
- emergency and security procedures,
- local shops and banks.

Electronic mail, if it can handle graphics, is a convenient way of sending out pre-work and joining instructions. Sending large volumes of pre-work electronically gives some electronic mail systems a headache, so check with your system expert before you do so.

Send attendee details to trainer

During the week before the course starts, the administrator should send the trainer the names of the attendees. This can be either a list or copies of the registration forms. The advantage of using the registration form is that the information is supplied by the trainee and so is less likely to be wrong. It also has information which will help the trainer decide on seating plans and sub-group arrangements.

Send attendee details to training centre

The week before the course, the administrator should send the hotel or training centre details of the attendees. This list includes the delegates' names, the nights they need accommodation, special requirements and whether they will be needing a meal the night before the course.

Post-course administration

Figure 7.8 shows the details of the post-course administration process.

Trainer confirms students' attendance

After the course the trainer should give a list of the attendees to the training administrator. Copies of the course critique should also be sent to the administrator.

Amend training records

Keeping the records accurate and up to date should be the responsibility of one named person. In our organization the responsibility for the records lies with the training administrator. Training administrators can only keep control if they are the only people given authority to access and amend the training records. Even training managers should merely be allowed to read the records!

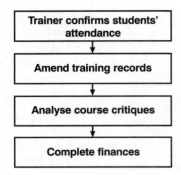

Figure 7.8   *Post-course administration process*

The training records should be amended as soon as the training administrator receives the confirmed list of attendees from the trainer.

When a person goes on an external course extra precautions should be taken to ensure that the training is recorded. The way to do this is to give the students a critique form to take with them. At the end of the course the student returns the completed form to the administrator. If the students do not return the form, the administrator contacts them to check whether they attended the course. Using a critique form in this way helps to control the quality of external courses.

The risk of incomplete records increases when training has been organized from within another department. It is a good idea to have all training requests pass through the training department and for the training department to hold the budget for all training.

The intention is not to control what functional training should be given to an individual. There is no way that anyone in the training department could have enough knowledge of all the professions to make any kind of sensible judgement. That decision is best left to the individual's manager. What the training department can do is to check whether good value for money is being obtained, co-ordinate separate demands for the same kind of training and ensure that the amount of training received is not being under-reported.

Analyse course critiques

The course critiques are analysed for trends in the students' perception of the course. Details on how to do this are given in Chapter 10, Validation. Keep the analysis and the critique forms on file for at least three years.

> Complete finances

After the course the administrator should pay the invoices that relate to the course. Re-charges should also be made for unfunded places, cancellations and work that has been completed for other organizations.

Controlling the budget

The amount you have spent needs to be checked at regular intervals so that you can detect deviations from your plan before they become an irrecoverable problem. How often the checks need to be carried out depends on the rate at which you are spending the money. It is unlikely to be more than monthly or less than quarterly. You will also need to check the accuracy of the invoices you receive.

If you find you are overspending you will obviously need to determine what the causes were so that the problems can be avoided in the future. However, do not spend a lot of time beating yourself up. Those problems are in the past and you can do nothing more to prevent them. The problems that you can do something about are in the future and that is where you need to concentrate your efforts. Come up with solutions which will allow you to meet your targets with the budget you have left.

You need especially to look out for the problem of invoices received after the financial year has finished. You need to be able to carry forward an amount of money into the next year to cover these charges, otherwise you will find either that there will be no money to pay for them or that you will have less money to fund the training plan.

Computers and administration

One of the things you will notice as you get more involved in training administration is that the same information keeps on cropping up in different circumstances. This means that the administrator spends a great deal of time typing, and perhaps correcting, the same information. It is precisely these circumstances which lend themselves to the use of computers.

Take the simple example of a student's name. This information appears in all of the following documents:

- course demand lists,
- course place notifications,
- course lists,
- registration forms,
- joining instructions,
- name cards,
- attendance sheets,

- drinks lists,
- sub-group composition,
- observation sheets,
- course certificates.

Not only does the student's name have to be typed or written on every one of these documents, the chances of getting the name wrong are considerably increased.

If the students' names and other information are kept on a computer database, standard letters and documents are produced quickly and accurately.

There are several training administration training programs on the market, but you may find that some of these programs have been developed for a particular industry sector. This makes it even more important that you have a demonstration to make sure that the program is suitable for your needs.

Facilities of a computerized administration system

To help you assess a particular system, the following is a list of facilities that you would expect a computerized administration system to provide:

Programme planning

- Proposed course schedule
- Trainer allocations
- Locations
- Budget allocation
- Schedule revisions

Course booking

- Course place status
- Vacancy details
- Reserves
- Block bookings (without specified student names if required)
- Unconfirmed bookings
- Waiting lists
- Notification letters
- Joining instructions
- Pre-work enclosure list
- Invoicing
- Cancellation fees

Accommodation

- Room allocation
- Daily register of residents' details
- Registration
- Invoicing
- Visitors' accommodation

Course documentation

- Certificates
- Name cards

- Lapel badges
- Delegate lists
- Seating plan
- Groupings
- Drinks lists
- Contact lists

Charging
- Internal re-charges
- Variable invoicing
- Separation of delegate-incurred expenses

Statistics
- Profit/loss statements
- Number of delegates
- Number of delegates per course
- Drop-out rate
- Resource utilization
- Hours of training per employee
- Cost of training per employee
- Cost per course place

Training records
- Employee training record
- Record of bookings, transfers, cancellations and fees
- Enquiry and report facilities
- Training records update

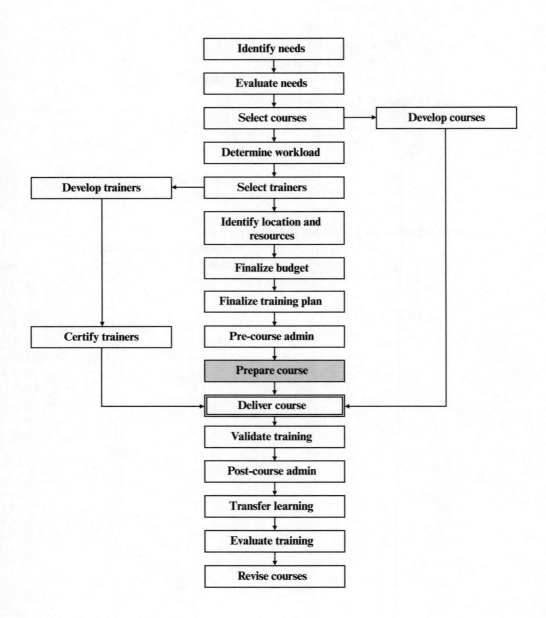

Figure 8.1   *Course preparation*

8 Course preparation

The more effort put into the preparation of a course, the more trouble free that course will be. Always plan to prevent (or at least have a contingency for) what you know could go wrong. As Murphy's law says: what can go wrong will go wrong, and at the worst possible time.

When you are dealing with these known emergencies you will be leaving no time for the hundreds of other gremlins that you didn't know about. Murphy's lesser-known second law – 'Murphy's law of time estimation' – also applies when you are preparing for a course. This law runs as follows: 'To determine the true time that a task will take, you should first make an estimate of the time. Double it and then move it up into the next time unit.'

For example, if you estimate that it will take five minutes to alter a document on your word processor, it will actually take 10 hours. If you estimate that you can write a one-day workshop in three days, it will probably take you six weeks to complete.

There is an inverse relationship between the amount of effort you put into preparation and the perceived difficulty of your job. The harder you work, the easier it seems. It is unfortunate that your strengths will always seem easy, simply because of smooth and professional execution. So don't be surprised when you are asked: 'When are you going to go back to doing a "real" job?'

Figure 8.2 shows that there are two parallel streams of preparation activity. Not only do trainers have to prepare, but students also have to prepare themselves for the course. For this reason this chapter has been divided into two parts: student preparation and trainer preparation.

Student preparation

Students do pre-work

If you were to take a survey of how many students do their pre-work before arriving at the training centre, you would

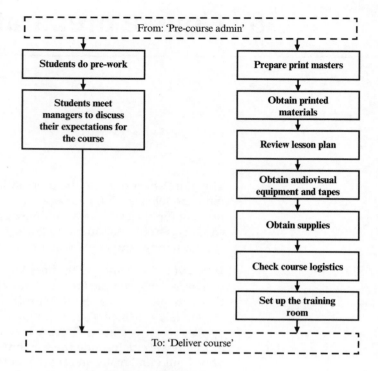

Figure 8.2 *Course preparation activity*

find the proportion to be less than 60 per cent. Of these, more than half would have left the pre-work to the last one or two days before the course.

Given these depressing statistics, it has to be asked why we bother with sending out pre-work. The usual reason for doing pre-work is to shorten the time it takes to do the course. This, by itself, is not a good reason.

However, there are activities which do not make the best use of course time. Examples of these activities are:

- background reading,
- collecting data,
- filling in questionnaires.

As students also vary widely in the time they take to complete these activities, it makes sense to set such tasks as pre-work.

The guidelines given in Figure 8.3 will help to ensure that the pre-work is done in good time.

- Always make sure that the pre-work is essential to the running of the course.

- Give an accurate estimate of how long the pre-work will take.

- Prioritize the pre-work tasks.

- Let the students know why the pre-work is necessary.

- Let them know how the pre-work is to be used.

- Let them know when the pre-work will be used.

Figure 8.3 *Guidelines for setting pre-work*

Students meet managers to discuss
expectations for the course

An important part of ensuring that training is effective is to make sure that the participants know why they are on the course, and how they are going to use the training after the course.

You would be right in thinking that this is a bit late in the day for the participants to find out why they are going on a course, but if you need convincing that this step is necessary, try asking your next group of students why they think they are on the course.

A certain proportion will know the developmental reasons for their attendance, but a significant minority will, after a few seconds of stunned silence, come up with some serious and some not so serious responses such as:

- 'I don't know.'
- 'I was told to come.'
- 'I came for the free lunch.'
- 'John couldn't attend, so I'm here as a substitute.'

The right time for people to know why they are on the course is at the time they are nominated. This is part of needs analysis, which is dealt with in detail in Chapter 2.

Once the participants have a clear idea of why they are attending the course they can discuss what their managers will expect them to do differently as a result of the course.

If the course is skills based it is a good idea for the participants and their managers to select tasks that can be practised during, and used for application after, the course.

For example, depending on the course, you could select:

- tasks that need to be delegated,
- projects that need to be managed,
- reports that need to be written,
- problems that need to be solved.

Not only does this concentrate the mind but it also provides a final check as to whether a person needs to come on the course. It is very difficult for people to justify their need for a project management course when they are unable to find any projects they need to manage.

Trainer preparation

> Prepare print masters

Some years ago the idea of the paperless office was much discussed. While there is a great deal of merit in having visions of the future, it will be a long time before people will feel comfortable without a piece of paper in their hands.

Undoubtedly computer technology has made tremendous strides already and will continue to do so. However, a computer's window on the world is still very small (about 200 words compared with an open book's 800). A computer prefers to act like a scroll rather than a book, and when it can be coaxed to turn pages it does so very slowly. It just cannot compete with leafing through a book. Surprisingly, even when supercomputers were used to simulate the speed and capacity of a book, people still found fewer errors in a proofreading experiment.

Computers do not like being folded up like a piece of paper and they always need more batteries and power than a book. Where computers do score is in their ability to search for a given word, present information in different ways (depending on the learning need) and link with other sources of information.

So, it looks as if printed documents (also known as hard copy) will be with us for some time to come. More and more materials will be prepared electronically but they will not be committed to paper until much later in the process. One of the main advantages of having electronic masters is the ease of revision and modification. There is no theoretical reason for the masters to be held in any form other than electronically.

However, electronic storage of information is always susceptible to being lost or corrupted. Surprisingly, a flimsy sheet of paper can take much more damage than an electronic file before it is impossible to retrieve the information. This is why computer users are always being urged to make 'backups' (additional copies) of their work. Although this has the effect of doubling the cost of storing information, it is still far cheaper than losing all your work.

I would still recommend keeping a paper version of your materials – if the worst comes to the worst you can always have the paper document scanned electronically.

In the future you could imagine a small terminal in the training room that prints the material as the students arrive and produces the handouts only when they are needed. In this way there should be no wastage whatsoever.

Currently most people make copies of paper masters that have been produced electronically. With this approach you can still produce the materials even if the whole of the computer system has 'gone down' because you can find a photocopier in nearly every office.

Another disadvantage of using electronic masters is that they may be compatible with only one word-processing program. However, most systems can read simple files on disks that are compatible with the MS-DOS format.

For this reason, it is advisable to keep a copy of your text files in the simplest format possible (usually called an ASCII file) or to make sure that you know how to convert your text to an ASCII file. Appendix 3 gives some tips on how to do this.

Although this seriously restricts what can be done (the document will be unformatted and you will not be able to have combined text and graphics), it does mean that you can access your text from almost any word-processor program. Convertibility between programs and even platforms (Windows and Macintosh, for example) is also becoming more common in the latest systems.

The other possibility is to keep an HTML (HyperText Mark-up Language) version of your documents which can then be read and printed from any computer with browser software. HTML can handle graphics and a wide range of formatting including tables.

Obtain printed materials

Be sure you have enough copies of the training materials ordered, printed or photocopied in time for the course. Ideally you would want the printed materials to arrive at the training venue on the day you set up the training room.

This ideal is risky unless your suppliers are of the highest quality. You will probably arrange for the materials to arrive a couple of days before the course as a contingency measure. What you don't want to do is have your office or storage area cluttered up with training materials months before you need them.

How many copies should you make?

In an ideal world you would have exactly the same number of copies as you have students. Yes, I know that, in spite of all the administrative systems we have put in place, it is still almost impossible to ensure full attendance. I also know that on occasions more students than you expect turn up. Sometimes the materials have defects and you need spare copies to replace them.

Assume that you order two extra sets of materials when you run a workshop for ten people. This may not seem a lot, but you are increasing the cost of the training materials by 20 per cent. This is a significant chunk out of your training budget. You may argue that having additional materials does not really matter as you can always use them on the next course. But when will the next course be? Where will you store the extra materials from this workshop and the materials from the other courses that you run? What happens if you revise the course? Will you have the time to 'rework' all the binders you have in the stores? Can you be certain that all your materials will have the same revision level? Can you ensure that the materials will not get dirty or be damaged while they are being stored? In fact, you might be better off throwing the spare materials away.

This might seem to fly in the face of today's emphasis on conservation and recycling, but it need not. First, concentrate on ensuring that the right number of people turn up to the course. Then have a really close look at the materials. Check to see whether they have been printed simplex or duplex (single sided or double sided). If the materials can be printed double sided, there will be a 40 to 50 per cent saving on paper usage and cost.

See if the materials can be printed on recycled paper. Rather than throwing excess materials in the bin, remove the sheets from their binders and arrange for a recycling company to come and collect the waste paper. Return the binders to your printer or copy centre or hold on to them yourself if you must. At least you can re-use them quickly because they will hold the materials for any of your courses.

If you have the impression by now that I am not in favour

of storing anything, you would be pretty close to the truth. This might seem counter-intuitive, because trainers find a certain amount of comfort in having large stacks of materials. They also have difficulty in throwing anything away – you never know when you might need it.

The trouble with storage is that you can never have enough of it. The quantity of materials you have to store will always increase to exceed the amount of storage space you have available. Good systems have to be in place to help you find the items you require and there is always a danger of damage to the materials while they are in storage.

Storage is very expensive. Ask your financial director how much a square metre of floor space costs your company. This money is locked up and doesn't earn a penny. The stored materials do not add any value to the business until they are removed from the store and are either used or sold.

Just-in-time materials
This concept of stock-less operation is called 'just in time' (JIT). It is one of the many ideas that have come over from Japan. The idea is that you train your suppliers to deliver the materials you need at the exact time you need to use them. So, in a supermarket, a new delivery of toothpaste would arrive just as the last tube was being taken from the shelf. Not only do your suppliers have to be well disciplined but you also have to be able to use the materials immediately. If you don't you will be buried under a mountain of stock.

This mode of operation seems to be a little strange to some British suppliers...

Komatsu, the Japanese manufacturer of bulldozers, took over a factory that used to be owned by the Caterpillar company in the north of England. In keeping with European Union regulations, the Japanese needed to use a proportion of locally manufactured parts in their bulldozers. One such part was the fuel tank. Komatsu asked one supplier when it could supply the tanks.
'Next week,' came the reply.
'No, you don't understand,' said the Japanese, 'Which day? Which hour?'

This does not mean that this kind of approach cannot be transferred to a Western culture. Neither does it mean that everyone has to do exercises and sing the company song before starting work in the morning. There are many Marks & Spencer stores in England that now have first-floor sales areas where their stockrooms used to be.

Applying the 'just-in-time' approach to training means that you have the materials copied just before you run the training courses. In this way you will only have to find storage space for about four boxes at a time. The clever bit about this is that it is your printer who has to find storage space for the paper and binder stocks.

Even if you copy the materials yourself, it is still better to print off what you need when you need it, because there is less money tied up in the raw materials than there would be in the final product.

There is always the temptation to order a whole year's worth of materials because you can get a better discount from the printer. Think very carefully before you do this. Are your training materials so good and your company so stable that the materials will need no revision during the coming year? It can be very expensive throwing away or 'reworking' half a year's stock.

Also compare the savings that you make with the discount with what you would have to pay for extra storage. Estimate the cost of stocktaking and damaged materials. Ask what else you do with the money that you have 'invested' in the stock.

Storing the masters

All this assumes that you have a superb system for storing, revising and retrieving the masters for your course materials. One of the first decisions you are going to have to make is where the masters are going to be stored. The major options are: with the trainers, with the training administrator or at the printers. The final choice of location depends on the security of the masters and the stability of the course. If a course is stable and run many times a year, it can be very convenient to store the masters at the printers and just make a phone call when you need some more copies printed.

Electronic storage of masters is becoming more practical. When copies of the materials are required the 'digital masters' are retrieved and the materials are printed off. It is also possible to create a document on a personal computer and send it electronically to a printer for printing and finishing.

Take the security of your paper and electronic print masters very seriously. Masters should be kept in file boxes, and the file boxes should be in a locked cupboard or stored on shelves in a secure room.

With paper masters, every handout or sub-section of a student binder should be in its own plastic document wallet. The wallet should have a label that identifies the master and gives instructions to the printer on how the masters should be copied and bound (see Figure 8.4).

> Module 7 **Visions**
>
> • Single-sided
>
> • 4-hole punched
>
> • White, recycled, A4

Figure 8.4   *Example of labelling a print master*

This should be sufficient for relatively simple jobs. For more complex materials you should also provide a printer's dummy. A printer's dummy is an example of the finished materials so the printers can see exactly how they should produce the materials.

When you have the handouts printed, ask the printer to put them straight into the file you will be using during the course. It will not take the printer much longer, but it will save you a great deal of time and bother.

Handouts v binder material   When I see a course that has a large number of handouts, I start to suspect that the course is becoming out of date (it is easier to produce another handout than to revise and reprint the student binder). This suspicion becomes stronger if the trainer does not make full use of the materials that are in the binder.

> Review lesson plan

Make sure that you have enough time to prepare yourself for teaching the course. If you are unfamiliar with a course this can take as much as a day of preparation for each hour of trainer presentation. For a familiar five-day course you may need no more than a hour to skim through the lesson plan.

No matter how familiar you are with the course, don't be tempted to miss out this step entirely. Familiarizing yourself with the course provides reminders of all the things you need to do before and during the course. Over-confidence leads to disaster.

> Obtain audiovisual equipment and tapes

The course specification should have a complete list of all the audiovisual equipment required for the course, such as:

- overhead projectors,
- flip-chart stands,
- cassette recorders,
- video recorders and cameras,
- computers and printers.

The technical specifications need to be very precise when you order or hire video equipment and computers. There are many different standards and, if the equipment supplied is not compatible with your tapes or software, you will not be able to use it.

The most common standards are VHS for video and IBM-PC for personal computers. I say standards, but even these popular 'standards' come with several different variations.

Overhead projectors

Most training locations supply an overhead projector as standard. There is not a lot to choose between the different makes of overhead projector, although there are a couple of features you should look out for. The first is an internal spare bulb that can be changed quickly and easily by turning a handle. The second is the ability to 'tune' the optics so that blue and orange colour fringes can be eliminated.

Flip-chart stands

Check to make sure that your transparency frames do not foul the column that supports the optics head.

Flip-chart stands seem to be innocuous pieces of equipment, but like deckchairs they can be a trap for the unwary. Here are some pointers to look out for:

Height

Check that the stand can be adjusted for both your shortest and tallest trainer.

Weight

If you have to transport your own flip-chart stands check the weight and bulk of the unextended stand.

Rigidity

Check that the stand does not move around or bend when you write on it.

Method for holding the paper

Look at the method for retaining the paper. This can be a spring-loaded jaw or a pair of pegs. Check that the pegs align with the holes in your flip-chart paper. (Why on earth isn't there a standard for this?) Many of these stands have screw-on clamps which make it difficult to tear off sheets cleanly.

The jaw method of retaining the paper has the advantage of not needing a particular spacing for the holes but it does not retain the pad so well. Some methods use a retaining bar and I have seen it take two people to insert the pad – one to hold the bar out of the way and the other to push the pad into the jaws!

Check to see whether the stand will retain single sheets, either by themselves or in addition to the pad. This feature is essential if you have sub-groups reporting back to the main classroom.

Video recorders VHS is the most popular format for video recorders but unfortunately it comes in three different standards: PAL, NTSC and SECAM depending on which country you happen to be in. (See the glossary at the end of the book for an explanation of these abbreviations.) Most European countries use PAL. France and the former Soviet Union use SECAM and the USA uses NTSC.

Unless you can buy or hire a multistandard video recorder which will play PAL, SECAM and NTSC, you will need to make sure that all your tapes are in the same format as the machine you are using. You can check this by looking at the label on the cassette or its case. If this doesn't give you a clue, try playing the tape on your machine. A different standard usually runs the soundtrack at a different speed and produces horizontal lines on the screen.

If your tapes are in a different standard you will need to get them converted by one of the specialist video houses. A word of warning – if your tapes are commercially produced, you will be breaching the owner's copyright if you have the tape converted. So when you buy a commercial tape make sure that it is in the standard you will be using.

The introduction of camcorders, i.e. portable video cameras with a built-in video recorder, has led to two new formats (plus variations): VHS-C and 8 mm. This isn't a problem if you are using video feedback that will be played back during the course, but it will cause problems if you want to give the students their tapes to take away with them. The VHS-C cassette has to be either copied on to a standard tape or clipped into a special carrier before it can be viewed on a domestic video recorder. 8 mm has to be copied on to a standard tape.

A more recent introduction is Super VHS. This has a cassette the same size as an ordinary VHS cassette. It achieves higher definition and picture quality. An ordinary VHS cassette can be played on a Super VHS machine, but a Super VHS cassette cannot be played on a standard VHS machine.

Modern video recorders are very reliable and the most common problems are dirty recording heads and damaged connecting leads. The main symptom of a dirty recording head is a snowy type of interference. This problem can easily be solved using a head-cleaning videocassette. Scotch makes a version that has a pre-recorded video message and audio tone. The cassette is played until the tone is clear and the message is legible.

Audiocassette recorders

Until the introduction of digital tapes, audiocassettes followed a universal standard. There is not a great deal to choose between the different makes of recorder. It is convenient if the recorders have an internal microphone. A battery indicator light gives an early warning of flat batteries and helps you prevent spoilt recordings.

The most common problems you are likely to get with an audiocassette recorder are:

- flat batteries,
- dirty recording head,
- dirty pinch roller and capstan.

If you have poor sound quality always check the batteries first, and then use a head-cleaning cassette. If the problem persists refer to the user manual and clean the capstan and pinch roller. The capstan is a metal spindle that turns to drive the tape. The pinch roller is a rubber wheel that holds the tape against the capstan.

Computers and printers

The situation with computers is very similar to the video situation – different standards with many variations. Always check that your computer matches the system requirements that are printed on the software packaging or in the software manual. Appendix 4 explains computer specifications in more detail.

> Obtain supplies

Supplies are consumables that you need for every course – and they have a habit of running out just when you need them. The trainers' checklists in Appendix 7 suggest a selection of supplies that you will need during a course. It is a good idea to use the checklists before each course to ensure that you have a sufficient stock of supplies.

Fixings

It is almost certain that every course you run will involve displaying charts or posters on a wall. If you are working in a purpose-built training room, there should be rails or pin-boards on the wall for displaying posters and charts. It is an unwritten law of the universe that you will always need more display area than is provided.

Masking tape is the best all-round method for sticking charts to walls. If you are careful, it should not pull off paint and wallpaper when it is removed.

Blu-tack is less satisfactory as it can be difficult to remove without leaving a mark. A tip for removing Blu-tack is to roll up another piece into a small ball, and then roll it over the wall so that it picks up the pieces like a snowball. Doing it this way decreases the likelihood of removing any paint.

Flip-chart pads The holes in the flip-chart pads should align with the pegs on your flip-chart stand. Some pads are stapled together which makes it difficult to tear off single sheets. One way to overcome this problem is to buy pads with perforations, but this leaves the holes behind which makes it difficult to put the sheets back on the stand. Another way around this problem is to buy pads which are held together by an adhesive rather like a note pad.

A square grid printed faintly on the sheets helps you draw diagrams and keeps your writing on the level. Considering the amount of flip-chart paper that is thrown away at the end of a course, it is a good idea to buy pads made of recycled paper.

Flip-chart pens Flip-chart pens or markers come in several different types: spirit based, water based and dry wipe. Black and blue are the best colours for reading from the back of the room, while red and orange are the worst. The pens' tips should have a minimum width of 5 mm.

Whiteboards should only be written on with dry-wipe pens. Too many whiteboards have been spoilt by writing on them with permanent pens. If this should happen to you, all is not lost because there are several methods that you can use for removing the marks.

First there are proprietary sprays. If you do not have any of these around when you need them, you can try Snopake or White-out thinners. An effective but lengthy method is to scribble over the permanent marks with a dry-wipe pen. Then use a dry cloth to remove both marks together. As this method is also quite tiring it teaches you not to use the wrong pens on the board. You could also try using a plastic eraser to remove the marks.

The manufacturers of some water-based pens say that these pens can be used on whiteboards. This is true but the marks have to be removed with a damp cloth. This can turn out to be a somewhat messy operation.

Some trainers take the preventive route by banning all pens except dry-wipe pens. The only problem with this is that dry-wipe pens are not very suitable for flip-chart work. The lines they draw are not broad enough to be read from the back of the class and the colours are not strong enough.

I prefer to use water-based pens for flip-chart work. If you do accidentally use them on a whiteboard, it is not too much hassle to remove the marks using a damp cloth. Another advantage of using water-based pens is that you do not spend all day breathing in fumes.

Throw flip-chart pens away as soon as they dry out. Repeatedly picking up the same exhausted pen is a frequent source of frustration. No amount of shaking or standing the pens on their heads will get more than a few extra minutes of life out of them. It is advisable to bring your own flip-chart pens with you as it is amazing the number of training locations that provide exhausted or unsuitable pens.

Overhead projector pens

There are two types of overhead projector pens: permanent and water soluble. Pens with a medium tip are generally the most useful thickness but you might find you will also need a set of fine pens. Red, blue, green and black stand out well on the slides.

Use permanent pens if you don't want them to rub off. Water-soluble pens are useful if you want to make corrections as you go along, or if you want to re-use the slide, but cleaning the slide can be a bit messy. Another option is to place a blank transparency on top and write on that with a permanent pen. I prefer to use this method even when I am using water-soluble pens because it is easier to throw the top sheet away than clean up the prepared transparency.

Whatever you do don't get the two types of pen mixed up. Buy pens that allow you to see easily which is which. For example, Staedtler makes permanent pens with a black barrel and water-soluble pens with a grey barrel. Permanent pens do not always write very well on some types of transparency material. If you have a problem, try a water-based pen instead.

Check course logistics

Some courses are more complex than others when it comes to preparation. Scanning through the lesson plan will remind you of what you have to do.

Course specifications

When you provide many different courses it is always difficult to remember exactly what has to be prepared. The kind of details you need to remember are:

- How many syndicate rooms does this course need?
- For what time should we order the coffee?
- What are the start and end times?
- What videos do we need to bring along?

This problem is compounded when you are training away from your home base. You may have to rely on somebody else to prepare the classroom and to make all the necessary arrangements.

As suggested above, you could scan through the lesson plan to answer these questions, but you need to attend to the logistics long before you start in-depth preparation of your sessions. The answer to this problem is to have a specification for every course you run. A course specification only needs to be two or three pages long at the most. Figure 8.5 gives an example.

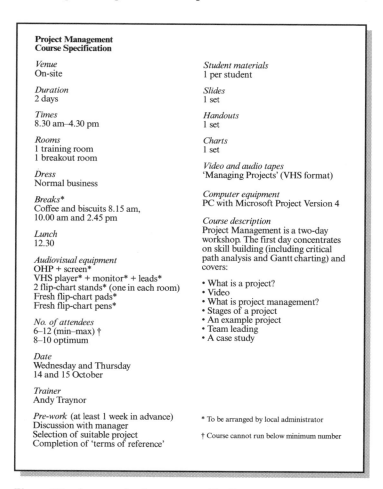

Project Management Course Specification

Venue
On-site

Duration
2 days

Times
8.30 am–4.30 pm

Rooms
1 training room
1 breakout room

Dress
Normal business

Breaks*
Coffee and biscuits 8.15 am,
10.00 am and 2.45 pm

Lunch
12.30

Audiovisual equipment
OHP + screen*
VHS player* + monitor* + leads*
2 flip-chart stands* (one in each room)
Fresh flip-chart pads*
Fresh flip-chart pens*

No. of attendees
6–12 (min–max) †
8–10 optimum

Date
Wednesday and Thursday
14 and 15 October

Trainer
Andy Traynor

Pre-work (at least 1 week in advance)
Discussion with manager
Selection of suitable project
Completion of 'terms of reference'

Student materials
1 per student

Slides
1 set

Handouts
1 set

Charts
1 set

Video and audio tapes
'Managing Projects' (VHS format)

Computer equipment
PC with Microsoft Project Version 4

Course description
Project Management is a two-day workshop. The first day concentrates on skill building (including critical path analysis and Gantt charting) and covers:

- What is a project?
- Video
- What is project management?
- Stages of a project
- An example project
- Team leading
- A case study

* To be arranged by local administrator

† Course cannot run below minimum number

Figure 8.5   An example of a course specification

I usually send my customers a copy of the course specification as soon as the course dates have been confirmed. You will notice that I give a detailed specification for computer and video equipment. This is to avoid the embarrassment of not being able to play the tape, or run the software, on your customer's equipment.

I also make it clear what equipment I will be bringing and what equipment needs to be supplied by the customer.

Fred's list The course specification is sufficient for short, straightforward courses. Courses that have complex logistics need the equivalent of a course specification, or a checklist, for every module. This checklist details the items that you need to prepare or obtain for the module.

We call the complete set of checklists 'Fred's list' in honour of a colleague of ours whose lists helped us through the logistics of a particularly tricky course.

You will still need a course specification for the course's general requirements. 'Fred's lists' are for trainers' eyes only – they are far too detailed to be of use to the customer.

Seating plans When students ask me how I choose the seating plan, they are disappointed to learn the simplicity of the criteria. (They suspect that I use some complex psychological method.)

There are two basic approaches for seating people on a course. The first is to have them sitting next to somebody they know, the second is to have them sitting next to somebody they don't know.

One of the advantages of a residential course is the opportunity to meet people with different backgrounds. To foster this, I often arrange the seating so the students sit next to someone they don't know.

If the course intends to do team building I would have the participants sitting in their natural work groups. This situation is one of the few times that I would have managers and their people in the same group. Having a manager and one of that manager's people on the same course can make it difficult for both parties to act naturally.

Before you can make any decisions on the seating plan you have to have some data on the students. The registration forms have information which indicates whether the participants know each other. Look to see whether they work in the same location, are part of the same organization or work for the same manager. Although this approach is no substitute for local knowledge, it does have a high success rate. In the absence of these data, a random seating plan is as good as any other. Having the students sit in sub-group order helps the logistics (and the trainer's memory) considerably.

If you know the students well enough, you may be able to avoid potentially explosive seating combinations. In practice, predicting the interactions of 20 people is just too difficult to get right. Having too many criteria makes it impossible to find a suitable seating plan.

Sub-group assignments The guideline of keeping the criteria simple also applies to sub-group assignments.

The composition of the sub-groups should match the objectives of the course. Diverse groups allow people to learn about other departments. Homogeneous groups permit delegates to share knowledge and experience.

Be careful if you use criteria of race, age, gender, religion or nationality for creating diverse sub-groups. You must have a good training reason for using these criteria. 'Let's split the girls up' is not a good reason. Giving people practice in managing diversity is a better reason. The safest selection criteria are experience, location and the delegate's job.

Mixing the sub-groups A good way to have a nervous breakdown is to change the sub-group composition for each exercise. For an even better nervous breakdown, try arranging the groups so that every student has worked with every other student by the end of the course.

After a few hours of brain bashing, you will come to the conclusion that only certain combinations of course and group size provide a complete solution.

> Set up the training room

Setting up a training room, checking the equipment, putting up posters and laying out materials for 20 people can take up to two hours. If the training room is free the day or evening before, I would recommend that you set up the room then – you still have all night to sort out any problems. There is nothing worse than trying to get the video recorder to work as the students are walking in. Even better, get somebody you can trust to set up the room for you.

Of course, having somebody set up the training room for you does not work this well every time. It takes several years to build up this kind of relationship with a supplier and you would not normally want to cut things this fine – even with your most trusted supplier. However, this

> One of the training venues I had been using for many years understood my requirements so well that they would lay out the training room exactly as I would have done it myself.
> This arrangement worked well for both parties. I did not have to book the room for the night before to lay out the materials, and the squash club could run profit-making functions into the early hours of the morning. All I had to do was give the manager a copy of the course specification and a drawing of the room layout, and make sure that all the materials were on site.
>
> To give you an idea of how well this worked, I was once delayed by a traffic jam and arrived at the training venue just as a team-building event was due to start. Everybody had helped themselves to coffee, as indicated by a notice on the flip-chart stand, and I was able to walk in, switch on the overhead projector and say, 'Good morning and welcome to ...'

episode does underline the importance of having the training room set up as early as possible.

Room layout Check that the tables and chairs are positioned so that everybody will get a clear view of you, the video monitor and the overhead projection screen. Walk round the room and look at the layout from every student's viewpoint.

If you want to encourage discussion between the participants, avoid having students sitting with their backs to each other.

Arranging the tables in a 'U' shape is a good layout, but don't get stuck with only one kind of layout. Try out some more interesting variations. You could use groups of tables, or you could have gaps to allow for freedom of movement in the room.

Audiovisual equipment Checking the audiovisual equipment should be one of the first things you do when you are setting up a classroom. This will give you the maximum time to have the equipment replaced, or repaired, in the event of a major malfunction.

Check the sound level of the video, but bear in mind that the soundtrack will appear louder in an empty room than in a room full of sound-absorbing students.

After you have checked the sound and picture, wind the tape back to the beginning. Cue the tape by playing it up to where you want it to start. You may have to experiment with the exact stopping point as some recorders do not restart at the same place as they were stopped. This should help you avoid showing a blank screen and the copyright notice. The few seconds that it takes for the video recorder to get itself started will give you time to turn out the lights.

People do not have a great tolerance for video recorders that do not show a picture as soon as you press the play button. It must be due to a basic mistrust of technology.

> This basic mistrust of technology was once demonstrated to me when I lent a videotape to a group of senior managers. The video was in two parts, separated by a period when the screen faded to blue.
> When the first part had finished the managers assumed that the video recorder had gone wrong so they switched it off. Later I timed the interval between the two sections of the tape. It was six seconds!

If you are using audiocassette recorders, make a test recording on every recorder to make sure that the batteries aren't flat and that the recorders are recording properly.

Switch on the overhead projector and, using one of your own slides, check that the projector is in focus and the optics are clean.

I usually remove the clamp from the flip-chart stand and remove the staples and cover sheets from the flip-chart pads to make it easier to tear off sheets. I also attach short lengths of masking tape lightly to the back of the stand so that I have tape readily available when I want to stick sheets on the wall.

Student materials

Lay the students' binders, pens, pencils and erasers on the tables. Use this opportunity to do a final quality check on the materials.

Locate the handouts in an easily accessible place. If you are training in your permanent location, consider investing in a wheeled set of hanging files. If portability is your first consideration then a card 'concertina' expanding file will be more convenient.

Name plates

Name plates are essential for the first few hours of the course so that you are able to learn the students' names. There are several types of name plates. The simplest is a sheet of A4 card folded along its length.

Other types use individual plastic letters. The letters have small pegs on the back so that you can press them into the holes on the name plate. Not only do these seem to take for ever to prepare, but they are also an irresistible temptation for the members of 'Anagrams Anonymous'. You will be amazed at their creativity. You will never catch them in the act because they strike when you least expect it.

A popular type of name plate has a shiny, white surface which can be written on with dry-wipe pens. These are quick to prepare but the name can only be written on one side and the lettering is easily smudged.

One of the best name plates that I have seen was made in-house by one of the large conference centres. The base was a piece of wooden moulding that had a groove cut into its length. A name card was held by a piece of perspex (Plexiglas) that had been bent in half along its length. The perspex fitted into the groove on the wooden moulding.

You can get the students to fill in their own names as part of the warm-up. This helps if you are not confident of who is going to turn up. It also helps if you are not sure whether the names are spelt correctly.

My preference is to have the names already filled in on the name plate. This allows you to decide where the students will sit and it also makes the students feel expected when they walk in.

Consider having the names printed or written on both sides of the name plate. If you can withstand the jokes about students not knowing their own names, you will be able to see who the students are from any part of the room. This also helps participants find their places when they first walk into the training room.

> There was one incident that convinced me that the names should be on both sides of the name plate. This was a course when some of the students knew everybody's names except those of the people they were sitting next to.

Prepare syndicate rooms

Visit each syndicate room to make sure that the correct wall charts have been put up. Check the lighting. See if there is enough flip-chart paper. Test the felt-tip markers to make sure they have not dried out.

Check that there are sufficient supplies of other consumables such as masking tape, 'Post-its' and drawing pins.

Trainer materials

Finally, set out the trainer's guide and transparencies at the front of the room. Check that all the supplies you need are close to hand. Make sure that you have the latest version of the student materials in front of you. In this way you will not have the embarrassment of referring to the wrong page or to an exercise that was removed three courses ago.

Final check

When you think you have finished setting up the room, take a few moments to look round the room and check that everything is in place. Make sure that you know:

- where the keys are kept,
- where the light switches are,
- how to control the heating,

- how to open and close the windows and the window blinds.

Then turn off all the equipment at the wall, turn off the lights and lock up the room.

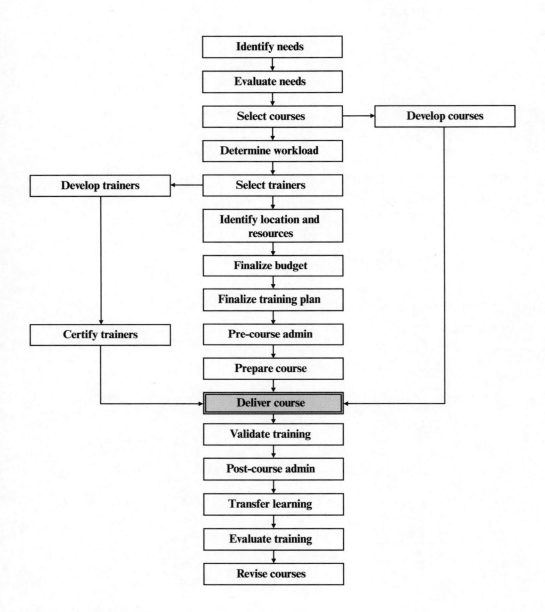

Figure 9.1   *Delivering the course*

9 Delivering the course

This chapter deals with the pivotal step of the training process:

- course delivery.

Because the thrust of this book is about managing the training process, rather than learning to be a trainer, the emphasis in this chapter is on the principles associated with the steps of the delivery process plus consideration of the following three topics:

- open and distance learning,
- training in other languages and cultures,
- the use of computers in the classroom.

Course delivery process

The process for delivering a course is shown in Figure 9.2.

Pre-course check

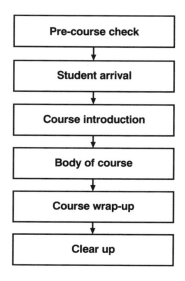

Figure 9.2   *Course delivery process*

Although you should already have prepared for the course, it is worth taking a few minutes to check that the following are still in order:

- lights,
- materials,
- overhead projector,
- video equipment.

The telephone You will already have asked reception not to put calls through to the training room. As an extra precaution I would also recommend diverting calls or disconnecting the telephone from the socket – it's amazing how persuasive some people can be in trying to contact their staff.

If you forget to disconnect the telephone and it rings while you are in the middle of a session, keep talking while you walk over and disconnect it. Ignore the gasps of amazement – some people are psychologically unable to resist the call of a ringing telephone.

Spike Milligan once drew a cartoon of a person who was tied, head to toe, to a post. The only part of this person's anatomy you could see was an arm sticking out between the coils of rope.
A ringing telephone was placed on a pedestal that was just out of reach of the arm. The cartoon was titled: 'Chinese telephone torture'.

Don't worry about the call being urgent – they seldom are and most things can wait for 45 minutes. If it were a matter of life or death you can be sure somebody will ring the alarm bells or run round to the classroom.

Make sure that everyone has turned off their mobile phones and pagers.

Student arrival

The impression the students get within the first few minutes can make all the difference to the success of the course. If the course is residential it is essential that registration goes smoothly and the rooms are clean and available. If you are not able to meet the students as they arrive, it is a good idea to leave a welcoming letter at reception. The letter can also include additional details about the course and its location.

Be in the classroom before the first student arrives so you are there to greet them. The important thing to remember about this step is that you want the students to feel comfortable about the training.

Coffee One way to help students feel comfortable when they arrive is to have coffee and other beverages available. This gives people a chance to relax and get to know each other.

Dress code The participants' joining instructions will have advised them of the type of clothes that are expected to be worn on the course. The recommended level of clothing is part of the course design and depends on where the course is being run and its training philosophy.

Some training courses are designed to have a more informal atmosphere so students are asked to dress casually. No matter what is put in the joining instructions, it is another one of those unwritten laws of the universe that at least one of the students will turn up wearing a business suit and will continue to wear a suit for the rest of the week. There is no problem with this as long as the person feels comfortable with what they are wearing.

Whatever the dress code, the cardinal rule is that trainers should not be dressed very differently from the students. If a trainer adopts a dress style which is the same as the most casually dressed student the more smartly dressed may start to feel uncomfortable, and vice versa. The best approach is for trainers to try to adopt a level of dress that is at about the middle of the students' range.

As the students arrive you will get a feeling for the level of dress. If the level of dress is biased towards one end of the dress code, you can subtly amend your own clothes. This can be as simple as removing a jacket.

Late arrivals Always insist that training courses start on time. I know there is a temptation to wait for late arrivals, but there is no way of knowing how long they are going to be or whether they are going to turn up at all. Waiting punishes the people who have been punctual and destroys the momentum that is required at the start of a course. Five minutes lost at the start of a course often translates into an hour's loss by the end.

When the latecomers arrive do not make any fuss and do not stop the course to bring them up to speed. Making a fuss just disrupts the course and could lead to strained relationships. Stopping to summarize communicates that it is all right to be late because the trainer will always bring you up to date.

Course introduction

The course introduction is for:

- you to get to know the students,
- the students to get to know you,
- the students to get to know each other,
- communication of the course aims and structure,
- validating student expectations,
- understanding the reasons for their being on the course,
- communicating course logistics.

If there are two trainers consider having both take part in the introduction as the co-trainer is often disadvantaged by having to sit at the back of the room.

Student introductions   The standard course introduction is to go round the room and have the students give a brief autobiography to include:

- name,
- job title,
- organization,
- how long they have been in the company,
- hobbies and interests.

This method is somewhat pedestrian and it often does not achieve what it sets out to achieve. People stop listening when they are thinking about what they are going to say. In a class of 20 this introduction can take up to an hour and each person is only directly involved for 5 per cent of the time. Here are some variations you might like to try:

Claim to fame   Most people have met somebody famous or have done something excitingly different – and most people like talking about it. So instead of getting people to do the standard introduction you could get them to relate their claims to fame.

The best claims to fame don't always come out during the course introduction, so have another session later in the course if you want to hear the juicier stories.

Paired interviews   Some people do not like talking about themselves in front of the class. In this type of introduction the students pair up with the person they know the least and interview each other. After about 15 minutes each person reports back with a brief biography of their partner.

A picture of my life   Provide coloured pens and sheets of A3 drawing paper. Ask the students to draw a picture of who they are and what they do – both at work and at home. You will find that, despite initial reservations, people really get into this exercise and disclose more about themselves.

Catch ball   Instead of going round the class in order, throw a ball (preferably a soft one) at one of the students who does the first introduction. This student then throws the ball to someone else. Challenge the class to complete the introductions without throwing the ball to the same person twice. It's probably a good idea to clear the coffee cups before starting this exercise.

Mugshot Ask the students to bring either a passport photograph or their identity badges to the course. Display the photographs on the wall along with an identifying letter (identity badges should have the names taped over). Supply each student with a list of identifying letters. The objective of the exercise is to write the names of the other students against their identifying letters on the list. This involves matching the people in the room with the photographs on the wall. When approached, people should only give their name. They should not say which photograph is theirs. The worse the photographs, the better this exercise works.

Course logistics At the beginning of the course only communicate the most vital course logistics – very little is remembered of an information dump. Obviously emergency procedures have to be given at the beginning, but coffee, lunch and dinner arrangements etc. can be communicated as they are needed.

Training course or assessment centre? It is important to communicate whether a report will be sent back to participants' managers.

Unfortunately, some managers expect training courses to assess how good their people are at doing their current job. Apart from the fact that this would be an abdication of one of the manager's prime responsibilities, training courses are not adept at and, for that matter, not designed for carrying out this task. The environment on a training course is very different to the work environment. If it were exactly the same, there would be no difference between formal training and on-the-job training. This difference in environment means that observed behaviour on a training course would not necessarily be a good predictor of behaviour back at work. The ability of a trainer to assess accurately 20 individuals on a week's course would also have to be questioned. It can take up to two days just to learn all the names!

If you assume that each student participates equally and that the exercises where behaviour could be assessed make up 60 per cent of the course, you would only have a maximum of one hour's data on each person – not a very efficient assessment process.

If the students work in sub-groups, it is the other members of the sub-group who are in the best position to make an assessment of a particular individual. I am not suggesting that students should 'spy' on their fellow students, but feedback from other class members can, if handled sensitively, be very powerful.

At this point it is worth pointing out the difference between training courses and assessment centres. Training courses are for increasing knowledge and the development of new skills. Assessment centres are designed to measure or assess existing skills.

In the development of new skills it is essential for a person to be able to reveal their current deficiencies and then to experiment and make mistakes without being punished. It follows that confidentiality is an essential part of a training course. If a person feels that everything they do is being reported back to the organization or their manager, they will be very reluctant to participate openly and the training will not be as effective.

With assessment centres the question of confidentiality does not arise because everybody knows and accepts that a report will be made.

It might be argued that it is essential for a person's manager to know whether that person has reached the desired standard in the skills that they were expected to learn. This is a reasonable request and complying with it need not be inconsistent with the principles outlined above.

With self-paced training a person could in theory remain on the course, receiving additional coaching until the desired level of expertise is attained. Thus completion of the course itself would be the indicator of meeting the required standards.

Of course, it would not be good business practice to allow everybody to stay on a course for an indefinite period, so most courses would have an upper limit on their duration. Above this limit it would be uneconomic to continue the training to completion. It would also probably indicate that the student concerned would be very unlikely to make the grade under any circumstances.

You should consider any failure to complete a course as an error in the process and a waste of your limited training resources. The cause of this kind of error is usually in the selection of the student for the course or the selection of the course for the student.

With trainer-paced courses the completion of the course does not give an indication of the standard reached. So how can the organization be assured that individuals have attained the necessary standards without reducing the effectiveness of the training? The answer is to make a distinction between the parts of the course where learning is taking place and the parts of the course which are assessed.

You would have to make this distinction very clear at the beginning of the course and assure the students that no reports are being made during the teaching phase. Under no circumstances should you imply that there is confidentiality where in fact there is none. Not only would this breach professional etiquette but it would quickly lose you all trust and ruin your reputation.

Expectations and reasons for being on the course

Take some time to understand what people are expecting from the course and why they are attending it. You will find that the course will meet most of their expectations, but there will also be some expectations that the course was not designed to meet. Be open about the extent to which the course will meet your students' expectations.

Understanding the reasons for the students being on the course will help you deal with any emotional issues that might arise during the course.

Course aims and structure

Describe the aims and structure of the course. Explain what will happen and when it will happen. Describe the linkages between the components. Take the opportunity to emphasize the parts of the course which best meet the students' expectations.

I like to have the course agenda displayed as a poster. (For a five-day course this could be as big as three sheets of flip-chart paper.) The students can then refer to this at any time to check where they are, and you can use it to reinforce the course structure as you move between components.

> Body of course

I believe that there are four main phases in teaching:

- presentation,
- assimilation,
- practice,
- testing.

Presentation

In this context presentation has a broader meaning than is usually understood. It includes any method that presents the skills and facts to the students. So, in addition to the trainer standing up and making a presentation, it would include videos, demonstrations, text and self-discovery exercises.

We learn through all of our senses (the usual five plus sense of movement and rhythm) yet training makes limited use of only two – auditory and visual. Try introducing more colour into your presentations. Have exercises that involve movement and people doing things with their hands. Try presenting a lesson to the accompaniment of baroque music.

Assimilation

After presenting the facts or demonstrating the skills, the temptation is to go straight on to the next set of facts without allowing an opportunity for learning to take place. Even if the skills are practised and the knowledge tested, the assimilation phase is often left out. By assimilation we mean the process by which students are given 'space' to make sense of what they have just heard and seen. It also allows them to fit this new knowledge into their existing model of the world. If the training proceeds before they have had this opportunity, it will be building on a very shaky foundation.

This opportunity can be provided in several ways. You can give students a couple of minutes to reflect, you can get them to jot down a few notes or you can give them the opportunity to ask questions. If you presented the lesson accompanied by music, you could replay the music to help the assimilation.

Practice

The third phase is for the students to practise what they have been taught. Practice is an absolutely essential part of learning, so it is a pity that it is the first thing to go when the pressure is on to reduce the duration of a training course. The only circumstance under which you should permit the removal of practice from a course is when you can guarantee that supervised practice will occur immediately after the course has finished.

There is sometimes a debate on whether skills should be practised on case studies or on real examples. The argument against case studies is that it is difficult to transfer the skills being practised outside the classroom because case studies are too simple and unrealistic. The argument against using real projects is that they are too complex and students will spend far too much energy on the detail to the exclusion of learning the concepts. As with many 'either/or' arguments, the answer is not 'either/or' but 'both'.

The process I prefer for courses where the appropriate teaching style is more 'directed' rather than 'discovery' is as follows:

- First give an overview of the concept, principle or process.
- Then demonstrate using a simple example. Don't worry if the example seems trivial – this will allow some humour to creep in and will make demonstration of the skills all the more memorable. You could use a 'tea-making' example for teaching critical path analysis and have a heated discussion about whether the milk should be poured into the cup before or after the tea!
- After the simple example the students can then practise on a more complex case study.
- Finally students can be coached on an example from their own work area. If they have any difficulties they can always refer back to the example and the case study.

Testing   Finally you should check the extent to which the students have learnt the skills and knowledge desired. This could be a formal pencil-and-paper test but more effective, and incidentally less intimidating, is observing the student applying the learning to a project or their own work. This also increases the chances of the learning being transferred back into the business.

Another way of testing is for the trainer to ask questions in class. Even better, get the students to write the questions themselves.

Instead of using 'pose then pounce' or 'pounce then pose' techniques, try asking the question as you throw a ball to the student ('throw and pose' technique). Throwing the ball is not a gimmick: the idea is to distract the student's conscious attention so that the answer can surface from the subconscious. Suitable balls for this exercise are either sponge balls or balls that have been constructed from strands of rubber in the fashion of a pompom.

I had some reservations about this 'catch ball' technique until I used it to help teach a dozen theories of motivation and leadership.

The lesson included a videotape which described all 12 theories in 40 minutes, obviously too much to take in at one go. I had already split up the tape with discussions about the theories and I also had 'stills' from the video on display. Despite this it was still apparent that the students had little confidence that they could remember the theories. I decided it might be worthwhile using the 'catch ball' technique.

After showing the video I called a coffee break to allow the students to relax and to give some time for assimilation. When they returned I named one of the theories and threw the ball to one of the students. Immediately the student explained what the theory meant. The ball was thrown from student to student, each student explaining one theory and naming another. To our amazement all the theories were accurately recalled.

Accelerated learning

Some of the techniques described above were first developed in 1956 at the University of Sofia by the Bulgarian psychologist Dr Georgi Lozanov. Colin Rose's book *Accelerated Learning* describes these techniques in more detail.

Level of intervention

One of the things that is most difficult to get right is the trainer's level of intervention in what students are doing. If students have problems with a task it is best if they can sort these problems out for themselves. If they can't sort out the problems for themselves, and the trainer does not intervene, they begin to flounder and lose confidence. If the trainer intervenes too early the students become frustrated and learn little. In extreme cases the trainer ends up doing the task for the student.

The best way to find the correct level of intervention is to identify the parts of the course where students are likely to have a problem, monitor them regularly and discreetly and err slightly towards intervening too late. (It is difficult to tell whether you intervened too early, because students might have got on to the right track if you had not intervened.)

The pudding shift

The pudding shift, otherwise known as the graveyard shift, is the session immediately following the lunch break. It is difficult to gain students' attention and concentration because they would rather be having a siesta. For this reason it is best to avoid presentations immediately after lunch and to have a participative exercise instead.

Course wrap-up

During the course wrap-up you should:

- check whether the students' expectations have been met,
- have students complete a course feedback form,
- thank students for their participation and share your feelings about the course,
- if applicable, distribute certificates,
- stand near the door to say goodbye as students leave.

> At the end of every course, a colleague of mine used to say that this was the best course he had ever taught and that he loved all the students!
> The amazing thing about this was that he really believed it – and, more amazingly, so did the class!

Clear up

The end of a course can be somewhat of an anticlimax, but you need to pack up the materials and take a few minutes to think about how the course went.

- Ask yourself how you feel. If you feel down, consider what you could do better next time. If you're on a high, the course might have gone exceedingly well, but check to make sure you were not playing games with the class. Feeling quietly pleased is a good position to be in.
- Look through the feedback forms. More on this in Chapter 10, Validation.
- Clear up the rubbish so the cleaners can distinguish between what should be thrown away and what should be kept.
- Pack up the materials that need to be sent back to the store.
- Send a copy of the feedback and attendance sheets to the appropriate administrator.

Open and distance learning

In Chapter 5 we discussed the 'Identify location and resources' step of the training process. An important part of this step is determining the type of learning environment. We usually think of the classroom when we talk about the learning environment. Although the classroom provides a controlled environment, it is usually more expensive and does not provide the flexibility of 'open learning' or 'distance learning'.

The terms 'open learning' and 'distance learning' are used interchangeably as this type of learning is usually 'open' to everyone (as with the Open University) and is carried out 'at a distance' from the creators of the material.

Learning can be at home, in the workplace or in specially adapted rooms known as 'learning centres'. These rooms are resource centres and usually come equipped with books, audiotapes, videotapes and computer programs – along with all the necessary equipment. The great advantage of open learning is that students can study at their own pace and at their own convenience.

The need, selection, development, administration and delivery of open learning courses should be given the same attention as any other type of course. If this is not done, the use of open learning will become haphazard and random and will fall into disrepute. The training process described in this book applies to open learning as much as it does to any other kind of learning. The principles of managing the training process remain the same.

Learning centres have variable success rates – some are over-booked while others are hardly utilized. Our research into learning centres has identified a number of factors which are critical to the success of the centre:

- Qualified tutors should be available all the time the centre is open.
- The centre should be open when it is needed, which means that it will probably have to be open both early morning and late evening.
- The centre should be located where it is easily accessible.
- The room should be purpose built.
- The organization's culture must be supportive of learning – people should not feel uncomfortable because they are perceived to be not working when they are in the centre.
- The programmes should be integrated with the organization's other learning activities.
- The materials and equipment must be up to date.

The need for a 'physical' learning centre will decrease as computers and access to the Internet become more widespread. This will enable time-of-need and point-of-need training.

Training in foreign languages and cultures

Unfortunately the British and Americans tend not to be fluent in any language other than their own. When compared to other nationalities such as the Scandinavians and the Dutch, we are truly put to shame. English is spoken widely, and few other countries speak Swedish or Dutch, which makes it easier for them and harder for us. However, this is not a good excuse for refusing to learn even a few words of someone else's language.

Whatever our level of linguistic expertise, most of us still have a problem when faced with a class of foreign students. Of course, the problem is minimized if all your students speak excellent English. In this case you should be able to train the course in the same way as you do for English students.

It is often assumed that the course should be presented in the students' own language and that all the materials should be translated if their command of English is less than perfect. Luckily, there are several levels of translation that can be applied and this can be critical when time or cost is at a premium. Table 9.1 shows the relationship between the level of translation and the standard of English.

When the language ability is very high, all the presentations, materials and exercises can be in English.

Where the command of the language is not perfect, but still very good, the presentation and materials can be in English

Table 9.1 *Relationship between language ability and the level of translation*

Ability	Exercises	Presentations	Materials
High	English	English	English
Good	Own language	English	English
Fair	Own language	Own language	English
Poor	Own language	Own language	Own language

but participants should be allowed to complete the exercises in their own language. It is still possible to use English trainers. If a translator is not available they will have to rely on their knowledge of the course, body language and tone of voice to understand what is going on. This is not as difficult as it might seem, because a trainer who has intimate knowledge of the exercises will soon be aware of any problems or difficulties. It is then just a matter of intervening and asking what is happening.

The next level is to have the course presented in the students' own language but still have the written materials in English. Videotapes would have to be over-dubbed. When producing videotapes that are to be used in other countries, make sure that the master has two soundtracks. The first track should have the music and sound effects, and the second track should have all the language-sensitive material. This makes dubbing in the foreign language very much easier.

As language ability decreases, more and more of the materials will need to be translated. However, not all of the written materials will need to be translated unless the language ability is very low. Articles and explanations of concepts would need to be translated but simple instructions may not have to be.

Some companies use a restricted vocabulary to write the service manuals for their engineers so that the time and cost of translation can be avoided. The author is asked to use only a vocabulary of about a thousand of the most commonly used words. The words in this vocabulary are carefully chosen and they are also defined to have only one meaning. If the user is taught the same vocabulary, the service manual can be understood by somebody with a minimal knowledge of the language.

The use of restricted vocabulary also makes computer-assisted translation easier. Computer translation has come a long way since the time when a computer translated 'The spirit is strong but the flesh is weak' into the Russian equivalent of 'The vodka is good but the meat is bad.'

However, the best use of computer-assisted translation is still as a translator's tool where the original and the computer's translation are shown side by side on the screen. The translator is then able to make adjustments for grammar, idiom and style.

Culture is a thin but very important veneer that you must be careful not to scratch. People from different cultures are basically the same and respond in the same way. However, make sure that you understand their basic customs and show an interest and willingness to learn the differences between your cultures.

> The meaning of Chinese words changes with the pitch of the voice. A word spoken at a low pitch has a completely different meaning to the same word spoken at a higher pitch.
>
> I was aware of this, but I was still caught out when I was teaching a class of Singaporeans.
>
> I was asking Tng a question but I didn't seem to be getting his attention. To make matters worse the whole class burst out laughing.
>
> When I asked what the problem was, they told me that I had been saying 'Tng' with a high instead of low pitch – I had been telling him to go home!

One of the most surprising things I have experienced is that there is often less difference between people of different nationalities who share the same profession than between people of the same nationality who work in different professions. The cultural differences between companies, between civilians and service people and between sales, marketing and manufacturing are fascinating and can easily catch out the unwary.

The use of computers in the classroom

A computer is a tool – no more, no less. Computers are excellent for running business simulations and can be used to present instructional material. There is some very effective computer-based training around.

When it comes to training, a computer is just one medium among many. Just like any other media, it is appropriate in some situations and less appropriate in others. The most effective training is usually a skilful blend of different media.

One of the most effective uses of computers is as part of a simulation. In this way it is possible to give students very fast feedback on their decisions and actions.

A computer is not only a useful tool for training but it can also bring large increases in the productivity of course administration. If you find yourself spending a great deal of time on a repetitive task, consider whether a computer could give you a productivity increase.

> Interpersonal skills observations involve categorizing people's verbal behaviour. Every time a person speaks the observer records the interaction as one of 11 types of behaviour.
>
> After the observation the observer has to perform a series of calculations which involve working out each type of behaviour as a percentage of the person's total number of behaviours. With a class of 20 this would typically require two hours to complete – even with the assistance of a calculator. Not only did this take up a lot of the trainer's time, but it also meant that the students would often not receive feedback until the following day.
>
> This time was cut in half by using a computer with a spreadsheet program. After the observation, data were fed into the computer and the spreadsheet performed the calculations.
>
> The time was cut even more dramatically by using a hand-held computer to record the observations directly. The hand-held computer was then connected to a printer and the students received a copy of their feedback within five minutes of the last observation being made!

The following is a checklist of activities where a computer may improve your productivity:

- preparing course materials,
- revising course materials,
- record keeping,
- presenting slides,
- making slides,
- course administration (delegate lists, sub-group composition, certificate lists, certificates),
- interactive skills observation and analysis,
- business simulations,
- analysis and presentation of course statistics,
- communication via electronic mail,
- access to centralized training records,
- computer-assisted learning,
- computer-assisted personality testing,
- computer-assisted career counselling.

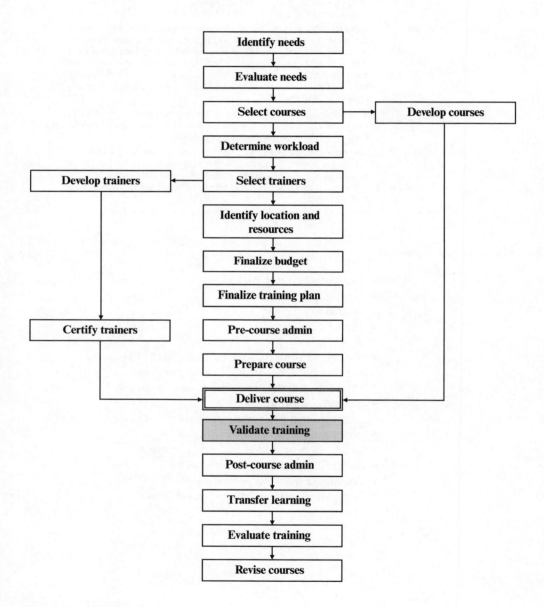

Figure 10.1 *Validation*

10 Validation

Validation ensures that the course meets, and continues to meet, the aims and objectives you set for it. Validation is an internal check on the course. The following is the definition of validation used in this book:

> 'A systematic analysis of data and judgemental information, collected during a training course, which is designed to ascertain whether the course achieved its specified aims and objectives.'

See Chapter 12 for a discussion of other definitions of validation and their origins.

Validation does not give you information on whether the students will use the skills and knowledge. It does not tell you whether those skills and knowledge contribute anything towards business effectiveness. Neither does it tell you whether the objectives were the right ones. I might have learned how to play Rachmaninov's Third Piano Concerto, but will this help me manage a group of sales people when I get back to work? It is evaluation, the subject of Chapter 12, that deals with these questions.

Validation is critical because learning cannot be transferred to the business unless the course has met its objectives. Good validation systems not only show us what needs to be changed, but they also prevent us from changing a course for change's sake. They give an early warning of a drift in the course's standards before disaster occurs.

Validation tells us whether the course has had the desired effect. There are two perspectives from which this can be done:

- validating against students' perceptions and comments,
- validating against the course objectives.

Validating against students' perceptions and comments

The first way of seeing whether the course meets its objectives is from the student's point of view. This is often done using end-of-course feedback sheets (sometimes called 'happiness sheets') comprising a questionnaire and a comments section. The questionnaire asks how much the students liked the course, whether they thought they met its objectives and what they thought of the trainer. It also gives them an opportunity to make open-ended comments.

Figure 10.2 is an example of a typical feedback sheet. Most courses have the students complete a feedback sheet at the end of the course.

The sheet could also have a space for the student's name. Some people feel that feedback should be anonymous so the students do not feel restricted in what they say. Unfortunately, anonymous sheets prevent you from

---

MANAGEMENT DEVELOPMENT PROGRAMME FEEDBACK

Directions: Please take a few minutes to respond to these statements about the course as a *whole* by placing a tick in the appropriate box to the right of the statement. Space has been provided for any comments you may wish to add.

1. Relevance of workshop to your present job   ☐ ☐ ☐ ☐ ☐
                                                    Very low   Very high
Comments: _____
_____
_____

2. Confidence in your ability to use the skills   ☐ ☐ ☐ ☐ ☐
                                                    Very low   Very high
Comments: _____
_____
_____

3. Usefulness of the pre-work   ☐ ☐ ☐ ☐ ☐
                                    Not useful   Very useful
Comments: _____
_____
_____

4. Overall satisfaction with the course   ☐ ☐ ☐ ☐ ☐
                                                Very low   Very high
Comments: _____
_____
_____

5. One change for improving the workshop   _____
_____
_____

6. One thing that should be left as it is   _____
_____
_____

THANK YOU FOR YOUR ASSISTANCE

Figure 10.2   An example of a course feedback sheet

following up comments to get further clarification or to clear up confusion.

Explain why it is useful to have the names on the feedback sheet, but let students know that their feedback can be anonymous if they prefer. If you have established trust and credibility during the course, the students should not feel that they need to withhold their names.

Feedback sheets give you data on how the students feel at the end of the course but they do not tell you much about how they felt along the way. This interim information is essential for continually improving the training process. Avoid giving the students a questionnaire to complete after every course module. You might get away with this on a pilot course, but under other circumstances students will rapidly become frustrated.

A technique we use is to provide the students with some cards. They write their comments on one of the cards whenever they feel they have some feedback to give us. A 'postbox' is provided at the back of the class. Once a day we review the comments, give responses to the feedback and, where necessary, clear up any misunderstandings.

Halo effect
The danger with perceptions is that many different factors affect them. The halo effect occurs when a student judges a course in terms of a general feeling.

For example, some trainers are skilled performers: they have the class eating out of their hands and they get amazingly good feedback regardless of how good or indifferent the course. The students are judging the course in terms of how they feel about the trainer.

The halo effect also works in a negative direction. Students might give a course poor feedback because they had a bad experience on a previous course or because they have had problems with accommodation, or they might not feel too good because of a hangover.

Despite this weakness, student feedback is essential. Student perception is one of the main factors that determine a course's credibility and reputation. Students' perceptions and comments are also essential for identifying unexpected effects of the training.

Validating against course objectives
The second way of looking at validation is to see whether the students met the course objectives. Checking whether the students have met the objectives can be either very difficult or very easy – it all depends on the quality of the objectives.

If the objectives meet the guidelines given in Chapter 3 you will know what behaviours to test, the conditions under which to test them and the standards that should be reached.

Testing or measuring is implicit in validating a course against its objectives. A test does not have to be a 'pencil-and-paper' examination. It can just as easily be an observed exercise where the trainer records the results on a check chart.

Reacting to validation data

Be careful how you respond to validation data. It is all too easy either to over-react or to rationalize problems away. Over-reaction can make the course lurch from one extreme to the other.

For example, an exercise receives some negative feedback the first time you run a course, so you decide to remove the exercise. The next time you run the course you find that important objectives are not being met, so you reinstate the exercise. On the third course the exercise receives more negative feedback...

This is similar to the way some people adjust the thermostat on a radiator. The room is feeling a bit cold so they turn the control up to maximum. After a while they start feeling hot, so they turn the control down to minimum. When the temperature drops...

They end up spending all day adjusting the thermostat while the room temperature lurches from being too hot to being too cold and back again. What they should do is to let the system settle down and then only make minor adjustments when necessary. What is needed is a light touch on the steering wheel.

Although one piece of feedback may not mean anything by itself, you shouldn't fall into the trap of ignoring obvious problems. Too often we avoid taking action because we don't have a 'statistically significant' sample.

How many plane crashes does it take for us to think that something is wrong? How many times does a coin have to come up heads before we suspect that something is wrong with the coin?

Deciding when to react to feedback or a deviation is a difficult judgement to make. After the course has run several times you will begin to get a feeling for what is normal and what is a significant variation. The decision then depends on the intuition and experience of the individual trainer.

The problem is similar to deciding when to adjust a machine on a manufacturing line. Until the introduction of total quality management the decision was either left to the operator's experience, or nothing was done until the product drifted out of specification. The entire batch would then have to be inspected and as much as 20 per cent of production would have to be scrapped.

Statistical process control   Manufacturing's answer to the problem of when to react to deviations is statistical process control (SPC). The idea behind SPC is to collect data on a process and to determine statistically what is an abnormal variation. These data are displayed on a control chart. The chart has two lines drawn on it, an upper control limit (UCL) and a lower control limit (LCL).

The operator takes no corrective action as long as the data remain between the two control limits. If the data go outside the limits, the operator knows that the variation is significant and requires action before the process goes out of specification. This is similar to a driver turning the steering wheel before the car hits the kerb.

Figure 10.3 gives an example of a control chart for the manufacture of a 10 mm disc whose diameter should be a minimum of 9.90 mm and a maximum of 10.10 mm.

Applying SPC to training validation   When you are running the same course many times (such as when you are training every employee) it is possible to collect sufficient data to apply statistical process control to the validation results.

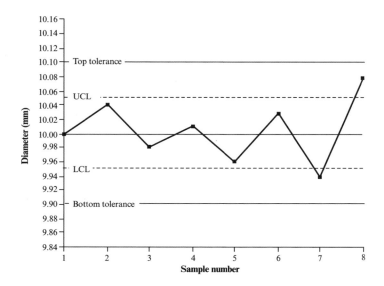

Figure 10.3   *An example of a control chart*

SPC allows you to detect changes in course performance that are due to significant causes. It allows you to check whether different trainers are training to the same standard. It shows you whether the course, in its present form, is capable of meeting the objectives. Most importantly, it gives you an indication of when you should not make changes to a course.

Measurements versus targets

The very act of measurement has the effect of distorting the data. If we are sensitive in how we carry out validation, the distortion should not make a significant difference to the results. Measurements are essential for maintaining the quality of our courses and we should do everything to reduce distortion to a minimum.

A single measurement is not a complete description of a course's quality. At best it is a prime indicator. The number of measurements required to define a course's quality completely would be so large as to make any validation system unwieldy. This need not be a problem as long as we take care in choosing the measurements we use as prime indicators of quality.

However, the moment a measure is turned into a target, the underlying weaknesses of using a few measures become apparent. (This is compounded when a trainer's pay increase is directly linked to measures such as student perception of 'trainer effectiveness'.)

Trainers will soon subconsciously realize which unmeasured indicators can be sacrificed to improve the measured ones. They will also learn which are the best times to make the measurements – such as just after telling the class that they are the best students they have ever trained, or after breaking open a bottle of champagne!

The way to deal with this is not to dispense with measures but to make the trainers responsible for their own quality. It is very unlikely that they would, even subconsciously, deceive themselves.

The validation process

Figure 10.4 gives an overview of the validation process. First, the data have to be collected throughout the course. Student perceptions, comments and test results are examples of validation data. A preliminary assessment is made at the end of the course while the course and any incidents are still fresh in the trainer's mind.

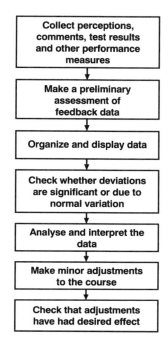

Figure 10.4 *The validation process*

Next the data have to be organized and displayed so that you can see whether the feedback is significant or just due to natural variation.

Then the data have to be analysed and interpreted so that you can determine the causes of the significant variations. Once you have understood the causes it is possible to make changes to the course. Always make the smallest adjustment consistent with solving the problem.

The next time you run the course you will need to go through the process of collecting and analysing the data again. This is to check that the changes have had the desired effect.

The remainder of this chapter looks at these steps of the validation process in detail.

> Collect perceptions, comments, test results and other performance measures

When collecting perceptions, it is common practice to use feedback forms with five-point response scales. The responses can be numbered or labelled. These responses have different labels depending on the type of questions asked.

Table 10.1 summarizes some of the more common labels

Managing the training process

Table 10.1 *Relationship of different labels to a five-point response scale*

		1	2	3	4	5
A	What opinion do you have of the course?	Very poor	Poor	Fair	Good	Very good
B	How satisfied are you with the course?	Very unsatisfied	Unsatisfied	Fairly satisfied	Satisfied	Very satisfied
C	What is the probability of you using the skills when you go back to work?	Very low	Low	Medium	High	Very high
D	The course is the best that I have been on.	Strongly disagree	Disagree	Neutral	Agree	Strongly agree
E	The length of the course is...	Much too short	Too short	Just right	Too long	Much too long

and relates them to the five-point scale. It also gives examples of the types of questions that are used with the different labels.

Deciding whether '1' represents 'very poor' or 'very good' is an arbitrary decision. I use the convention of 'higher equals better'. The exception to this is the last scale in Table 10.1 where the best score is '3'. ('The length of the course is just right.') Be careful when you are using this type of scale as it can lead to confusion.

I also have the numbers run from '1' on the left-hand side to '5' on the right-hand side. This corresponds to the way Western cultures read across the page. It also makes it easier to use graphical display programs because this is the convention used for graphs.

Always stick to the same convention, no matter which one you decide to choose. And always give a warning when the scale changes.

People have varying views of what 'very poor', 'poor', 'fair', 'good' and 'very good' mean. You get better consistency when it is possible to frame the feedback questions in the form of opposites (see Figure 10.5).

This format produces a five-point continuum and the students put an 'X' in the column that best matches their perception.

The wording used in Figure 10.5 can have the effect of grouping the responses around the middle because of the 'all or nothing' nature of the extremes. One way round this

	1	2	3	4	5	
The trainer did not give satisfactory answers to any of my questions by the end of the course				X		The trainer gave satisfactory answers to all of my questions by the end of the course

Figure 10.5 *Using opposites as feedback questions*

is to use a seven-point scale so that there is more definition around the middle.

Another way to avoid the problem is to reword the questions. Don't make the wording too weak as this will introduce the problem of inconsistent definition. Figure 10.6 gives an example of weak wording. (Does 'most' mean 50 per cent, 60 per cent, 80 per cent?) Figure 10.7 gives a better example.

Make sure that the questions used are true opposites, otherwise this format becomes very confusing. Figure 10.8 gives an example of questions that are not true opposites.

Collecting comments Although feedback on a five-point scale is easy to display and analyse, it is restrictive because you will only get feedback on what you asked for. Neither does an 'X' on a

	1	2	3	4	5	
The trainer gave unsatisfactory answers to most of my questions			X			The trainer gave satisfactory answers to most of my questions

Figure 10.6 *Example of weak wording for feedback questions*

	1	2	3	4	5	
I was very unsatisfied with the answers the trainer gave to my questions				X		I was very satisfied with the answers the trainer gave to my questions

Figure 10.7 *Example of stronger wording for feedback questions*

	1	2	3	4	5	
The trainer did not seem to care about whether I learnt		?		?		The trainer was very enthusiastic about the course

Figure 10.8 *Example of questions that are not true opposites*

one-to-five scale give many clues to the reasons for the response. To overcome this each question should have a comments space for the students to expand on their responses.

Also leave space at the end of the questionnaire for general comments that will give you feedback on aspects you never dreamt about when you were designing the questionnaire. Good questions for stimulating a response are:

- Is there anything that should be left out of the course?
- Is there anything that should be put into the course?
- What should be kept as it is?
- Is there anything that should be done differently?
- Any other comments?

Collecting test results

A test is a measure of whether the behavioural objectives of the course have been met. As tests should be based firmly on the objectives, your students should not be surprised by any of the test items.

The objectives should also give you the required standard, as in:

'Given a list of 20 countries you will be able to name the capital cities of at least 17 of those countries.'

Many objectives, like the one above, lend themselves to written tests. Others are best tested through observations of practical exercises. The observations can then be compared to a checklist or a profile of behaviours.

Good trainers constantly validate their training by asking questions as they go along. Although you can get a feeling for the level of knowledge by noting how many students want to answer, you can only be sure that one person knows the correct answer. One way round this is to ask multiple choice questions. Each student is given a device which allows them to display their response to the question. A Cosford responder (see Figure 10.9) is an example of such a device.

A Cosford responder is a cardboard, plastic or wooden tetrahedron which has a different colour on each of its faces. Each colour represents a different response to the question. In this way the trainer can easily see which students responded correctly.

Collecting other performance measures

Look out for other indicators which tell you how the course is progressing and whether you need to make any adjustments as you go along. Be as creative as you can. The following are some suggestions.

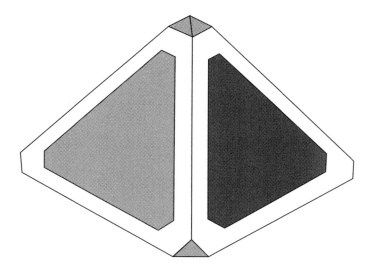

Figure 10.9 *A Cosford responder*

Room tidiness   A colleague of mine once said that the success of a course is inversely proportional to the tidiness of the room. At first I thought this was just a clever remark, but the more I think about it the more I am convinced that it has a relationship to the participants' energy level.

Smiley charts   A smiley chart (see Figure 10.10) is used to collect students' perceptions during a course. The chart is drawn on flip-chart paper and at the end of the day the students are asked how they feel. The trainer makes a mark or puts the student's initials in the appropriate square. These feelings are then explored by the trainer.

Stress level chart   A stress level chart (see Figure 10.11) works in a similar way to a smiley chart but it is based on the premise that everyone has an optimum stress level. If the stress level is too low, people become lethargic and are not motivated to learn. Too high a stress level interferes with learning. The stress level chart allows you to monitor the parts of the course that are too challenging and those parts that are too easy.

Working on   A measure of students' interest and motivation is whether groups continue working on projects after the 'official' end of the day. This does not mean that they have to 'burn the midnight oil' every night.

Talking on   On a residential course see whether your students make jokes or talk about the course content in the bar. This will give you a useful indication of interest and retention. An even better indicator is if they impose cash penalties on each other for talking about the course!

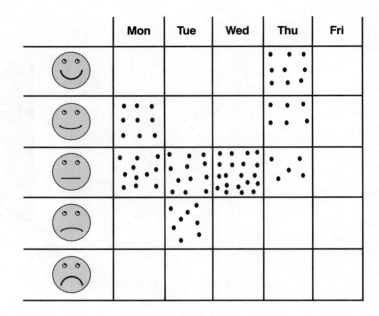

Figure 10.10   *Smiley chart*

	Mon	Tue	Wed	Thu	Fri

Figure 10.11   *Stress level chart*

Alertness   Note when the students start to drift off, are distracted or their eyelids start to droop.

Quiz challenge   Asking questions is a good method of measuring learning. A variation on this is to split the class into three or four groups and ask them to write questions for each other. The number and quality of the questions will give you an additional measure.

Make a preliminary assessment of the feedback data

At the end of the course you should collect all the evaluation sheets and test results. Immediately count the feedback sheets to make sure that you have received one from every person. Also check to see if there have been any omissions – sometimes people forget to complete part or some of the questions. It is much easier to collect the missing data now rather than after your students have returned to work.

Incidentally, you should initially suspect that omissions are caused by the feedback form rather than being a 'student problem'. For example, we should not blame the students for failing to complete the second side of a feedback sheet if we have not printed 'continued on other side...' on the first side of the sheet.

Scan through the sheets and look for obvious patterns and messages. Don't delay doing this – even if it means spoiling your evening or weekend! Timely feedback is the most effective feedback. Some comments are difficult to understand at the best of times. By the time you get back to the office, you will have even more difficulty understanding the comments.

Preliminary assessment of comments

Read the comments and try to recall any incidents that might have triggered the comment. Look for the same comment coming from different people. Make a mental note of those comments that will need further clarification, and those people to whom you will need to give additional explanation of the concepts.

Preliminary assessment of perceptions

Look at the scores that have been given for the feedback categories. You won't be able to make many conclusions without doing further analysis, but make a mental note of those scores which stand out as being very high or very low. Check to see if these scores have comments associated with them.

Preliminary assessment of test results

Look through the test results to see if the class was having the same type of difficulty throughout the course. (You should already have checked the individual test results immediately after each test to see what changes you needed to make during the course.) Detailed analysis of the test results can wait until you get back to the office.

Organize and display data

It is difficult to draw conclusions about data when the information is spread over a dozen or more evaluation sheets. The raw data need to be organized and, where possible, displayed graphically.

Organizing and displaying perceptions

The usual way of organizing this type of data is with a frequency chart. Figure 10.12 gives an example.

The process for constructing a frequency chart is as follows:

- Work through the evaluation forms and count the number of students who gave the course a relevance score of 1 (i.e. very low relevance).
- Enter this number (if any) in the '1' (Low) column on the relevance row.
- Count the number of relevance scores of 2, 3, 4 and 5.
- Enter these numbers in the '2', '3', '4' and '5' columns.
- Add up the number of responses to make sure you have not missed any out. This number is put in the 'Total' column.
- Calculate the average relevance score and put it in the 'Average' column. The calculation for the example given in Figure 10.12 is:

$(2\times2)+(9\times4)+(5\times5)$ divided by 16

- Follow a similar procedure for each of the response questions.

A computer with a spreadsheet program such as Lotus 1-2-3 allows you to make the calculations quickly and easily. Appendix 1 gives instructions for constructing this spreadsheet.

Although it is possible to draw conclusions directly from the frequency tables, it is much easier when the information is displayed graphically. The best tool for displaying distributed data is the histogram. A histogram is a set of vertical bars which represent the number of responses for each category of feedback. Figure 10.13 is a histogram for item (a), 'Relevance'.

Organizing and displaying comments

Qualitative data, like the feedback comments, are the most difficult to organize and display. The simplest way of

	Low			High			
Question	1	2	3	4	5	Tot	Ave
a. Relevance		2		9	5	16	4.1
b. Ability to apply			4	9	3	16	3.9
c. Probability of using		1	8	6	1	16	3.4
d. Overall satisfaction				10	6	16	4.4
e. Trainer effectiveness				6	10	16	4.6

Figure 10.12 *Using a frequency chart to organize student feedback*

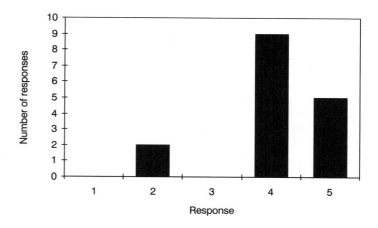

Figure 10.13   *Histogram of relevance scores*

organizing comments is to list them by question. Figure 10.14 gives an example of this. This is better than having the comments spread over all the evaluation sheets, but it is still difficult to detect patterns in the feedback.

Be careful when you group similar comments because there is a temptation to interpret the comments to fit into one of the existing groups. This has the effect of moving away from the original intent of the comments.

COMMENTS

1. **Relevance of workshop to your present job**
   — Very relevant, having recently acquired the responsibility for tracking projects.
   — Not for most day-to-day activities, but useful for two projects just starting.
   — Useful reminder, will be able to use positively in the future.

2. **Confidence in your ability to use the skills**
   — Only doubt is retaining correct skill level when I have a project to work on.
   — Useful revision of work previously covered at college.
   — I would now like to practise these skills.
   — My confidence will increase as I use these skills.

3. **Usefulness of pre-work**
   — Not completed as I have no project to work on.
   — Not relevant on this occasion.
   — Useful having a project in mind to increase relevance etc.
   — Would have helped if manager had given me proper terms of reference.
   — I received no pre-work.

4. **Overall satisfaction with the workshop**
   — Excellent workshop, especially with introduction of case study and monitoring.

Figure 10.14   *Organizing student feedback comments*

Where the same or similar comments are given by more than one person, it is possible to display this graphically as shown in Figure 10.15.

Organizing and displaying test results

Much of what has been said about organizing and displaying perception data can be applied to test results. As with students' comments, a histogram gives a good display that assists in interpretation.

A histogram takes a long time to produce so the temptation is to use a straight average. The problem with an average is that it does not give any information on the variability of the result. A good compromise is to display the average along with the lowest and highest scores (see Figure 10.16).

The distance between the highest and lowest scores gives an indication of variability and the position of the average indicates how the results are skewed. As the results are displayed in a compact format this method is ideal for showing trends over a number of courses (see Figure 10.17).

> Check whether deviations are significant or due to normal variation

It is essential that you make a judgement about whether deviations are significant and require action to be taken, or whether they are due to normal variation and can safely be ignored.

Checking comments for significant variation

When you read the comments there will be some feedback that 'rings true'. You know that it reflects a real problem and you won't need much more data before you do something about it. There will be other comments that are not so clear cut – others will be totally confusing. When you get confusing comments, go back to the students and ask for clarification. They might be surprised but you will be demonstrating that you take their comments seriously.

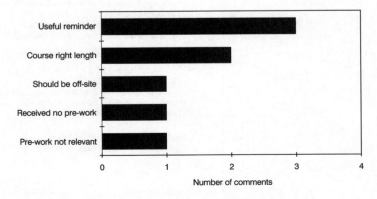

Figure 10.15 *Displaying student comments graphically*

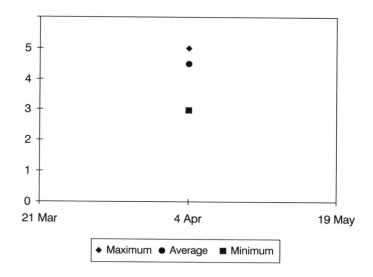

Figure 10.16   *An average displayed with maximum and minimum scores*

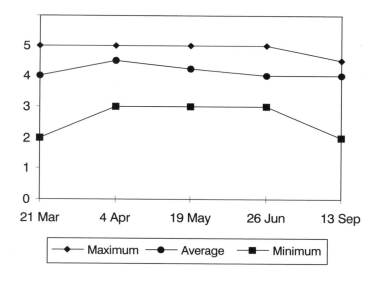

Figure 10.17   *Tracking the results over a period*

Checking perception scores for significant variation

You will need to run a course several times before you can definitely tell what are normal and abnormal responses for the perception scores. As it can take many months to gather statistically significant data, I use the following assumptions when I am making a preliminary assessment of significance. The assumptions are based on a five-point scale.

- Many people are reluctant to give a very high or a very low score. They do this on the basis that nothing is perfect and nothing is totally useless.
- People are more reluctant to give a '1' (very low) than a '5' (very high).
- '3' is a neutral score. It means that this aspect of the course had little effect on that person. Always consider a '3' to be a defect if you are aiming for your courses to have a high reputation.
- Taking the above into account, Table 10.2 indicates the significance that should be attached to individual responses.
- The average score gives an indication of how the course performed. It also allows you to track how course performance changes from course to course. Table 10.3 gives you an indication of the significance and acceptability of averaged scores.
- Do not use the average by itself: it smoothes out the scores and hides problems. It's like the person whose average temperature is just right – but his hair is on fire and his feet are in a bucket of ice!
- Always check the spread (range) of the scores as well as the average. The range is the lowest score subtracted from the highest. It shows how closely the students agree on their perceptions of the course. A small range indicates a stable learning process. A large range indicates an unstable process. Table 10.4 gives an interpretation for all the possible ranges on a five-point scale.

Table 10.2   *Significance and acceptability of individual scores*

Score	Significance	Acceptability
1	Very poor score	Totally unacceptable
2	Poor score	Unacceptable
3	Neutral score	Not acceptable
4	Fair or good score	Acceptable
5	Good or very good score	Very acceptable

Table 10.3   *Significance and acceptability of averaged scores*

Score	Significance	Acceptability
1.0–1.9	Very poor score	Totally unacceptable
2.0–2.4	Poor score	Unacceptable
2.5–3.4	Neutral score	Not acceptable
3.5–3.9	Fair score	Fairly acceptable
4.0–4.4	Good score	Acceptable
4.5–5.0	Very good score	Very acceptable

Table 10.4 *Interpretation of a score's range*

Range	Agreement	Training process stability
0	Extremely high	Extremely stable
1	High	Very stable
2	Good	Normally expected level
3	Low	Getting unstable
4	Very low	Unstable

Note: A course can be stable at the low end of the scale as well as at the high end. This is why the range should be taken into consideration along with the average.

- 'Overall satisfaction' and 'Trainer effectiveness' usually score higher than other questionnaire items.
- 'Relevance' and 'Probability of using' often score lower than the other items. 'Relevance' scores lower than other items because of poor needs analysis and student selection. 'Probability of using' often has a low score because we do not pay enough attention to learning transfer.

The above assumptions reflect what are generally regarded to be normal responses. We shouldn't be content with these. We should aim for zero defects (i.e. every student giving every feedback item a score of 4 or 5).

Checking test results for significant variation

Every test should have a standard attached to it. Any failure to meet that standard should be considered to be a defect. At this stage we are not assigning causes to the deviation. The cause might be that the student was not able to reach a sufficient standard or there might be a defect in the teaching of the course. We are simply noting that a significant deviation has occurred.

> Analyse and interpret data

Analysing and interpreting comments

It is always difficult to receive negative feedback about one of your courses – doubly so if you wrote the course. A course is part of you. Feedback can feel like personal criticism.

These feelings are natural but misguided. You should seek and welcome feedback. Students are your customers. Like other customers, they are reluctant to complain. Instead, they usually stop using your services and then loudly let their friends and neighbours know about it. You are the last person to find out, often too late to save your business from damage.

When people complain, it is for one of two reasons. The first is when their frustration with the product or service overcomes their reluctance to complain. The second is when they respect you enough to want to help. You should always pay attention when people take the trouble to give you feedback. Good feedback is very rare.

Reacting positively to a problem enhances your reputation. Customers are impressed by suppliers who correct mistakes quickly. Curiously, suppliers who never make a mistake are thought less of. Don't let this tempt you into making deliberate mistakes! There will be sufficient real mistakes to give you enough practice.

Always consider negative feedback as a symptom of a problem you need to solve. Remember, no matter how trivial you think a problem is, it is always significant to your customer.

Guard against rationalizing the feedback away. 'That person shouldn't have been on this course anyway' is a typical rationalization. Even if this were true, it's not the student's fault – it's a failure of our process. I find that the principle of 'guilty until proven innocent' helps me rationalize less.

When I receive a piece of criticism I make the assumption that something is wrong with the course or the way it was run. This doesn't mean that I will change the course every time I receive criticism. This would throw the course into confusion and cause even more problems. Instead, I keep the feedback in mind and collect more evidence until I can reach a clear verdict.

Criticism often comes in the form of a solution. An example of this is: 'I think you should scrap the session on company objectives.' Taking this at its face value will lead to a poor training decision. Removing the session from the course will stop the negative feedback but the course will fail to meet its design objectives.

There was obviously something wrong with the session on company objectives. You need to investigate further and find out what is causing the negative reaction. Could it be that students sit without a break for two hours listening to a presentation? Is the presenter unprepared? Perhaps the session makes no link between the company objectives and students' own objectives.

Analysing and interpreting perceptions   The shapes of the perception histograms are useful in analysing and interpreting student perceptions. The following is a discussion of what the different shapes indicate.

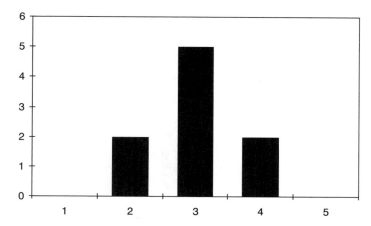

Figure 10.18   *Normal distribution*

The most common shape is the normal distribution, which is symmetrical and bell shaped (Figure 10.18). Most of the results are close to one value. Provided that the histogram does not have a large spread it indicates a consistency in student perceptions.

A negatively skewed distribution (Figure 10.19) shows that the feedback from the majority of students is positive. (I know this sounds contradictory but you'll have to argue that one with a statistician.) The trainer or training has had a significantly positive effect on the students.

A positively skewed distribution (Figure 10.20) shows that the feedback from the majority of students is negative. (Again, have a word with the statistician about the apparent inconsistency.) The trainer or training has had a detrimental effect on the students.

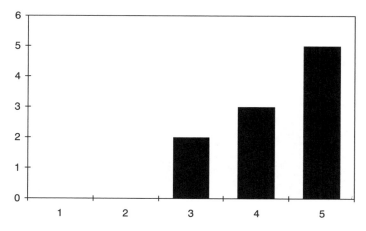

Figure 10.19   *Negatively skewed distribution*

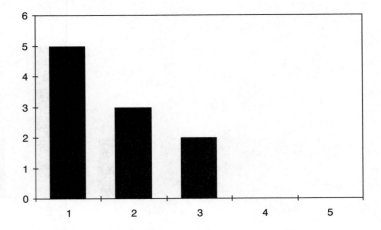

Figure 10.20   *Positively skewed distribution*

A negatively skewed distribution with a wide spread (Figure 10.21) is often seen as a reaction to a trainer who has charisma but whose style is not liked by some of the population. We find that videos starring business 'evangelists' often have this effect. The majority of the class is carried along with the energy of the presentation but some are 'turned off' by being shouted at.

An isolated peak distribution (Figure 10.22) indicates the inclusion of a small number of people from a separate population. For example, if this graph represented a relevance score it would indicate that the problem is more likely to lie with the process for selecting students than with the course itself.

The twin peak distribution occurs when the results of two

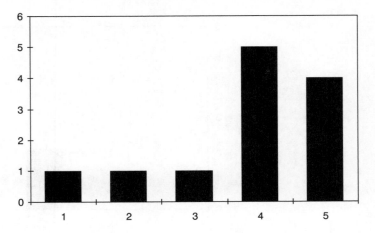

Figure 10.21   *Negative skew with wide distribution*

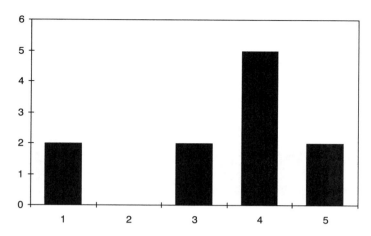

Figure 10.22 *Isolated peak distribution*

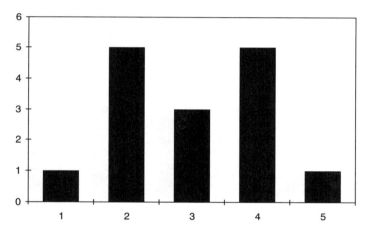

Figure 10.23 *Twin peak distribution*

distinctly different populations are mixed. For example, you might get this result when a course originally designed for sales people is given to a mixed sales and engineering class.

This interpretation can be checked out by stratifying the data. Stratifying the data involves displaying the data so that the two different populations can be easily identified. Figure 10.24 shows one way of doing this.

A flat distribution (Figure 10.25) usually results from a mixed reaction to the course. It can also mean that there are several different populations of students in the class. This is not a problem if you believe that the advantages of having a diverse group of students outweigh the disadvantages, and if the histogram does not have a wide spread.

Managing the training process

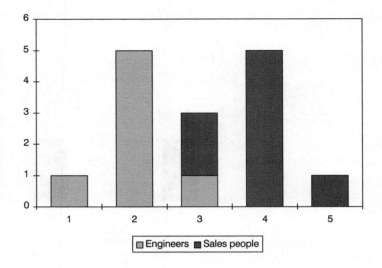

Figure 10.24 *Stratified twin peak distribution*

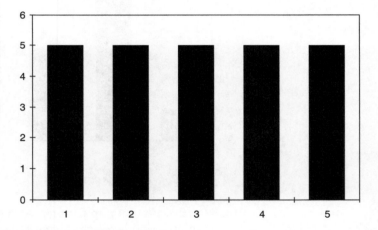

Figure 10.25 *A flat distribution*

Analysing and interpreting test results

A normal distribution means just what it says. It is the kind of distribution you would normally expect when things are left to themselves. If we get a normal distribution it may mean that our training has little effect on the students. Some examination results force the results into a normal distribution so that 50 per cent of the students pass, 25 per cent get credits and 25 per cent fail. As trainers we should be aiming for all our students to pass and to get the highest possible score. We want the distribution of our results to be skewed towards the top end (see Figure 10.26).

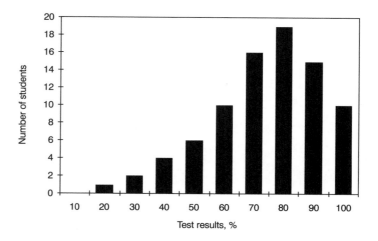

Figure 10.26 *An example of a positive effect on test results*

| Make minor adjustments to the course |

After you have assessed all the validation data you will be in a position to know what alterations to make the next time you run the course. Don't try to change too many things at once, otherwise you won't know what changes caused which results.

Corrections to printed materials

Many of the minor adjustments will involve making revisions to the printed materials. These could be typographical errors, changes to exercises or minor rewording of the text. You should correct these errors immediately or as soon as the course is finished.

If the materials are held electronically, make the corrections and then make sure that you replace the affected pages in the print masters. All this sounds obvious, but failure to make revisions while they are still fresh in your mind is one of the main reasons for the same mistakes turning up on every course.

| Check that adjustments have had the desired effect |

The next time you run the course you should collect exactly the same data as those which led you to make the change. This will give you confidence about whether the changes have had the desired effect. You should also check the other validation data to make sure that your changes have had no unexpected side effects – it has been said that the biggest causes of problems are solutions.

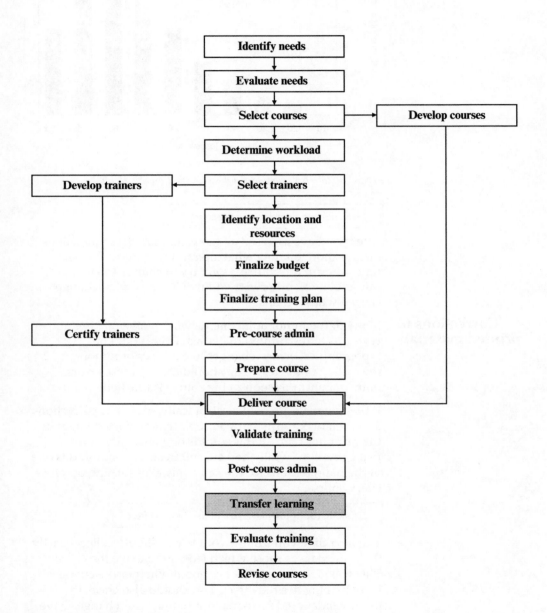

Figure 11.1   Learning transfer

11 Learning transfer

Training, no matter how good, is a waste of time if it does not help improve the business. Training will have no impact on the business unless the skills are used back at the workplace. Unused skills are soon forgotten: within six months it will be almost as if the training had never taken place.

As learning transfer is so important you would think that companies would put considerable effort into making it happen. Yet surprisingly few training organizations give learning transfer the priority it requires. Perhaps they think that learning transfer is a natural outcome of training and, as such, does not need nurturing.

Nothing could be further from the truth. New learning soon withers without constant attention. Unless considerable effort is put into learning transfer the effect on the business will be, at best, random and haphazard. Even companies that are aware of the importance of learning transfer find difficulty in making it happen.

In this chapter we will look at:

- the definition of learning transfer,
- what prevents learning transfer from taking place,
- what assists learning transfer,
- who is responsible for learning transfer,
- putting learning transfer into practice.

What is learning transfer?

The definition of learning transfer that I use is:

'The post-training application of the newly acquired knowledge and skills to improve the business.'

You may think this definition too lenient because the skills and knowledge could be used once and then promptly be forgotten. You might also argue that transfer is complete only when the students use the new skills and knowledge naturally, skilfully and automatically.

This stiffer definition should always be the ideal to aim for even though it is much more difficult to measure and attain.

What prevents transfer from taking place?

Given that learning is not efficiently transferred to the business, the next step is to understand the causes of the problem. Assuming that the students are not bothering to use the skills over-simplifies the problem. It just leaves us imploring them to use the skills. Unless we understand why the students are not using the skills, we will make very little progress towards solving the problem. Only understanding the root causes will allow us to remove the barriers.

The following is a selection of potential causes for poor learning transfer. You will need to check whether they apply in your situation and whether there are any additional causes.

Poor needs analysis

Curiously enough, the seeds of this problem are sown long before the training ever takes place. If there is to be any chance of the students using what they have learnt, there must be a need for the skills and knowledge.

This takes us right back to the beginning of the training process – needs identification and analysis. Far too many people are put on to the wrong course, for the wrong reason, at the wrong time. Typical of these misguided reasons are: 'It's a long time since that person's been on a course', 'It's the next course in the series' and 'We had a few spare places to fill.' If the training has little or no relevance, it should come as no great surprise if it is not used.

Skills not used immediately after the course

If the needs analysis has been done correctly, the next aspect to look at is the initial use of the learning after the course. There should be an opportunity to use the skills.

Ideally the students should use the skills and knowledge immediately after the course. However, significant transfer still occurs if the skills are used within three weeks. If this were to happen after every course, there would be a lasting impact on the business.

The work environment

There can be an aspect of the environment that 'punishes' people who use their new skills when they get back to work. This is known as the 'charm school effect'. It is particularly prevalent in management and behaviour training.

A person returns to the workplace, experiments with the skills and uses a new vocabulary. Other people in their work group, faced with strange and new behaviours, start to feel uncomfortable. Although they didn't like the old behaviours, at least they knew what to expect. This nervousness prompts them to make jokes like: 'Look who just got back from charm school!' In this way people are taught not to use their new knowledge.

Even if the returning trainee does not suffer verbal abuse, the work group's lack of training in the skills can still provide an impediment. Many skills need to have a critical mass of people using them before they can take root in an organization. If this critical mass is not reached, the skill becomes extinct. Once the critical mass has been exceeded, even those who were sceptical about the skills will be swept along with the rest.

The culture of the company often reinforces the behaviours we are trying to change. We take people out of this environment, train them to use new behaviours, and then put them back into the environment that caused the problems in the first place. We then wonder why the learning hasn't been transferred.

Little control over the transfer process   Another reason for poor learning transfer is loss of control over the process. When the students are in the classroom they are a captive audience. You can monitor and give feedback, you can coach and counsel. But once the course is over that responsibility passes to the students' managers.

One way to gain more control over learning transfer is to spread the learning experiences. For example, in the BBC's 'Managing Change' course the delegates meet a few days before the course. They do the introductions and get to know each other. The course runs for five days. At the end of the course the students are given projects to do when they return to work. Three months later the delegates meet again to review how their projects are proceeding.

This approach goes a long way towards enhancing learning transfer. However, waiting three months to check a project is too long. It does not allow for the monitoring, feedback and coaching that are required in the early days of learning transfer. Another problem with projects is that the students see them as additional work and a burden that gets in the way of their priority tasks. Consequently, it is put off and the bulk of the project work is done in a rush, just before it is due to be checked.

Using a trainer to coach a student through the early stages of learning transfer is an effective but expensive method. It also has the disadvantage that it is usurping the manager's role. Managers can only fulfil their role if they have coaching skills and they become partners in the training process.

Skills not learnt on the course   No transfer can occur unless the students develop the skills in the first place. Some training is of the 'hosepipe' variety.

The trainer sprays knowledge and experiences in the hope that all the students will grow.

Ideally, we should measure each student's performance, give feedback and coach until every student reaches the required standard. As we will never have the time or resources to do this, we need to understand what can be done with the resources we have.

Courses that intend to teach a specific skill, or set of skills, range from half a day to two days. Although the length of a course depends on the skill and knowledge complexity, the following guidelines will give you some idea of what can be done in a fixed time.

Half a day   You can teach some basic concepts, models and terminology. There will be little or no time for practice. Unless the students practise the skills very soon after the course, there is little chance that the learning will be transferred. However, half a day of theory in the classroom combined with coached practice in the workplace is a powerful combination.

One day   A full day's course allows time for some practice but not enough time for a significant amount of learning to take place. As there is only enough time for one practice session, the students end the course on a low note. The practice will give them feedback on what they cannot do. They will not have confidence that they can perform the skills correctly.

One and a half days   An extra half-day sees significant skill improvement so the chances of effective learning transfer are greatly enhanced. The intervening evening also helps because the students can reflect on what happened during the day. Learning still goes on even after the practice has stopped.

Two days   Two days of training also allow the students to start a post-course project or to rehearse an application.

Complex skills need to be taught in stages. When there is time pressure on a course there is a temptation to move on before the basics are thoroughly understood. Students who are confused early on in a course get and remain hopelessly lost. They will neither hear nor understand anything that follows.

Longer courses have modules which cover different subject areas. Again, time pressure forces us to move on before the students have had time to breathe.

Assimilation time is important for both learning and its transfer. The students need to check whether they have understood the information and how it fits into what they already know. They need to consider how they would use the learning back at work. Figure 11.2 gives an example of an assimilation aid.

Time also has to be given for the trainer to summarize what has gone before and to introduce what is coming next. There also needs to be constant reinforcement of where the modules fit into the overall scheme of the course.

Difference between work and classroom environments

Another reason for poor learning transfer is the difference, and sudden transition, between the classroom and work environment. The classroom can be compared to a gymnasium: its purpose is to develop skills. Work is like a sporting event – skills have to be used in a complex environment to produce results.

An athlete works out in the gym, practises on the field and then enters a competition. No athlete would go straight from the gym to the Olympics. Yet this is what we do with our students. We give them the skills, send them back to work and expect them to perform like champions.

We need to manage the transition from the classroom to the workplace. We need to create a transition environment that is more challenging than the classroom and safer than the workplace.

The transition between the two environments is not helped by the common perception that training is not work and work is not training. Training and learning need to be seen as a continuous process, an unending journey. The type of

---

Learning Assimilation Aid

1.   What do you consider to be the main learning points of the module?

2.   How do you currently behave when you find yourself in the situation described in the module?

3.   Given what you have learnt from the module, as well as what you have learnt about yourself, what will you do differently in the future?

Figure 11.2   An example of an assimilation aid

organization where the distinction between learning and work becomes blurred is a learning organization.

> The European design managers of a large multinational organization were to be trained in counselling.
>
> The training started with a four-hour introduction to counselling and its techniques. Soon after the course each manager had a meeting with a facilitator to prepare for a real counselling session.
>
> Facilitators observed the managers carrying out their first counselling session. The facilitators explained to the counsellees that they were solely to observe the managers.
>
> After the session the facilitators gave the managers feedback and, where necessary, further coaching in counselling techniques.
>
> One of the benefits of this training was that more appraisals were completed on time than ever before.

Trying to do too much

A journey of a thousand miles starts with a single step. It should not start with a giant leap. Trying to cover too much ground too soon risks injury and exhaustion.

The same is true for learning transfer. Too many people return to their workplace and try to change the world overnight. Not only does this contribute to the 'charm school effect' but it is also a recipe for failure.

The first application of the skills and knowledge should be chosen very carefully. People need to succeed and to see the value of what they are doing.

> Major-General Jeremy Moore, commander of the British land forces during the Falklands War, was asked what should be the first objective for a newly arriving battalion of paratroopers. 'A battle you are going to win,' he replied.

What assists learning transfer?

The lessons to be learnt from what hinders learning transfer help us understand what assists the transfer of learning. These are:

- Training people from the same work group together aids learning transfer.
- Post-course project work assists learning transfer, but it is only effective if it is suitably supported and controlled.
- Some skills can only be transferred successfully if there is a cultural change in the company.
- Involve the managers before, after and, in some cases, during the training.
- Ensure that managers have the necessary coaching skills to assist learning transfer.
- Ensure that competence is demonstrated at one level of difficulty or complexity before proceeding to the next.

- Ensure that there is enough time to practise the skills on the course.
- Have at least two practice sessions. Complex skills require up to five practice sessions over a week's course.
- Allow time for assimilation between different subjects.
- Advise the students to be selective about what they apply the training to when they get back to work. Advise them against trying to do too much too soon.
- Manage the transition from the classroom to the workplace.
- Reduce the perception that training is not work and work is not training.

Vocational qualifications

Vocational qualifications can be used to assist in both learning transfer and the evaluation of the course. Vocational qualifications measure a person's effectiveness in the workplace rather than in the artificial environment of the classroom. A person is not awarded the qualification for passing a course. A course provides the background skills and knowledge that allow someone to demonstrate competence in the workplace.

If you design a course so that it is consistent with vocational qualifications you have an automatic link with the workplace. The skills are practised, managers function as mentors and competence is assessed.

Accrediting learning

Accreditation of your courses by an academic establishment rewards the effort put into learning and gives students a recognizable, transferable qualification. Students have to satisfy the requirements of the qualification and usually have to complete a project, thesis or dissertation which further facilitates learning transfer.

The Rover Body and Pressings Business, based at Swindon in the UK, is a good example of an organization using this type of accreditation. Students studying their 'Total Quality Leadership' programme have obtained qualifications at certificate, diploma and master's degree levels.

It is essential that a good relationship exists between your company and the accrediting body so that accreditation supports the course objectives rather than the other way round.

Who is responsible for learning transfer?

The people who are responsible for learning transfer are, in order of importance:

- the student,
- the manager,
- the trainer.

It is often thought that learning transfer is most affected by what the trainer and student do during the course but, in reality, what is done by the student and manager before and after the course have a far greater effect.

Putting learning transfer into practice

As you can see, transferring the training into the business can be both difficult and complex. Figure 11.3 shows a process for putting learning transfer into practice.

> Train managers, coaches and assessors

The essence of learning transfer is support for the student before, during and after the training course. You would normally expect the trainer to provide support during the course. Support before and after the course is often a chance occurrence.

A process has to be installed and a support network has to be established and trained. Coaching and counselling are essential skills for managers and coaches. If you are linking your training with vocational qualifications, you will also need to have assessors trained and accredited.

> Student/trainer selects skills and knowledge for initial application

Time is given during the course for the student to decide which skills and knowledge they should use during the initial application of the training.

> Student identifies initial application opportunities

Students should have a clear idea of the situations where they can use the skills and knowledge. The initial application will not happen unless they have a vivid mental picture of the situation. They should be able to imagine what it will look like and how it will feel.

For this reason a student should not leave the course without being sure of when the application will happen and who will be involved. Do not accept a fictitious or generalized situation.

> Student discusses practice opportunities with manager

For learning transfer to be successful the manager must support the skills and knowledge application. This step of the process happens more than once. Potential application opportunities should be identified before the course as part of the student's preparation.

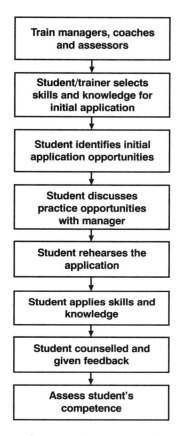

Figure 11.3 *A process for putting learning transfer into practice*

The discussion that occurs after the course is to let the manager know what is going on and to enlist their help and support.

Student rehearses the application

Rehearsing the application in a simulated but safe environment is a powerful way to make a bridge between the classroom and the workplace. It allows the new skills and knowledge to be tried out, mistakes to be made and feedback to be given.

Student applies skills and knowledge

By this time students should be fully prepared for their first application of their training. Where possible a coach should observe this initial application. The coach can be the person's manager or someone from a specially trained network of coaches. An alternative is the 'buddy system' where the students pair up and provide support, coaching and feedback to each other.

| Student counselled and given feedback |

As soon as the students have completed their first application, they should review their own performance. They should ask themselves what they did well and what they could have done better. Give them feedback to cover what they might have missed. Then provide any additional coaching and practice that they might require.

| Assess student's competence |

When both the student and coach feel that the correct standard has been reached, the student's competence should be assessed. If you have been following the vocational qualifications path the job will done by an internal or external assessor.

An alternative method is to give the student a project book to complete after the course. The project book would have questions and exercises that allow the trainer to assess the extent to which the skills were applied after the course.

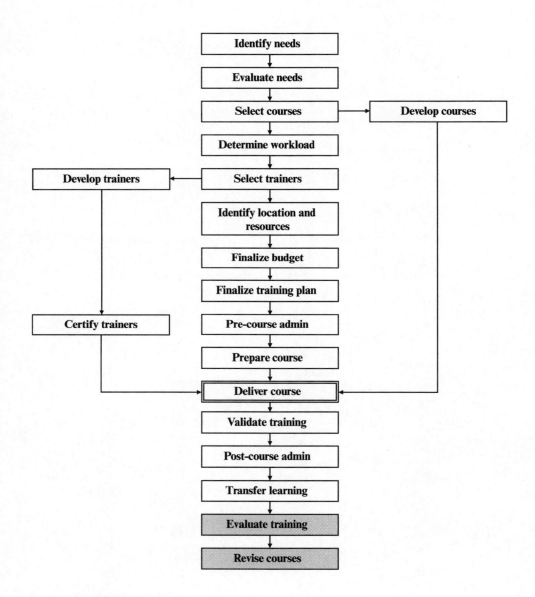

Figure 12.1   *Evaluation and revision*

12 Evaluation

This chapter covers the two final steps of the training process:

- evaluation,
- revision.

Chapter 11 described a process for facilitating the transfer of learning from the classroom to the business. Evaluation checks whether transfer has occurred and makes sure that the training has had the desired effect.

Validation (Chapter 10) is an internal check, it assesses whether the students have reached the required standard before they leave the course. Evaluation is about determining the effect of the course after the students return to the workplace.

A course might have the objective of being able to ice a cake. Validation would show that the students were able to ice a cake before they left the course, but you would have no idea of whether they would continue to ice cakes to the same standard or whether icing cakes is a skill that enhances the business.

In addition to covering the evaluation of training programmes we will also consider how to evaluate our training process. One outcome of evaluation is the identification of changes and additions to the training courses and process.

Evaluation versus validation

In my research for this book I came across many different definitions for both evaluation and validation. None of these definitions seemed to be satisfactory for the practical purpose of managing the training process.

The *Glossary of Training Terms* (Department of Employment, 1971) defines evaluation as:

'The assessment of the total value of a training system, training course or programme in social as well as financial terms. Evaluation differs from validation in that it attempts to measure the overall cost-benefit of the course or programme and not just the achievement of laid down objectives. The term is also used in the general judgemental sense of the continual monitoring of a programme or of the training function as a whole.'

The two problems with this definition are to do with 'the total value in social terms' and 'overall cost-benefit'.

From a practical point of view I have absolutely no idea of how to measure the total value of a course in social terms. Even if I did, I have a feeling it could be a lifetime's work.

It is also not always possible to translate all the benefits of a training programme into financial terms. Even benefits which lend themselves to mathematical analysis involve complex calculations and the validity of the conclusions is nearly always suspect. Every outcome has more than one cause, so it is very difficult to apportion financial benefit to one activity rather than another. I have a suspicion that if you were to add up all the cost benefits claimed for training and other activities in a company, the total would exceed the annual revenue!

The *Glossary of Training Terms* defines two types of validation: internal and external. Internal validation is defined as:

> 'A series of tests and assessments designed to ascertain whether a training programme has achieved the behavioural objectives specified.'

The definition of external validation is given as:

> 'A series of tests and assessments designed to ascertain whether the behavioural objectives of an internally valid training programme were realistically based on an accurate initial identification of training needs in relation to the criteria of effectiveness adopted by the organisation.'

Many writers reject these definitions as being too narrow. Validation also needs to reflect the perceptions of the participants and consider other, perhaps unintended, effects of the training. From a practical perspective, I have great difficulty in drawing the line between where external validation ends and evaluation begins.

Peter Bramley, in *Evaluation of Training* (BACIE, 1986), suggests that it is better to take evaluation as a general term to cover the whole area rather than splitting it into three parts. He offers Goldstein (1980, p 237) as a broad definition:

'Evaluation is the systematic collection of descriptive and judgemental information necessary to make effective training decisions related to the selection, adoption, value and modification of various instructional activities.'

This approach certainly simplifies the business of defining evaluation. However, in my view there is a world of difference between checking whether a course does what you expect it to do on the day and the long-term effects of training on the individual, the department and the organization.

For the practical purposes of managing the training process, I have arrived at the definition of validation already given in Chapter 10:

'A systematic analysis of data and judgemental information, collected during a training course, which is designed to ascertain whether the course achieved its specified aims and objectives.'

This definition corresponds most closely to the definition of internal validation given in the *Glossary of Training Terms* but it also covers participants' perceptions of the course. Validation is primarily at the individual level – individual performance and reaction to the course. My working definition of evaluation is:

'A series of tests, assessments and investigations designed to ascertain whether training has had the desired effect at individual, departmental and organizational levels.'

Each of these three levels of evaluation can be further divided into quantitative and qualitative measures. See Table 12.1 for the types of quantitative and qualitative questions that can be asked at each of the three levels.

Figure 12.2 is a simplified diagram showing the relationship of evaluation to the rest of the training process. It shows evaluation taking a 'helicopter view' of the process. An evaluation strategy needs to take account of:

- the original aims of the course as identified in the needs analysis,
- the behavioural objectives as identified during course development,
- the validation data collected during and at the end of the course,
- assessment data taken during and after learning transfer.

Table 12.1   *Quantitative and qualitative measures for each evaluation level*

Level	Quantitative	Qualitative
Individual	Do the individuals still have the knowledge they gained on the course? Are they still able to perform the skills?	Do the individuals still believe the training to have been worthwhile?
Departmental	Have the desired improvements or changes occurred at the departmental level?	Does training have a good reputation in the participants' departments?
Organizational	Has the organizational aim been achieved? (e.g. profitability, productivity, flexibility, morale, commitment, achievement of business plan)	What is the organization's attitude towards training?

Our definition of evaluation covers the effect of training as a whole and includes two broad areas:

- evaluation of training programmes,
- evaluation of the training process.

Evaluating training programmes

When should training be evaluated?

Evaluation, according to the definition given in this book, is carried out after the end of the course. The question is how long after the course this should be.

Evaluation would not be done after every course. With a new course you would want to make a check three to six months after the first course. When a course is established there is little need to do evaluation. Validation is normally sufficient to let you know that the course has not wandered off track and is still delivering to the required standard.

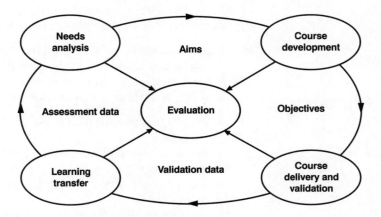

Figure 12.2   *Evaluation and its relationship to the training process*

Another time evaluation is required is when there has been a significant change in the organization or when the course is due to be revised or replaced by a new course.

Ideally, evaluation of training should also occur annually when the organization is assessing the success of its business plan.

How should training be evaluated? The way evaluation usually works is that the person doing the assessment goes into the workplace, sees the problems and successes that the organization, departments and individuals are having, questions whether training has helped them and then determines what additional training is required.

This type of evaluation is usually qualitative and also involves sending out questionnaires. The questionnaires and their analysis follow a similar format to that used for validation (see Chapter 10).

I prefer interviews to questionnaires. With questionnaires people can only answer the questions they have been asked. Questionnaires assume that the originator already has a good idea of what the problems with the course might be.

However, the problem with free-form interviews is that they do not have a structure. This raises questions about the validity of the data because different people are answering different questions. It certainly makes analysis of the data very difficult.

Structured interviews give the best of both worlds. In essence, they are interviews based on a questionnaire that includes all the basic questions that need to be covered. A sensitive interviewer will also be able to pick up and probe for any other feedback on the course.

A half-way house between free-form and structured interviews is to start the interview with a series of open questions such as: 'Tell me about any problems you have in doing your current job.'

Evaluation is not only done with the students. Their managers should also be asked if the course met the objectives from their point of view. With large-scale programmes feedback should also be sought from organizational and departmental heads. This ensures that the training is evaluated at all three levels. Different techniques are used depending on the level of evaluation and whether a quantitative or qualitative investigation is being carried out. Table 12.2 shows some of the techniques that can be used.

Table 12.2 *Techniques for use at different levels of evaluation*

Level	Quantitative techniques	Qualitative techniques
Individual	Tests Observations Vocational assessment	Interviews Questionnaires
Departmental	Production indices Quality indices Staff turnover	Interviews Questionnaires Attitude surveys
Organizational	Assessment and diagnosis of business results Financial results	Interviews Questionnaires Customer satisfaction

A process for evaluating training

The intuitive way of evaluating training programmes is to start at the first level of evaluation (individual level) and then proceed to the other two levels (departmental and organizational). This is the way in which most evaluation is carried out, except that few investigations get beyond the first level.

If you start evaluating at the lowest level, the process becomes training centred rather than business centred. It is difficult to assess whether the course's objectives are the right ones because you are actively looking for examples of the course objectives being met in the workplace.

Starting at Level 1 also makes it difficult to prove that training is an essential contributor to the business, because this narrow focus does not allow you to identify and isolate the other contributory factors.

Starting at Level 3, the organizational level, is more difficult but it is the only way to prove whether training has contributed to the business. Figure 12.3 shows a process that, when used with this 'top-down' approach, is an effective method for evaluating training.

> Review aims

In Chapter 1 we talked about the importance of training being aligned with the business. All training should support the maintenance or improvement of the business. When we evaluate at the organizational level (Level 3) we need to look at the original business aims that the training was meant to support.

> Have aims been met?

Evaluating whether business aims have been met is not something that can, or should, be done by the training

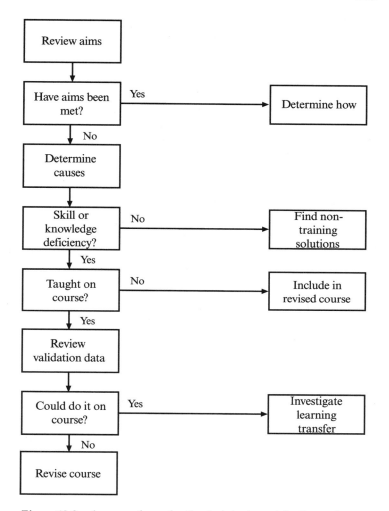

Figure 12.3 *A process for evaluating training's contribution to the business*

department alone. Well-run businesses assess the success of their strategies regularly – certainly at least once a year.

The assessment should be carried out by representatives of the company's main functions. Traditionally, the training function is not involved in these assessments. If we are serious about training being an integral part of the business, however, this is a critical omission.

Determine how

If the answer to 'Have aims been met?' is 'Yes', we should understand how we met our aims. A good result without understanding is just luck. There is no guarantee that we will be able to repeat our success. This step is often missed out because we are so pleased and amazed by our success.

Determining how the aims were met is really a type of problem solving. (Would that all problems were like this!) Instead of determining the causes for something going wrong, we identify the factors that contribute to success; instead of implementing a solution to correct a problem, we carry out an action plan to capitalize on our success.

Determine causes

If the aims were not met, we need to carry out an investigation to determine the causes of this. This is straightforward problem solving. Notice, we are still starting at the organizational level. The causes at this level are likely to be either strategic problems or widespread deficiencies such as skill, knowledge or motivation.

With any complex problem there are likely to be several causes. The root causes will often be found further down the organization. Tracing the problems down to their root causes is easier if the process of policy deployment (see Chapter 1) is followed when the business plan is put together.

Policy deployment is the process of cascading and translating corporate visions and directions throughout the organization. For each corporate direction, there is a series of supporting goals and strategies at the next level down. This process is repeated until we get down to objectives and work processes at departmental and individual levels. You can see how policy deployment lends itself to our model of evaluation.

If an important corporate aim has not been met, we can see which of the supporting goals are contributing to the problem. We can look at the supporting goals that we have not achieved and see which work processes are not meeting expectations.

Provided that the training plan was put together as part of the original policy deployment, this process gives us a method of evaluating training's contribution to the business. It also allows us to evaluate the training process as well as the individual courses.

Skill or knowledge deficiency?

Skill and knowledge deficiencies can be in terms of quantity as well as quality. If qualified individuals are not meeting the course objectives, the course needs to be revised. If we have not trained the numbers of people we said we would train, the training process needs to be investigated.

Skill and knowledge deficiencies should be investigated at all three levels of evaluation. Deficiencies in the number of people trained are first investigated at the organizational level. We then need to determine the extent of the deficiency across all relevant departments. Finally, we should identify the individuals who have not been trained and ensure that they are included in the next revision of the training plan. Deficiencies in the quality of skills and knowledge are handled in a similar manner.

Find non-training solutions

If the causes of a problem cannot be attributed to a skill or knowledge deficiency, we have to look elsewhere for solutions. Chapter 2 describes a process for finding alternatives to training. This process was designed for use during needs analysis but it can also be used at all levels of evaluation.

Taught on course?

If one of the contributing factors to a business problem is a skill or knowledge deficiency, the next step is to check whether it was included in the course. This can be done by reviewing the course objectives.

Include in revised course

If the deficient skills and knowledge were not taught in the original course, we need to make sure that they are included when we revise the course.

Review validation data

The next step is to review the validation data collected at the end of each course. These data should already have been analysed and displayed graphically as described in Chapter 10. It is during evaluation that you realize the benefits of having a good filing and retrieval system for your validation data.

> Could do it on course?

The purpose of reviewing the validation data is to see whether the students were able to demonstrate the skills and knowledge while they were on the course.

> Investigate learning transfer

If the students were performing to the required level on the course, their performance must have deteriorated after the training. The next step is to look at the output of learning transfer.

Chapter 1 (The process of training) recommended that every job should have a description of the competencies needed to perform the job. It also recommended that everyone should have their competence assessed before being allowed to do the job by themselves.

Chapter 11 (Learning transfer) showed how vocational qualifications could be used to carry out this assessment. Without job certification evaluation becomes a time-consuming and costly additional exercise.

If you do not have access to assessment data, you will need to re-test a selection of students to see whether they are still able to meet the course objectives in the workplace. This underlines the importance of having objectives that are meaningful in both the classroom and the workplace. For example, an objective that states:

> 'By the end of the course you will have participated in three simulations'

is not useful because it cannot be measured in the workplace. It is more a description of the training content rather than an objective.

If your objectives are meaningful, you can use exactly the same approach as described in Chapter 10 (Validation). In this case the only difference between validation and evaluation is *when* you carry out the investigation.

If your investigation or assessment data show that there has not been a successful transfer of learning, you will need to find the causes of this and modify the learning transfer process. Chapter 11 (Learning transfer) considers the most common causes of poor learning transfer.

The assessment data may show that learning was transferred successfully but that it waned after a period of use in the business. In this case it is unlikely that you will need to modify the original course. The usual response in these cases is a demand for refresher training.

Be cautious about making an immediate response to demands for refresher training. First look for environmental or cultural reasons for the decline in skills. If an environmental or cultural cause is prevalent, no amount of refresher training will overcome these factors.

If refresher training is appropriate, don't put people through the same course again. You will only be 'telling them what you told them' and it is unlikely that you will get better learning transfer. As a colleague of mine says: 'If you always do what you always did, you'll always get what you always got!'

The answer is to run a different course which covers the same skill and knowledge from a different angle or at a different level. Another approach is to run a simulation which requires skilful application of the skills and knowledge.

> Revise course

If the students were not able to do what was required on the course, the course will need revising. However, it should be said that if you reach this step as part of evaluation, you should look at the other parts of the training process.

Poor performance on the course should be picked up during validation. If the needs analysis and course development were done properly, you should need to make only minor adjustments between courses.

As an example of how this process works in practice, consider a company whose customer satisfaction ratings are disappointingly low.

The managing director calls a meeting to assess and diagnose the problem. The data suggest that there is a widespread lack of skill in dealing with customers. Customer satisfaction training had not been given to any of the people who have direct contact with the customer.

This evaluation at the organizational level led to customer satisfaction training being included in training of sales people, customer representatives, service engineers, telephone operators and receptionists.

Further investigation of the data showed that manufacturing defects, administration errors and service engineer response time all contributed to customer dissatisfaction.

Investigations continued by looking at each of these departments in detail. For example, in the manufacturing area most of the defects were attributed to materials problems. Only a few defects were attributable to workmanship. These workmanship defects were eliminated by minor modifications to the training.

Measuring training effectiveness

One of the best ways of evaluating your training is to benchmark yourself against companies who have a known high reputation for their training. To do this you will have to decide which are the important indicators you wish to measure yourself against.

Training measures can be divided into four categories:

- financial,
- utilization,
- time,
- process.

The first three categories are quantitative. They are relatively easy to measure but can be perceived as bureaucratic. Quantitative measures have to be used with caution – one of the most popular time measures is the number of hours of training received by each employee per year. Many companies have a blanket target of 40 hours. Although this is useful as a guide, it is possible to imagine a situation where a highly skilled workforce would need only two hours of training per year. Training should always be related to the need.

Financial measures

The two types of financial measures are costs and earnings.

Costs

The following are some examples of training cost measures:

- total annual budget for providing training,
- training investment per employee per year,
- training investment per manager per year,
- cost of providing a day's non-residential training,
- cost of providing a day's residential training,
- cost of employing a trainer per day,
- cost of hiring a consultant per day,
- annual training budget expressed as a percentage of the company's total employment costs,
- annual training budget expressed as a percentage of the company's revenue.

The annual cost of providing training can include or exclude the students' wages while they are being trained, depending on the convention used in the benchmark company.

Earnings

If you are running your training organization as a budget centre, you will also be interested in measurements that allow you to compare your earnings with those of similar organizations. The following is a selection of measurements you can use:

- earnings per trainer per year,

- earnings per trainer per day,
- earnings as a percentage of the training budget,
- earnings per day of developed course,
- earnings per square metre of training space.

Utilization measures

The main two areas of utilization are trainer utilization and facility utilization.

Trainer utilization

- Face-to-face ratio – the percentage of time a trainer spends in front of the class.
- Delivery to preparation ratio – how much time is spent delivering a course compared to the time spent preparing for it. Often expressed as a percentage.

Facility utilization

Facility utilization is simply the percentage of time that the training rooms are in use. If you have an open learning centre, you will need to express the utilization as the percentage of time that the learning stations are in use.

Time measures

Time measurements include:

- hours of training per employee per year,
- time between identification of training need and delivery of the training,
- number of hours to develop one hour of training,
- percentage of training completed within agreed time limits (the target should always be 100 per cent).

Process measures

Measuring training effectiveness promises to be a fruitful line of research from a process point of view. Process questions allow an assessment of training effectiveness to be made without getting bogged down in numbers.

One of the main questions would be whether the organization has a training process. Other possible questions are:

- Do all employees receive training for their job role?
- Is their competence certified on the job?
- Do you have people whose job roles specifically include:
  – training management?
  – training delivery?
  – training administration?
- Have training staff been accredited as:
  – professional trainers?
  – trainers of the subject matter?
- Are you using accredited training courses?
- Has a training needs analysis been completed?
- Where do the training needs come from:
  – individual requests?

    – manager requests?
    – corporate mandates?
    – job requirements?
    – organizational needs?
    – departmental needs?
    – individual development plans?

- Are training needs linked to the business plan?

- How do you validate these needs to ensure that training is an appropriate solution?

- How do you prioritize these needs?

- Do people have 'living' development plans?

- Do you have an overall training plan for your business?

- To what extent is the training plan achieved?

- How do you select new courses?

- How do you assure the quality of these courses?

- If you develop your own courses, what process do you use to develop them?

- How do you select trainers?

- How do you assure the quality of these trainers?

- Do you have a training budget?

- How often are courses cancelled because of other priorities?

- To what extent are people withdrawn from courses?

- Do you have a dedicated training room?

- If you use external training facilities, how do you ensure that they are of sufficient quality and suitable for your needs?

- Do your courses have behavioural objectives?

- Are these objectives tested?

- Do students complete an end-of-course questionnaire?

- Are these questionnaires kept on file?

- How are they analysed?

- Who receives the analysis?

- What other validation methods do you use?

- Is evaluation carried out after the course is completed?

- Does each employee have a training record?

- Does the record include:
  - required courses?
  - planned dates?
  - date courses completed?
  - test results?

Part Two

Extending the Process

13 Training quality

Training should be considered to be no different to any other business process – and as such it should be subject to the same rigorous quality controls as any other critical process. As more organizations outsource the delivery of their training, assuring training quality is assuming a higher profile and importance.

Many businesses talk about being 'world class' without really knowing what it means – apart from being the best in the world, which brings us back to where we started and does not really tell us how we are going to achieve it.

For me, being 'world class' is simply doing the basics, and doing them right. This might seem very easy – but how many organizations do you see getting the basics consistently right?

The elements of 'world-class training' are:

- a quality training process,
- certified courses,
- certified instructors.

This chapter describes an audit process that was designed to assure the quality of training suppliers by making sure that the basics were done consistently well. The audit is used to:

- clarify standards of training development, administration, delivery and evaluation,
- assess the standards currently provided by suppliers,
- facilitate supplier development,
- examine the relationship between the business and its suppliers,
- examine the training process in terms of determining training needs, learning transfer and evaluation.

The process described here can be used for internal as well as external suppliers.

Minimum standards of performance

The performance of training suppliers is assessed in six areas:

- business relationship,
- communication and administration,
- course development,
- course materials,
- course delivery,
- training evaluation.

The minimum standards shown here are only given as examples and should be modified to suit the circumstances in your own business.

Business relationship
Invoices

- The supplier should raise invoices two weeks before the start of the programme.
- The customer will settle payment within 30 days.

Cancellation and substitution

- The customer can replace any delegate with a substitute at any time without charge.
- Cancellation within four weeks of the start of the course incurs a 25 per cent charge.
- Cancellation within two weeks incurs a 50 per cent charge.
- Cancellation within one week incurs a 100 per cent charge.

Pricing

- Pricing and discount structures are subject to negotiation.
- The supplier will allow the customer to preview and evaluate training materials before purchase.

Expenses

- Additional expenses such as travel, subsistence and accommodation costs are to be agreed with the customer before the event.

Communication and administration
Enquiry handling by supplier

- The supplier's office should be staffed during normal working hours.
- Answering machines should be available at other times.
- Specialist enquiries should be answered by the appropriate consultant within 24 hours.

Course and service information

- Course and information brochures should be revised regularly and distributed to the business units.
- 'Training directory' entry should be revised annually.

Joining instructions

- These include details and map of the venue, the course timetable, the learning objectives and any pre-course reading.
- Joining instructions reach the delegate at least two weeks before the course starts.

Course development
Process

- New programmes should be developed using a recognized course development process.

- Programmes should have precise, behavioural learning objectives.
- Progress checks should be included in the course design to ensure that the learning objectives are being met.
- Existing programmes should be continuously developed in a manner which reflects the changing business need.
- Programmes should be tailored to the local need.

Case studies and syndicate exercises

- Case studies and syndicate exercises should have clearly recognizable learning outcomes in line with the objectives of the programme.
- They should reflect current company policies and initiatives where relevant.

Course materials
Training manuals and handouts

- A course manual is to be provided to the delegates for each programme.
- The style and format of the manual should be appropriate for the learning objectives.
- The content of the manual should faithfully reflect the content of the course.
- Delegates should be able to use the manual as a post-course reference document.
- The overall impression of the manual should be one of neatness and clarity.
- The manual should reflect current company policies and initiatives where relevant.

Overheads

- Overhead projection slides should be clear and legible, and avoid information overload.
- They should be appropriate to the size of room.
- Diagrams should be used wherever possible.

Training delivery

Ensure that each individual obtains the maximum possible learning from the programme by:

- motivating and coaching people in a way that facilitates learning,
- identifying and supporting those participants experiencing difficulty in learning,
- recognizing and adapting the course to the needs of the group,
- displaying a sympathetic and caring attitude.

Provide opportunities for participants to:

- learn from each other,
- demonstrate their learning,
- relate their learning to the workplace.

Training evaluation

Suppliers will be expected to work with their clients to evaluate the contribution of the training to individual, organizational and business performance.

End-of-course review
- A written end-of-course review form should be completed by each participant.
- The design of the form and the questions asked should be specific to the learning objectives.

Post-course transfer of learning
- A continuous sampling process, including telephone surveys, questionnaires and interviews, should be introduced to assess the transfer of learning to the workplace.
- The size of the sample should reflect the amount of investment involved. For programmes in excess of four days or where there has been a significant financial investment, a sample size of 25 per cent would be appropriate. For the remaining programmes, a sample size of 10 per cent would be more realistic.

Training audit process

Although this audit process (see Figure 13.1) was designed to ensure the quality of training we receive from outsourced suppliers, it can easily be adapted to assess internal training suppliers.

As you get into the detail of the audit you will come to realize, as we did, that this audit is as much about assessing your own training process as about auditing your suppliers. The reason for this is that suppliers can only provide you with world-class training if your needs analysis and post-course follow-up are also world class.

In addition it is important to understand that the purpose of the audit is to develop your suppliers and your relationship with them. It isn't about finding reasons for dumping your current suppliers and finding new ones. Constantly changing suppliers can only lead to an unstable training process.

However, the process does allow for parting company with a supplier if the supplier, despite being given every chance and encouragement, still fails to meet your stringent standards.

Select course to be audited

The full audit is a long process so you will need to be selective about which courses you audit. The following are criteria which would increase a course's priority for audit:

- a new course,
- an important course that has not previously been audited,
- a course that is part of a company-wide initiative, e.g. 'Finance Training Framework',
- a course that has given cause for concern.

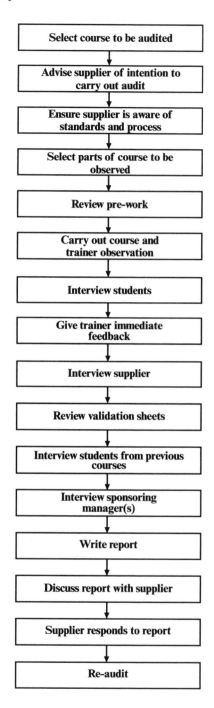

Figure 13.1   *Training audit process*

Advise supplier of intention to carry out audit

The supplier should be advised of the intention to carry out the audit and a suitable date for the audit should be chosen.

Ensure supplier is aware of standards and process

If the supplier is not aware of the audit standards and processes, arrange a meeting with the supplier to explain the approach. A copy of the process and standards should be given to the supplier.

Select parts of course to be observed

The supplier should provide the assessor with a copy of the course agenda and objectives so that a decision can be made on which parts of the course should be observed. Normally, short courses (one to two days) are observed in their entirety. Longer courses would require a minimum sampling of two days.

Review pre-work

The supplier should send the assessor a copy of the pre-work at the same time as it is sent to the students.

Carry out course and trainer observation

The course is observed by keeping a log of comments and the trainer is observed against a number of attributes. The 'trainer observation form' (see Figure 13.2) has a 1–5 rating check box and a comments section for each of the attributes. The ratings are defined as follows:

1. Not acceptable
2. Poor
3. OK
4. Good
5. Master performer

The target rating is 4 or 5 for each of the criteria. The performance of your assessors should be moderated by having new assessors observing the same course as an experienced assessor until rating consistency is achieved.

Interview students

While you are observing the course, take the opportunity to interview the students on their impressions of the course.

Give trainer immediate feedback

Give the trainer feedback at appropriate points throughout the course and summarize the feedback at the end of the course. Feedback is most effective if it is as close to the behaviour as possible. The written report should contain no surprises.

Interview supplier

Interview the supplier using a supplier questionnaire as a guide, similar to the one shown in Figure 13.3. The purpose of these questions is to determine the quality of the supplier's training process and to ascertain whether the supplier has met the standards for:

Trainer:	Date:
Session:	Observer:

(1) = Not acceptable   (2) = Poor   (3) = OK   (4) = Good   (5) = Master performer

Behaviours	**Assessment and comments**
<u>Preparation</u> — Rehearsed lesson — Administration — Classroom layout — Materials and equipment prepared — Arranged to be free from interruptions	(1) (2) (3) (4) (5)
<u>Presentation</u> — Introduced subject — Communicated objectives — Communicated agenda — Followed logical sequence — Summarized — Checked students' understanding — Kept to time — Kept to subject	(1) (2) (3) (4) (5)
<u>Manner</u> — Showed commitment — Showed enthusiasm — Created interest — Sensitive to group — Credible — Knowledgeable	(1) (2) (3) (4) (5)
<u>Technique</u> — Voice — Questioning — Pace — Movement — Eye contact — Mannerisms — Use of audiovisual aids	(1) (2) (3) (4) (5)

Figure 13.2   *Trainer observation form*

Supplier Questionnaire

Course:

Supplier:	Interviewer:
Interviewee:	Date:

1. How did you determine the objectives for this course?

2. How did you determine the length of the course?

3. How do you evaluate the effectiveness of this course?

4. Can you give me an example of how you have changed this course as a result of end-of-course feedback?

5. How do you evaluate the effectiveness of your training in terms of on-the-job performance?

6. Can you give me an example of how you have changed a training programme as the result of feedback on work-related performance?

7. How often do you run this course?

8. Who is your contact with the company and can you describe your working relationship with them?

9. How do you ensure that the course meets the specific needs of your students during the course?

10. How often do you revise the training materials?

11. What action do you take when a student fails to meet a course objective?

Figure 13.3　*An excerpt from a supplier questionnaire*

- business relationship,
- communication and administration,
- course development,
- training delivery,
- training evaluation.

Review validation sheets　Review validation sheets to see what additional insights can be derived from the students' perception of the course. A guide to interpreting validation sheets is given in Chapter 10, Validation.

Interview students from previous courses　The purpose of this step is to check the effect of the course three or more months after the student has left the course. Use a student follow-up questionnaire, similar to the one shown in Figure 13.4, as the basis of a structured interview. The questionnaire can also be sent out to graduates of the course to obtain a larger sample.

Student Follow-up Questionnaire

Course:	Date(s):
Venue:	Trainer(s):
Student:	Interviewer/date:

1. How good were the joining instructions? ☐ ☐ ☐ ☐ ☐
   Very poor — Very good

2. How good was the course pre-work? ☐ ☐ ☐ ☐ ☐
   Very poor — Very good

3. Did you discuss your personal development objectives with your manager prior to the course? ☐ ☐ ☐ ☐ ☐
   No — Yes

4. What was your overall impression of the course? ☐ ☐ ☐ ☐ ☐
   Very poor — Very good

5. How would you rate the effectiveness of the trainer(s) in the following categories:

   a. Subject-matter knowledge ☐ ☐ ☐ ☐ ☐
   b. Presentation skills ☐ ☐ ☐ ☐ ☐
   c. Enthusiasm for the subject ☐ ☐ ☐ ☐ ☐
   d. Personal coaching ☐ ☐ ☐ ☐ ☐
   e. Balance between lecture and practice ☐ ☐ ☐ ☐ ☐
   Very poor — Very good

6. How would you rate the quality of the course materials? ☐ ☐ ☐ ☐ ☐
   Very poor — Very good

7. How would you rate the relevance of the course to your work situation? ☐ ☐ ☐ ☐ ☐
   Very poor — Very good

8. How would you rate the duration of the course? ☐ ☐ ☐ ☐ ☐
   Too long — Too short

9. Did the course cater for your own preferred learning style? ☐ ☐ ☐ ☐ ☐
   No — Yes

Figure 13.4 *An excerpt from a student follow-up questionnaire*

Interview sponsoring manager(s)

The students' attendance on a course will have been sponsored by their immediate managers. Interview a sample of managers to see whether they have observed an improvement in performance as a result of course attendance. Also interview the organization's training manager to gain additional data on the effectiveness of the course.

Write report

Structure the report around the supplier standards and provide copies of questionnaires and observation forms.

Discuss report with supplier

Always meet the supplier to discuss the report and to communicate your recommendations. Sending the report without a meeting or an explanation is not as effective and it misses an opportunity to strengthen the customer–supplier relationship.

Supplier responds to report   Ask the supplier to make a written response to the report which will include their reaction to the observations and their plans for improving their performance.

Re-audit   If the initial audit was satisfactory, it may not be necessary to carry out a complete re-audit, but it will be necessary to assure yourself that your recommendations and the supplier's action plans have been carried out.

The audit will have to be repeated in its entirety if the initial audit was unsatisfactory. The supplier will be given every chance and assistance to reach the required standards, but you will have to look for alternative sources of supply if the second audit is unsatisfactory.

14 Training networks

Many large companies are concerned that they are 're-inventing the wheel' all over their organizations, with the consequent duplication of effort and loss of efficiency. A common solution to this problem is the formation of networks which allow learning to be shared across the business. This chapter looks at the purpose of networks, the characteristics of successful networks, and how to make the most of technology including e-mail and the Internet.

Networks come in two forms:

- physical networks – meetings of representatives from different parts of the organization,
- virtual networks – where members don't meet physically but use information technology to keep in touch.

Irrespective of whether they are virtual or physical, networks typically produce the outputs shown in Figure 14.1.

Physical networks

As most networks are physical networks, I am going to use a fictional example to illustrate the purpose of networks and why some networks function better than others. This example assumes a business with a fairly complex organizational structure:

- a large parent company,
- a central headquarters staff (including training and development staff),
- six or more relatively independent businesses (with their own headquarters),
- over 100 locations around the world.

The company established a training network whose main activity was a series of meetings which were held once a quarter at four different regional locations. Meetings were attended by training staff from sites within a 200 km radius but did not include representatives from the site's parent businesses.

The meetings were organized by headquarters' training staff who took the same agenda to each of the four regions.

Networking was limited to the parent company's home country and was thought of in terms of physical outputs such as network meetings and training directories rather than activities or results to be achieved. The network meetings, and hence the network, were calendar led rather than purpose driven. There were very few 'processing' and 'workshop' activities at the meetings.

After the initial novelty, attendance at the network meetings fell dramatically and only two or three stalwarts (plus a similar number of the central training staff) continued to attend each of the regional meetings.

The main sources of information sharing were a 'round table' session at the network meetings and the information contained in the training directory.

One of the root problems of this approach was that the network meetings were being run for their own sake. Although there was a purpose – to share learning – it was far too general to hold the network together and to provide a clear agenda for the meetings. The network only started to fulfil its initial promise when it was realized that its real purpose was to support a set of broader objectives:

- Training will be identified, delivered and evaluated to world-class standards by world-class processes.

- Maximum use will be made of the existing training resource.

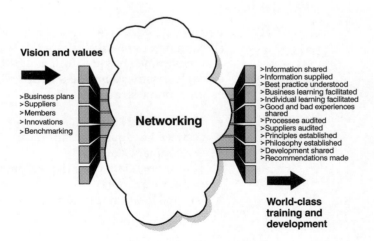

Figure 14.1   Input–output diagram of a training network

- Training will be a significant contributor to business success.
- Our employees will receive appropriate, timely training which will be admired and recognized throughout the world.
- Our businesses will have a shared training philosophy and principles.

Other problems that can be identified in the example are:

- Very little of the networking activity extended to the overseas parts of the business.
- The network meetings were held every three months irrespective of whether there was a real need.
- The majority of the meeting time was given over to 'information sharing'. This restricted the time that could be spent on 'information-processing' items such as discussion and problem solving. This was further compounded by trying to cover too much in the time allowed.
- Some of the network's members had influence on training and development at their own site but were not able to influence their parent business directly.
- The network's structure did not have representation from the people who ran the main businesses.

Factors which contribute to a successful training network

Taking the lessons of this example into account, we can summarize the factors that contribute to the success of a training network.

Definite purpose

The network should have a definite purpose, preferably in support of a broader set of objectives. All network activity should support the aim of providing your employees with world-class training and development. There should be no 'sacred cows'. Elements of the training network should be continued only for as long as they are useful.

One of the main purposes of a training network is to ensure that training plans are aligned to the business strategies. Having the chief executive officer make a presentation to the training network early on in the business planning cycle is a powerful means of achieving this. (See Chapter 2, Training needs, for a detailed description of this process.)

Appropriate ownership

The network should be 'owned' and driven by someone who has access to, and influence with, the chief executive officer and personnel director.

The network owner should try to visit individual network members, at their own locations, at least once every two years. This helps to flush out issues which would not normally surface in network meetings.

Appropriate membership

It is essential that the right people (those who have the power to implement change in their own organizations) are members of the network. Don't ignore important levels within the structure of the company when selecting members for the network.

Appropriate structure

In a multinational company, the network should extend internationally – not just cover the organization's home country.

When the size and geographical spread of the network increase, having everybody attend the same network meetings starts to become unmanageable. One approach is to run duplicate 'regional' meetings around the country, but this involves the network owner in an unacceptable amount of wasted time and travel.

A better solution is to have self-directed 'daughter' networks (with representation on the main network). These can be formed on a business or regional basis. You can still have occasional conferences when you can get larger numbers of people together.

Remember, a network is far more than a series of meetings, so encourage members to interact outside the structure of the network meetings.

Effective sharing of resources

One of the main reasons for forming a network is to improve resource utilization. This can be achieved by:

- sharing development of new training programmes,
- negotiating discounts on a national and international basis,
- co-ordinating applications for national awards,
- co-ordinating responses to surveys,
- sharing materials, people and other resources.

Effective dissemination of learning

An essential function of the network is to disseminate learning to the different parts of the business. Rather than trying to capture all the learning itself – which would take an enormous resource – the network should concentrate on recording where the learning can be found, and on bringing together people with complementary needs. This can be done through a paper-based training network directory. The section on virtual networks describes an electronic training network directory.

The network can also co-ordinate benchmarking and conference attendance. A network member makes a benchmarking visit to an external company or attends a conference and reports back to the network and other parts of the business.

Effective meetings Don't just plan network meetings for every month or once a quarter. Time them to coincide with and support significant events such as the production of the business plan.

The majority of the time spent at network meetings should be used for discussion, decision making and problem solving. Don't waste time sharing information which could be communicated better by other means such as newsletters. (See the section on virtual networks for other methods of distributing information.)

It is better to have one or two 'information-processing' items covered thoroughly than to rush through a crowded agenda.

Attendees, location, timing and duration of network meetings should be determined by the purpose and content of the meeting.

Meetings can be made more interesting by having presentations from high-profile speakers and demonstrations by suppliers.

Virtual networks

Many of the problems associated with physical networks are caused by the separation of their members in time and distance. Fortunately, these are problems which can be overcome by the use of a virtual network.

A virtual network is one whose members do not meet physically. Of course, this does not mean that the members would *never* meet physically – successful networks use a combination of physical and virtual networking.

As virtual networking has been made a great deal easier with the introduction of e-mail and the Internet, you could overlook the fact that virtual networks have been with us for many centuries, with members keeping in touch via letters, newsletters, magazines and books.

The following are a number of additional methods which can be used to support a virtual network.

Voice mail Voice mail allows people to leave recorded messages when they telephone you. The messages are usually recorded digitally and can be accessed from any telephone that has tone dialling. Telephone answering machines were the original form of voice mail.

It is possible to leave a detailed message, so voice mail allows you to communicate with people who are rarely at their desk or who work in different time zones.

Dial-a-fax   Many commercial companies distribute information to their customers by fax. A refinement of this is where the customer requests and automatically receives the information by fax. This has obvious applications in a network where, instead of deluging your members with every single piece of information, reports and papers can be requested when needed.

Electronic mail   Electronic mail (or e-mail) is another system which allows you to communicate with people independently of time and geography. You will need a computer that can be linked to either a commercial service provider or your company's own e-mail system. The service provider will provide you with all the software you need.

Messages addressed to you are held at your service provider's computer until you make a connection. The messages can then be read immediately or transferred to your computer. If you are linked to your service provider via a telephone connection, it's cheaper to transfer the messages to your computer, break the connection and read the messages later.

When you send a message, you will need to know the e-mail address of the person you want to contact. E-mail addresses can look a bit strange. For example, mine is:

    mikewills@compuserve.com

The characters to the left of the '@' sign identify the recipient of the message. These characters can be letters, numbers or a combination. You can also use some other characters, provided that their use has not been restricted.

The characters between the '@' and the '.' identify the service provider and the characters after the '.' identify the type of organization. For example, 'com' indicates commercial, 'co' is company, 'gov' is government, and 'ac' is academic. Many addresses also have a country identifier tagged on the end, as in '.uk'.

E-mail addresses have to be typed exactly as they are written. For example, in my address there should be no space between 'mike' and 'wills'.

The space is one of the restricted characters, so you will find that people either run the words together (as in 'mikewills') or replace the space with a dot or an underline character, as in 'mike.wills' or 'mike_wills'.

You type the message in exactly the same way as if you were using a simple word processor, and when you have finished you instruct the computer to send the message. It is sent to your provider's computer and is then transferred to the recipient's service provider. The transfer will not be instantaneous as there is unlikely to be a direct connection between the two service providers' computers. The message will have to travel round the world in a series of 'jumps' from one computer to another.

The same message can be sent or copied to several recipients at the same time, which makes e-mail an ideal medium for communicating with network members. You will also find that because there is a culture of informality surrounding the use of e-mail, many people will use e-mail in circumstances in which they would be reluctant to write a letter.

Electronic newsletters

Newsletters are a traditional method of keeping network members in touch, but their use can be restricted because of printing and distribution costs (including addressing and filling envelopes). Other methods of distributing a newsletter while keeping your printing costs to a minimum are to use e-mail or a fax machine.

If you have a large network, standing by a fax machine for a couple of hours is not the best use of your time. Try to use a fax that can keep all the network members' fax numbers in its memory so you can get on with something else while it does the dialling. Using fax can be quite expensive, especially when you have overseas members, but it is still comparable to the cost of surface mail and is certainly much quicker.

The quality of a faxed newsletter can be improved if your computer has fax software. Compose the newsletter using a word processor and, instead of printing it out and feeding it into a fax machine, fax it directly from your computer. This is usually done by 'printing' the document to the fax software instead of the printer.

The cheapest way of distributing a newsletter is using e-mail – it costs the same and takes the same amount of time no matter how many copies you are sending out. You may be able to 'attach' the newsletter to a memo. The recipients can then save the newsletter to their hard disk and, provided that they have the same word-processing software, can either read it on screen or print it. The look of the received newsletter may vary if the recipients have different printers connected to their computers.

If you can't be certain about the software being used at the receiving end, it's probably safest to send the newsletter as plain text within the body of the memo – but this does mean there will be no graphics and you will have to use a very simple format. A guide on how to convert a word-processor file to a plain text (or ASCII) file is given in Appendix 3. Or, since most people who have e-mail also have an Internet browser, you can save the newsletter in HTML format that can be viewed using any browser software.

Electronic network directory

Many networks have directories which list the network's members and the expertise that they can share with other members of the network. Paper-based directories share the same problems as traditional newsletters in that they are expensive to print and distribute.

An electronic directory can be distributed either as an e-mail attachment or on a lightweight computer disk. It also provides links to other parts of the directory and allows you to search for the information you require. Figure 14.2 shows the first screen of an electronic network directory.

This directory was constructed by collecting the data in a database and then writing a program for viewing the data which could be used by people who had no previous experience of databases.

Internet home pages

An Internet home page is just like having a noticeboard that anyone in the network can access at any time they want. A well-designed home page will also have links to related information and other home pages, building a 'web' of useful information.

If you have e-mail it is likely that you already have the software (called a browser) for connecting to the Internet. You can pay to have a home page designed for you but it really isn't too difficult to do it yourself. A good book on the subject is *Teach Yourself html* (Bride, 1996).

You need to know the location of a home page (called a URL) before you can access it. The location of my home page (which you are welcome to access to see how a home page can be used to support a virtual network) is:

http://ourworld.compuserve.com/homepages/mikewills

URLs are constructed in a similar way to e-mail addresses, but may be much longer. However, some may be quite simple, such as http://www.bt.com for telephone company BT.

Networked computers

If the members of the training network are connected to the same computer network, you can make use of shared files for collaborating on projects and distributing information.

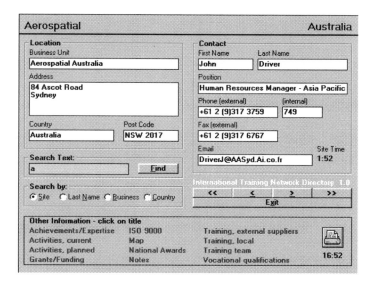

Figure 14.2   *An example of an electronic directory*

A private network may also have its own version of the Internet (called an intranet) where you can set up home pages that can only be accessed by people connected to your computer network.

Telephone and video conferencing

Instead of travelling to network meetings you could set up a telephone or video conference. Although these conferences can never be a complete substitute for a person-to-person meeting, they work remarkably well if there is a simple, prepared agenda and the participants know each other already.

A telephone conference for up to three people is relatively easy to set up using an ordinary telephone – contact your telephone company for details.

Once you get beyond three people it is best to use video conferencing so that you can keep track of who is talking. You will need to use a dedicated video link to get good quality and this can prove to be expensive – but not as expensive as flying everybody around the world.

Electronic conferences

Some Internet service providers have forums where people can 'talk' to each other electronically. It's rather like sending and receiving a series of e-mail messages where the response is almost immediate so long as members are on-line at the same time.

15 Using managers and others to deliver training

Along with other business functions, the training function is becoming leaner and flatter. Where once large, central training departments covered all aspects of the business, training is now being delivered by external suppliers, line managers and subject-matter experts in addition to in-house trainers.

Some organizations have the majority of their training delivered by external consultants. Although this is flexible, it can be a very expensive option. Many other companies are opting for the route of using line managers and subject-matter experts to deliver their training, not just because it is less expensive. Using your own people as instructors brings credibility to the subject matter and allows you to tailor the training to your exact needs.

Whatever method you choose for the primary delivery of your training, it is probably safest to keep your options open by not 'putting all your eggs in one basket'.

Using only in-house trainers can lead to over-resourcing and inflexibility. Depending on external consultants can drive up your costs enormously. Having only part-time instructors will eventually lead to lower quality standards.

The training professional's role

The trend towards using part-time instructors has implications for the role of the training professional. Rather than being responsible for the delivery of training, the role becomes more concerned with quality assurance and ensuring that the people who develop and deliver the training have the necessary skills.

You may decide to continue doing the training administration yourself or, depending on the organization, you may decide to devolve the administration as well.

Taking the empowered approach to training even further, you might even decide to set up 'faculties' which are aligned to specific 'disciplines' (such as engineering or sales) within the organization. The faculties would be responsible not only for developing, administering and delivering training in their areas, but also for research and capturing learning.

Assuring the quality of training

In Chapter 13, Training quality, I said that: 'Training should be considered to be no different to any other business process – and as such it should be subject to the same rigorous quality controls as any other critical process.'

This is just as true – perhaps even more so – when you are using managers and subject-matter experts to deliver your training. There is absolutely no reason why you should settle for standards which would be unacceptable if a full-time trainer or external consultant were delivering the material. Of course, you wouldn't necessarily expect them to be 'master performers', but you would expect them to be able to score '4' on a 1–5 scale.

The quality assurance process described in Chapter 13 can easily be adapted to audit internal rather than external suppliers. The only difference is that, as you will probably not be paying for the training, you won't need to examine the business relationship.

Developing part-time trainers

Chapter 4, Trainers, covers the development of full-time trainers. The process of developing part-time trainers is essentially the same but there are some additional factors which have to be taken into account.

The development needs to be more practical than theoretical and, because the instructor will not be training every day, the principles need to be simple and explicit.

When I was coaching a new part-time trainer, I remember giving advice similar to the following:

Training courses should have objectives and a method for checking that these objectives have been met. Putting it another way – if it doesn't have objectives and if it doesn't have a test, it isn't training!

Another consequence of this is that training does not have to take place in a training room but it does have to:

- be planned,
- be certified,
- be delivered by a certified instructor,
- be entered in the training records,
- have a record kept of the test results.

In other words – if it has objectives, and those objectives are tested, it *is* training!

Each objective should have an associated test item, and each test item should have an associated objective.

The course should also have been reviewed by colleagues of the author and at least one pilot course should have been run.

To begin with, part-time instructors will only need to understand the basic elements of a quality training process, which are:

- identifying the training need,
- developing the course,
- delivering the course,
- evaluating the training.

It is essential that trainers attend a recognized train-the-trainer course. For full-time trainers it is probably best that they attend train-the-trainer courses early on in their career so that they have the foundations of a strong theoretical framework that will allow them to make sense of the experiences they have during their development.

For part-time trainers, I have found it better to work very closely with them on a one-to-one basis during the development and presentation of their first course.

The section on 'Developing your own courses' in Chapter 3 will provide you with good reference material when you are coaching instructors on the development of their first course.

Similarly, the course delivery process described at the beginning of Chapter 9 will help trainers when they come

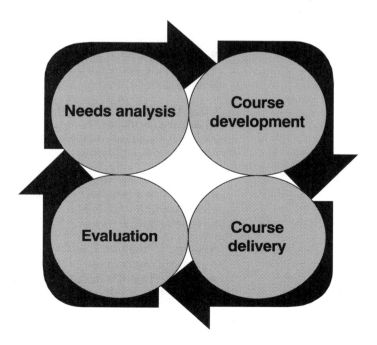

Figure 15.1   *The basic elements of a quality training process*

to prepare and present their first course. I would also provide them with a copy of the trainer observation form. Not only will this let them know how they are going to be assessed, but it is also a very useful summary of how to conduct yourself in the classroom.

When they present their first course, under your supervision, you should carry out a trainer observation as described in Chapter 4. This allows instructors to understand the need for the training and to concentrate on their development areas. It also allows you to have the train-the-trainer course tailored to the exact needs of your instructors based on objective observational data.

Based on previous experience, the content of a course for a part-time instructor is likely to include:

- presentation techniques,
- use of audiovisual equipment,
- learning principles,
- encouraging participation,
- questioning skills,
- facilitation skills,
- demonstrating,
- coaching,
- discussion leading,
- needs analysis,
- behavioural objectives,
- developing lesson plans,
- preparing visual aids,
- preparing handouts,
- evaluating training.

It will probably take several more observations after the train-the-trainer course for the instructor to reach the required standard of at least '4' out of '5' for all the criteria on the observation form.

Although the standard is stringent, it is possible for every instructor to attain the required standard because every element of the standard is behavioural and the criteria can be met by one or more of the following strategies:

- doing something that they are not currently doing,
- ceasing one or more of their current behaviours,
- doing more of what they do now,
- doing less of what they do now.

When the instructors reach the required standard, you should recognize their achievement, perhaps by issuing a certificate. Even better if the training can be accredited and put towards the award of a recognized qualification.

Don't forget to carry out observations after the trainer has been certified to ensure that the standards are being maintained.

The line manager's role

With the devolution of training development and delivery to the business, the line manager's role in identifying training needs and determining whether training is appropriate becomes even more critical.

When I was introducing this type of training approach into a US aerospace manufacturer, it rapidly became apparent that we would have to run a workshop to make line managers aware of what training can and cannot do, as well as underscoring the importance of the manager's role in the overall training process.

Although this workshop was run to support the strategy of training being delivered by non-trainers, it wouldn't be a bad idea to run a similar workshop for managers in any organization that values training and development.

An outline for such a workshop is given in Figures 15.2 to 15.5. Of course, you will need to extend and modify the outline to meet your local needs.

'Welcome to this presentation on the training process and your role in ensuring that we have world-class training in this organization.'

**Managers' overview
of the
training process**

[Review the session's objectives]

Objectives

By the end of this workshop you will be able to:

- Define training
- Identify the factors which contribute to world-class training
- Identify when training is appropriate
- Recognize the importance of course and instructor certification
- Describe a process for evaluating training

[Review the session's agenda]

Agenda

- Training quality
- Definition of training
- Getting the basics right
- Training process
- Identification of training and non-training solutions
- Alternatives to training
- Course and instructor certification
- Evaluating training

Figure 15.2   Managers' overview (page 1 of 4)

'Training should be considered no different to any other business process – and as such it should be subject to the same rigours as any other critical process.'

Training quality

Training is a critical process within the business. The quality requirement for training is no different from the quality requirement for all other critical processes.

'From this definition it can be seen that training activities should have objectives and a method for checking that these objectives have been met. Putting it another way – if it doesn't have objectives and if it doesn't have a test, it isn't training!

'Another consequence of this is that training does not have to take place in a training room but it does have to:

• be planned;
• be certified;
• be delivered by a certified instructor;
• be entered in the training records;
• have a record kept of the test results.

'In other words – if it has objectives, and those objectives are tested, it *is* training!'

Definition of training

Training is the transfer of defined and measurable knowledge or skills.

'For me, being world class is simply doing the basics, and doing them right. This might seem very easy – but how many organizations do you see getting the basics consistently right?

'The elements of world-class training are a quality training process, certified courses and certified instructors.'

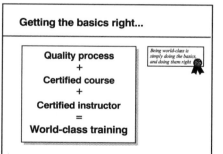

Figure 15.3   Managers' overview (page 2 of 4)

'The basic elements of a quality training process are:

• identifying the training need;
• developing the course;
• delivering the course;
• evaluating the training.'

[Refer participants to Chapter 1, The process of training, for a more detailed description of the training process.]

Training process

'There is a tendency to assume that every business problem can be corrected by training. In reality training forms only 10 per cent of the solution – but this is a vital 10 per cent. If a person has not been trained properly, everything else that follows is built on sand.

'The questions shown in this slide will help you decide whether training is, or is not, an appropriate solution.'

[Go through the questions using the explanation and example given in the following sections in Chapter 2, Training needs:

• Check that training is an appropriate solution
• Check queries with managers]

Is training an appropriate solution?

• Is there an important business or strategic need for this training?
• Does the individual already have the knowledge and skills?
• Is the individual willing to use the knowledge and skills?
• Has the individual received this training before?
• Does the individual have the ability to be trained?

'If training is not an appropriate solution, then we have to find alternatives to training.'

[Go through these suggestions using the explanation given in the following section in Chapter 2, Training needs:

• Find alternatives to training]

Alternatives to training

• No action required.
• Remove barriers.
• Arrange coaching.
• Arrange practice.
• Arrange counselling.
• Re-design job/procedure.
• Look at recruitment standards.
• Move person into another job.

Figure 15.4   *Managers' overview (page 3 of 4)*

'A certified course will have objectives and tests. Each objective should have an associated test item and each test item should have an associated objective.

'The course should also have been reviewed by colleagues of the author, and at least one pilot course should have been run.'

[It should not be necessary to go into the details of how a course is developed at this stage, but if managers are interested you can refer them to Chapter 3, Training courses.]

'The training manager will work closely with the instructors during the preparation of their first courses.

'We will provide them with a train-the-trainer course which will be followed up by observation and feedback.

'Instructors will be certified when they score at least "4" out of "5" for every observation criterion.'

[See Chapter 4, Trainers, for a copy of the observation form and a detailed description of the instructor certification process.]

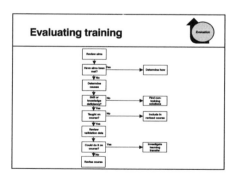

'Evaluation of training is essential for ensuring that the learning has been transferred into the business, and that we are providing the right kind of training to meet the business needs.'

[Go through the algorithm shown on this slide by referring to Chapter 12, Evaluation.]

Figure 15.5   Managers' overview (page 4 of 4)

16 Competencies

Organizations are increasingly using competencies to help them identify and develop the characteristics in their staff that they need to be successful. Competencies provide a common language for describing performance. They help identify and prepare successors, allowing 'surprise fits' to be included while avoiding 'poor fits'; facilitate the selection process; and allow managers to have objective development discussions with individuals based on capabilities that the business needs.

There are many approaches to the use of competencies and this has resulted in much confusion. The purpose of this chapter is to provide an explanation of:

- what competencies are;
- their relationship to the training process;
- how they can be identified;
- how they are used.

What are competencies?

There are two types of competency (or competence):

- threshold (or essential) competence;
- distinguishing competency.

Threshold competences are characteristics that are causally related to effective or average performance. In terms of the training process, threshold competences are essentially the same as the skills and knowledge that are used in training needs analysis.

Distinguishing competencies are characteristics that are causally related to superior performance. In other words, they separate the superior performer from the average performer. (See Figure 16.1).

In a work context it is possible to evaluate an individual using a continuum of characteristics (see Figure 16.2). These range from results (what a person 'does') to innate characteristics (what a person 'is').

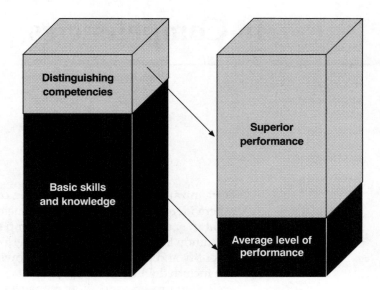

Figure 16.1   *Distinguishing competencies*

Knowledge and skills are relatively easy to develop (see Figure 16.3) but rarely differentiate outstanding performers from average performers. They are job dependent and usually indicate the minimum requirements (threshold competences) for doing a job adequately.

Although motives, traits, attitudes and values are hard to develop, it is often these which make the difference between average and superior performance. They are more generic, which means that they are less likely to be job dependent.

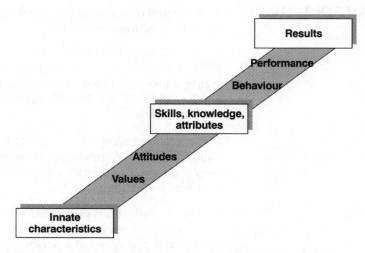

Figure 16.2   *Continuum of personal characteristics*

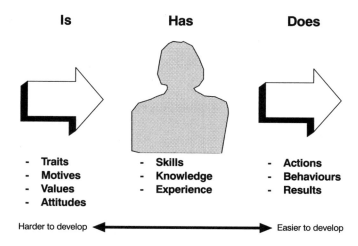

Figure 16.3   *Ease/difficulty of developing personal characteristics*

These ideas have profound implications for training because they imply that, although training courses may be excellent at developing threshold skills and *competent* performance, they may not be the best method for developing *superior* performance in an organization.

Using competencies

There are a large number of uses for competencies. Maximum benefit is gained by using competencies within key processes such as:

- selection,
- appraisal,
- personal development planning,
- training needs analysis,
- objective setting,
- training evaluation,
- succession planning.

Competencies are extremely powerful tools for shaping organizational culture. They help to change individuals' behaviour in directions required by the business by focusing their attention on 'what it takes to be successful' (e.g. 'has a broad business perspective'). Once businesses have identified and articulated the competencies they need, they can begin to focus employee development activities on acquiring them.

Identifying competencies

There are three main ways of deriving competencies:

- adopting an existing set,
- adapting an existing set,
- identifying a unique set of competencies.

Adopting an existing set

The advantage of this option is that it can be quick and easy to implement and, with careful selection, provides a high degree of actual as well as face validity. Some existing sets of generic competencies (such as McBer's) have an empirical basis and should be broadly applicable.

Using competencies that have been derived from an existing set saves time because you don't have to start with a blank sheet or an unprocessed list of characteristics, but you do need to make sure that they are appropriate for your application. An expert panel can be used to check whether the competencies are relevant to the needs of the business.

The disadvantages associated with this option are:

- It might be difficult to find a generic set of competencies that fit your business.
- Isolating the differentiating competencies might be more difficult.
- You might miss some of the unique aspects of the roles you are considering.

Adapting an existing set

Existing sets of competencies can be modified to reflect the needs, priorities and plans of the business – leading to an increased sense of ownership. An expert panel can be used to adapt the existing set, adding, deleting or modifying competencies where necessary.

Identifying a unique set of competencies

The advantage of this option is that the competencies will be developed by the people closest to the critical business issues and will therefore be driven by the specific business situation.

A potential disadvantage of this approach is that some of the processes used to identify competencies can be rigorous and time consuming. This is why many companies use external consultants to design and implement such processes. This approach should be considered when:

- businesses need to redefine job requirements to meet new demands and needs,
- when the jobs in question are 'key' roles,
- significant numbers of people are in these roles,
- a significant recruitment requirement exists for these roles.

The process outlined in Figure 16.4 is typically used to develop a set of tailor-made competencies.

Determine performance standards

As competencies are used to differentiate between average and superior performers, we need to know what constitutes superior performance. An effective way of doing

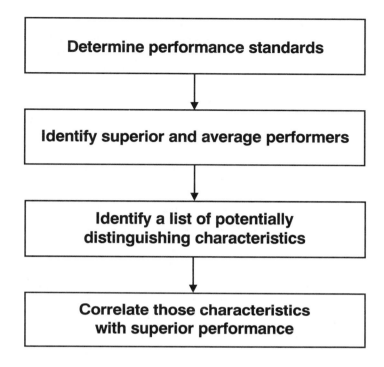

Figure 16.4 *Process for identifying competencies*

this is to have an expert panel determine the performance standards of the roles that are to be analysed.

Identify superior and average performers

The expert panel can now select a sample of superior and average performers. The sample should have at least 20 subjects: 12 superior and 8 average performers. If you are forced to use a smaller sample, make sure that you have twice as many superior performers as average performers because you will always learn most from your 'high fliers'.

Identify a list of potentially distinguishing characteristics

Use behaviour event interviews, job element analysis or a repertory grid (all described below) to identify potentially distinguishing characteristics.

Correlate those characteristics with superior performance

Distinguishing competencies are those that are shared by the superior performers but will not be in evidence for average performers. Use another sample to check whether the identified competencies can distinguish superior from average performers.

Tools for identifying competencies

The following is a description of the tools that are commonly used for identifying competencies.

Behavioural event interviews

The behavioural event interview is a technique developed by McClelland and Dailey that is used to identify competencies by getting detailed descriptions of a sample of individuals' performances. The sample includes both average and superior performers, but the interviewers are unaware of interviewees' performance records.

Examples of questions used in behavioural event interviews are: 'Describe a time when you had to work as part of a team to achieve a goal' or 'Tell me about a time in the last 18 months that was really a high point for you.'

The characteristics which emerge are coded, categorized and correlated to performance criteria.

Expert panels

An expert panel is a group of knowledgeable human resource specialists, managers and superior performers who are used to identify competencies.

Job element analysis

Job element analysis was developed by Boyatzis and uses a weighted list of characteristics that managers perceive as important in distinguishing superior from average performers.

Repertory grid

The repertory grid is a technique developed by Kelly that takes three individuals at a time from a sample that contains both average and superior performers. An expert panel is then asked in which way two of the individuals are similar to each other and different from the third. These similarities and differences form the basis of a set of competencies which are related to superior performance.

Assessing competencies

The two most common ways of assessing competencies are:

- assessment by the individual's manager,
- attendance at an assessment centre.

Assessment by the individual's manager

This usually takes the form of an appraisal or counselling session. It is at its most powerful when the manager and individual agree on the assessment.

Both the manager and the individual should make separate assessments of the individual's competency levels (usually on a 1–5 scale) before the session starts. The session can then concentrate on reconciling differences of opinion.

The process is made much easier if there is a description of the expected behaviour for each level of the competency.

An extension of this method is 360-degree appraisal, where the competencies are assessed by peers and subordinates as well as the individual's manager.

Attendance at an assessment centre

At an assessment centre individuals' levels of competency are measured by a series of tests and exercises. The scores and results of the exercises have to be converted to competency levels. Typical assessment tools are described below.

Tools for assessing competencies

The following is a description of tools commonly used for assessing competencies:

Personality questionnaires

Personality questionnaires usually take the form of self-reporting tests. A series of statements is rated or scored on the basis of how well they describe the person being tested. The results of the tests rate the individual against a number of factors on a 1–10 scale (stens).

The personality factors have to be correlated to the competencies you are measuring and the sten score has to be converted to the competency level.

Aptitude tests

There are a number of aptitude tests that cover areas of ability such as verbal and numerical reasoning. They are more objective than self-reporting personality questionnaires. The results are usually expressed in percentiles. A percentile score indicates a person's ranking in the group of people for whom the test was designed. For example, a person whose test results were in the 75th percentile in a test designed for senior managers would be ranked in the top 25 per cent of senior managers.

Aptitude tests have to be chosen to represent the competencies you are looking for and the percentile score has to be converted to the competency level.

In-tray exercise

This is a simulation exercise in which participants work through a typical basket of items. This includes 'big picture' items as well as looking at more detailed issues. Items include memos, data analysis and problems which require urgent attention. It is a timed exercise that most participants will not finish. They are expected to prioritize their responses and to complete a written review of how and why they made decisions about items in the exercise.

A scoring key has to be constructed that relates the in-tray items to the specific competencies. The person scoring the exercise looks at the decisions for evidence of the particular competency. The evidence is collated and each competency is given a rating.

Focused interviews

Focused interviews are used to assess competencies and involve using the same techniques as behavioural event interviewing. The purpose of the focused interviews is to elicit evidence of the required competencies. For example, a question that could be asked to elicit evidence of 'customer orientation' would be: 'Tell me about a time in the recent past when you personally have had to deal with a customer.'

Interviewers are provided with an interview guide for them to record and summarize the candidate's replies. Time is allocated at the end of each interview for completion, matching interview evidence with descriptions of the competency levels.

Although the questions target specific competencies, individuals would still be credited with other competencies if strong positive evidence of them emerged during the course of the interview.

Interviewers should compare notes at the end of each session to ensure consistency of their ratings.

Appendices

- Appendix 1 Spreadsheet examples
- Appendix 2 Public holidays
- Appendix 3 Hints for converting a word-processor file to ASCII format
- Appendix 4 Computer specifications
- Appendix 5 An example of course development
- Appendix 6 Using criteria to determine course content
- Appendix 7 Trainers' checklists

Appendix 1 Spreadsheet examples

The following examples of spreadsheets are provided so that you can use them as a basis for programming your own spreadsheets. The formulae are Lotus 1-2-3 compatible but you should have no difficulty in converting them for use on your own spreadsheet.

If you don't want to have the bother of typing in the formulae, please e-mail the author (mikewills@compuserve.com) for details of how you can obtain electronic versions of the spreadsheets.

Course cost calculations

This spreadsheet shows how Table 6.6 in Chapter 6 (Training plans and budgets) was put together.

- Set Default Currency to £
- Set width of column A to 20
- Set width of column B to 16
- Set range B11..B21 to Currency Format, 0 decimal places
- Type the following into the cells indicated:

A1: 'Middle Manager's Course

A3: 'Type of Training:
B3: "Residential

A4: 'Duration (days):
B4: 5

A5: 'Number of Students:
B5: 20

A6:   'Number of Trainers:
B6:   3

A7:   'Type of Trainer:
B7:   "Own

A8:   'Location:
B8:   "Off-site

A9:   'Additional rooms:
B9:   4

A11: 'Trainer cost/day:
B11: 300

A12: 'Materials/student:
B12: 50

A13: 'Main room hire/day:
B13: 0

A14: 'Seminar room hire:
B14: 50

A15: 'Accomm/student:
B15: 120

A16: 'Equip hire/day:
B16: 250

A17: 'Simulation costs:
B17: 9000

A19: 'TOTAL COST:
B19:
+(B11*B4*B6)+(B12*B5)+(B13*B4)+(B14*B4*B9)+(B15*(B5+B6)*B4)+(B16*B4)+B17

A20: 'COST/STUDENT:
B20: +(B19/B5)

A21: 'COST/STUDENT/DAY:
B21: +(B20/B4)

Spreadsheet for analysing student feedback
- Set the width of column A to 27
- Set the widths of columns B, C, D, E and F to 4
- Set the width of column G to 6
- Set the width of column H to 5
- Type the following into the cells indicated:

A1:   \-
A2:   'Question
A3:   \-

B1:   \-
B2:   "1
B3:   \-

	A	B	C	D	E	F	G	H
1	---							
2	*Question*		1	2	3	4	5	*Tot*	*Ave*
3	---							
4	a. Relevance							0	ERR
5	b. Ability to apply							0	ERR
6	c. Probability of using							0	ERR
7	d. Overall satisfaction							0	ERR
8	e. Trainer effectiveness							0	ERR
9	---							

Figure A1.1 *Spreadsheet for analysing student feedback before data entry*

C1: \-
C2: "2
C3: \-

D1: \-
D2: "3
D3: \-

E1: \-
E2: "4
E3: \-

F1: \-
F2: "5
F3: \-

G1: \-
G2: "Tot
G3: \-

H1: \-
H2: "Ave
H3: \-

A9: \-
A4: 'a. Relevance

B9: \-
A5: 'b. Ability to apply

C9: \-
A6: ' c. Probability of using

D9: \-
A7: 'd. Overall satisfaction

E9: \-
A8: 'e. Trainer effectiveness

F9: \-
G9: \-
H9: \-

G4: @SUM(B4..F4)
H4: (B4+(C4*2)+(D4*3)+(E4*4)+(F4*5))/G4
G5: @SUM(B5..F5)
H5: (B5+(C5*2)+(D5*3)+(E5*4)+(F5*5))/G5
G6: @SUM(B6..F6)
H6: (B6+(C6*2)+(D6*3)+(E6*4)+(F6*5))/G6
G7: @SUM(B7..F7)
H7: (B7+(C7*2)+(D7*3)+(E7*4)+(F7*5))/G7
G8: @SUM(B8..F8)
H8: (B8+(C8*2)+(D8*3)+(E8*4)+(F8*5))/G8

You can save time when entering the formulae by:

- Copying cell A1 to range (B1..H1)
- Copying cell A3 to range (B3..H3)
- Copying cell A9 to range (B9..H9)
- Copying cell G4 to range (G5..G8)
- Copying cell H4 to range (H5..H8)

Using the spreadsheet   This spreadsheet is used to analyse the end-of-course evaluation forms. The ERR which appears in the 'Ave' (Average) column stands for ERROR. The error is caused by the spreadsheet dividing something by zero. The ERRs will disappear as soon as data is entered on each line.

- Working through the evaluation forms, count the number of students who gave the course a relevance score of 1 (i.e. very low relevance).
- Enter this number in cell B4.
- Then count the number of relevance scores of 2, 3, 4 and 5.
- Enter these numbers in cells C4, D4, E4 and F4.

The 'Tot' column will show you the total number of responses that you received for course relevance. This number is used as a check on the counting. The average score is shown in the 'Ave' column.

Follow a similar procedure for each of the response questions.

Appendix 2
Public holidays

These dates are only given as a guide to help you identify when your training dates would coincide with a public holiday in the UK. The government has the final say on when public holidays occur each year. This is especially so when a public holiday falls on a Saturday or Sunday. Typically it would be held over until the following Monday.

Fixed holidays

New Year's Day — 1 January (Scotland also has a holiday on 2 January).

Saint Patrick's Day — 17 March (Northern Ireland only).

May Day — The first Monday after 1 May.

Spring Bank Holiday — The last Monday in May.

Orangeman's Day — 12 July (Northern Ireland only).

Summer Bank Holiday — The first Monday in August (Scotland only).

Late Summer Bank Holiday — The last Monday in August (not Scotland).

Christmas Day — 25 December. If Christmas Day falls on Sunday, an additional holiday is normally given on the Tuesday.

Boxing Day — 26 December. If Christmas Day falls on a Saturday, Boxing Day is usually moved to the Monday and an additional holiday is given on the Tuesday.

Moveable holidays

Good Friday — The Friday before Easter Sunday. Falls between 20 March and 23 April. Not always taken by some British factories who will often take the following Tuesday instead.

Easter Sunday — The first Sunday after the first full moon on or after the vernal equinox. Falls between 22 March and 25 April. Table A2.1 is a list of dates for Easter Sunday that will take you well into the twenty-first century:

Table A2.1   Dates for Easter Sunday

Year	Date	Year	Date
1999	4 April	2009	12 April
2000	23 April	2010	4 April
2001	15 April	2011	24 April
2002	31 March	2012	8 April
2003	20 April	2013	31 March
2004	11 April	2014	20 April
2005	27 March	2015	5 April
2006	16 April	2016	27 March
2007	8 April	2017	16 April
2008	23 March	2018	1 April

Easter Monday	The day after Easter Sunday (UK but not Scotland).
Ascension Day	Celebrated in some continental countries. 40 days after Easter, counting Easter Sunday as the first day. Falls between 30 April and 3 May.
Whit Monday	Celebrated in some continental countries. The Monday following the seventh Sunday after Easter. Falls between 11 May and 14 June.

Appendix 3
Hints for converting a word-processor file to ASCII format

Hint 1: Check to see if your word processor has a facility to convert documents to standard ASCII text files. If it has such a facility, use it to create an ASCII text file. Many programs identify ASCII files as 'Text only' files. On a Macintosh system the term is also 'Text only'.

Hint 2: If this doesn't work, see if your word processor will allow you to create a print file on a floppy disk. Use this option to create a print file from your original document.

Hint 3: Many word processors and computers have a facility for creating and editing computer programs. If you use this facility to create your text files, you can usually use the normal word-processing mode to edit the files and add formatting commands.

Appendix 4 Computer specifications

When you buy software to use on a course or for training administration, it is important to make sure that it will work on the computers that you are using. If possible, try to see the software working on a computer system that is exactly the same as yours. Failing that, check that the system requirements shown on the software's packaging or in its manual conform to the specification in your computer's manual. Figure A4.1 shows an example of a typical set of system requirements.

System requirements

The things that you have to look out for are:

- the type of machine on which the software will run;
- the type of disk that the computer accepts;
- the amount of memory the program needs;
- the type of display it requires;
- the type of pointing device, if any, it requires;
- the operating system required.

Type of computer

There are many types of computer. Software written for one type of computer will not work on a different type of computer, although commercial programs are available in different formats.

The software shown in Figure A4.1 requires an IBM-compatible computer. Your computer's manual will tell you whether your machine is IBM compatible. The glossary at

---

System requirements

• IBM compatible PC

• 386SX or higher processor

• CD-ROM drive

• Audio board

• Headphone or speakers

• SVGA resolution monitor, 256 colors or higher

• 4MB RAM

• At least 3.5 MB of hard disk space

• Microsoft Windows version 3.1 or above

• MS-DOS operating system version 3.1 or later

• Microsoft mouse or compatible pointing device

Figure A4.1   Typical computer system requirements

the end of this book gives an explanation of many of the terms you will come across.

Disks When you buy a computer program it usually comes on flexible magnetic disks called 'floppy' disks or on plastic disks called CD-ROMs. It is essential that you buy the program on a disk that your computer will accept. A hard disk is a magnetic disk that is permanently installed inside the computer. If a program requires a hard disk (as most commercial programs now do), you will need to transfer the program from the floppy disks to the hard disk as part of the installation procedure. It is also possible to run some programs directly from a CD-ROM.

Memory This is known as RAM (random access memory) and is measured in kilobytes (Kb) or megabytes (Mb).1 Kb is approximately the memory it would take to store 1000 characters. Letters, digits and spaces are all characters. 1 Mb is 1000 Kb. As programs become more demanding, the amount of memory needed increases. Currently the minimum memory required for a machine running the Windows 95 operating system is 24 Mb.

Type of display A computer's display looks like a television screen and is called a VDU (visual display unit). Early computers were unable to display pictures (graphics) and were only able to display text. Today computers can display graphics in full colour and high definition. The development of graphics displays evolved over a number of years and consequently the number of different displays that a computer can have is quite bewildering.

Always check your computer manual to make sure that your 'graphics adaptor' is one of those supported by the software. The software shown in Figure A4.1 needs an SVGA display. See the glossary for an explanation of this abbreviation and other abbreviations you are likely to come across.

Pointing device Most programs require a pointing device to work properly. A pointing device allows you to access any part of a computer's screen faster than you can with the cursor (arrow) keys.

The most popular type of pointing device is called a mouse, so called because its plastic body approximates to the shape of a mouse and the lead looks like a tail.

Operating system When a computer is switched on it is like a new-born baby: all the wiring is in place and it can carry out basic functions but it needs to be 'educated' to carry out more complex functions. This 'education' is carried out by a program called an operating system.

The most popular operating system for IBM compatibles is Microsoft Windows. It is essential that the software you are using has been written not only for the operating system but also for the correct version of the operating system, for example Windows 95 or the earlier Windows 3.1. The version is usually indicated by a decimal number, e.g. 2.0, 3.3, 6.0. A program that has been written for an early version will normally work on a later (higher-numbered) version, but it is unlikely that a program written for a later version will work on an earlier version.

Other operating systems include Macintosh and Unix.

Appendix 5
An example
of course
development

The following is an example of how a course was developed using the process described in Chapter 3. The chosen course is simple and straightforward but it illustrates all the relevant points.

Defining the subject

A company had embarked on training all its full-time employees on total quality management. As the culture and language of total quality started to embed themselves into the fabric of the company, it was realized that contract staff were becoming increasingly isolated from the rest of the company. They had no understanding of the language or processes of quality. It was not possible to justify giving them the six days of training that full-time employees receive. What was needed was a one-day overview that explained what total quality management was all about.

Describing the aims

The aim of running a one-day introduction to total quality management was to allow medium-term contractors to participate in 'quality circles'. They would not be expected to take a lead but they should not be confused when the company's permanent employees talked about total quality.

Obtaining subject-matter expertise

In this case the training analyst assigned to the development of this course had been training the full course for two years, so they already had subject-matter expertise. If the analyst had not had this previous experience, a considerable amount of time would have been required to bring them up to speed. Given the complexities of the subject, it could take about six months to gain sufficient subject-matter experience and knowledge. Without this experience the analyst would not be able to determine the critical content that should be included in the course.

Describing the students

The students were to be medium-term contractors. They would want to know what total quality is all about. Contractors may have concerns about being treated differently from full-time staff. They would also be concerned whether there would be another contract after the current one expires. Medium-term contractors may not have the same loyalty to the company as full-time staff but they have a professional approach and would be able to see how the concepts relate to their own businesses. In fact, it might be easier to communicate 'customer awareness' to these people than to permanent staff who rarely see an external customer.

Most of them would be designers with electrical/electronic, software or mechanical backgrounds. They would not appreciate a 'wordy' approach or put up with a significant amount of reading.

A significant minority would be translators with an arts background. Although English was not the mother tongue of many of the translators, the nature of their work obviously meant that they would not have any language difficulties. Reading would not present any problems.

All the contractors identified for the course were in good health with normal hearing and sight. Colour vision would normally be good for engineering people, but this would not usually be a requirement for translators.

Although some of the contractors may have done business studies at a university or college, the subject matter would be new to most of them.

Identifying the course content

In Chapter 3, I described how 'mind mapping' could be used to identify the content of a course. To apply this technique to the one-day 'Total Quality Management Overview', first draw a shape in the middle of a sheet of paper.

In this shape write 'TQM Overview', the subject of the course. Attached to branches radiating from this central shape are the main categories of topics that will make up the course. The categories come from thinking about the student description and the goals for this overview.

In this example the main categories were based on the questions the students would ask about total quality management and what the company would expect them to be able to do after they had completed the training. The

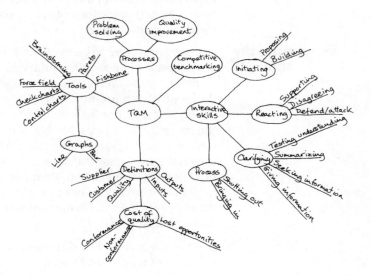

Figure A5.1   *A mind map for the TQM overview*

detailed topics radiate from the main category 'bubbles'. Although these detailed topics will form the content of the course, there are two other aspects that need to be considered before finalizing the content.

The first is to determine the level of the students' current knowledge. Teaching topics with which they are already familiar will be a waste of time. These familiar topics can be crossed out on the mind map. In the case of the 'Total Quality Management Overview' all of the topics will be new to the vast majority of the contractors, so no topics are omitted for this reason.

The other consideration is whether any of the topics are too advanced for the level of the course. In the example given in Figure A5.1, 'The use of control charts' was thought to be too advanced for a one-day overview.

Structuring the content

The modules chosen for this course were:

- Tools of the trade
- Why did we introduce total quality management?
- Quality is free?
- Who's the customer?
- What is quality?

The main course modules are to be found in the body of the course. The body needs to be sequenced so that there is a logical flow from one module to another. We used the 'Post-it' note method described in Chapter 3. The structure chosen for this course is given in the agenda shown in Figure A5.2.

Choosing the methods and media

Given the potentially wide range of students, we decided to base this introductory session on trainer presentations and student exercises. Short excerpts from existing videos would also be used.

We also had a tape/slide presentation put on to video. This was done to increase reliability and to keep the number of different media down to a minimum.

Writing the objectives and tests

After each module the students should be able to do something they could not do before. Objectives are best written by considering what this change of behaviour should be. For example, after completing the 'Tools of the trade' module the students should be able to 'Describe the basic tools of quality and their uses.'

You should keep the aims of the course in mind when you are writing the objectives. Although describing the tools and their uses would be a sufficient level for our target

```
┌─────────────────────────────────────────────────┐
│ AGENDA                                            │
│                                                   │
│ Introduction                              9:00    │
│ — Introductions                                   │
│ — Expectations                                    │
│ — Agenda                                          │
│                                                   │
│ Why total quality management?             9:20    │
│ — The need                                        │
│ — Initial steps                                   │
│ — Quality gurus                                   │
│ — Birth of a strategy                             │
│ — Key elements of the strategy                    │
│                                                   │
│ What is quality?                          9:40    │
│ — Definition                                      │
│ — Standard                                        │
│ — System                                          │
│ — Measurement                                     │
│                                                   │
│ Quality is free?                          11:00   │
│ — Cost of quality                                 │
│ — Conformance                                     │
│ — Non-conformance                                 │
│ — Lost opportunities                              │
│                                                   │
│ Who's the customer?                       11:20   │
│ — Suppliers                                       │
│ — Internal customers                              │
│ — External customers                              │
│                                                   │
│ Tools of the trade                        12:00   │
│ — Problem-solving process                         │
│ — Quality improvement process                     │
│ — Process capability                              │
│ — Fishbone diagram                                │
│ — Pareto analysis                                 │
│ — Forcefield analysis                             │
│ — Interactive skills                              │
│                                                   │
│ Where do we go from here?                 16:00   │
│                                                   │
│ Review                                    16:30   │
└─────────────────────────────────────────────────┘
```

Figure A5.2   *Structure for the TQM overview*

population, it would not be suitable for people who lead quality circles. They would need to demonstrate competence at using the tools. Figure A5.3 shows the objectives for the TQM overview.

Once the objectives have been written, tests become relatively easy to design. For example, the fourth objective is for the students to be able to identify customers and suppliers in a given situation. To test this we showed a video clip of a scene in the restaurant. There were four main characters:

● the paying customer;
● the waitress;

OBJECTIVES

After completing today's session you will be able to:

• State why the company introduced 'total quality management'

• Define quality

• Explain the basic concepts of quality

• Identify customers and suppliers in a given situation

• Describe seven basic tools of quality and their uses

Figure A5.3   *Objectives for TQM course*

• the cook;
• the owner.

Using the form shown in Figure A5.4, the students were asked which of the four characters was the customer and who was the supplier in the given situations. We developed the other tests in a similar manner.

Writing the trainer's guide and student materials   The trainer's guide and student materials were developed together. The student materials included a booklet which had a section for each of the modules. We also developed a set of cards that had objects, or pictures of larger products, glued to them. These cards were designed to help the students define quality. They would have to decide whether they considered the product to be a quality product. They would also have to give a reason for their decision.

Preparing the visual aids   Many of the visual aids were developed as the trainer's guide and the student materials were being written. We saved some development time by using artwork we had

OUTPUT	SUPPLIER	CUSTOMER
• Order taken		
• Order delivered		
• Dinner cooked		
• Dinner served		
• Money taken		

Figure A5.4   *Example of a test based on a course objective*

prepared for the student's guide as masters for overhead transparencies. The videotapes were already available as they had been developed for the full-length course.

Peer assessment   The materials were given to a new trainer to review. It is a good idea to have one of your colleagues review the course at every stage of its development. The development of this course was also used to teach a new trainer the basics of course development.

Running the pilot course(s)   We decided to use a group of 12 'target population' students for the pilot course. The maximum number of students for this course was 18 but we decided to restrict the numbers for the pilot course. I conducted the course and the new trainer made observations of the training process and the students' reactions. We asked the students to complete the feedback forms and then we had a debriefing session.

Appendix 6 Using criteria to determine course content

The following is a description of the process we used when we were asked to reduce a technical training course from 15 days to 5. At first sight this seems to be a particularly brutal reduction, but you should bear in mind that this condensed course was needed for a different population of students.

We would use this shortened course to train maintenance engineers. Maintenance engineers were recruited at a lower skill level than the service engineers for whom the original course had been designed. Their duties involved regular cleaning and maintenance of the machines as well as repairing some of the more frequently occurring faults. It was always expected that these maintenance engineers would not be able to repair every single fault they came across. From time to time, they would have to call in a service engineer for assistance.

So, giving maintenance engineers the same training as the service engineers, with all the associated travel and accommodation costs, was not a good investment. Service engineers would still need to have the full three weeks of training.

The criteria we chose for selecting the tasks were:

- frequency (how often would the task have to be done?);
- difficulty (how hard was it to do the task?);
- criticality (what is the impact of poor task performance?).

Frequency was the most important of the criteria because the strategy was to have the maintenance engineers performing the most commonly occurring tasks. The temptation might be to decide on the basis of frequency alone, but this approach would lead to difficulties. For example, if we decided to teach all tasks that occurred within a certain pre-determined period (say six months), we would find we would also be teaching tasks that are so easy that they need not be taught. Clearly, practising these tasks would be a waste of valuable teaching time.

Incorrect performance of other tasks, although infrequent, might lead to disastrous consequences. We would not want to take the risk of omitting them even though the task was performed infrequently.

The criteria of difficulty and criticality were introduced to overcome these problems.

Having determined the decision criteria, a method of rating the tasks against the criteria was required. We needed an objective method for determining how frequent, difficult or critical a task was. Tables A6.1, A6.2 and A6.3 show the ratings we used for our three criteria.

Table A6.1   *Frequency ratings*

Task interval (months)	Frequency rating
1–6	1
7–12	2
13–18	3

Table A6.2   *Difficulty ratings*

Difficulty rating	Definition
1	Without prior training, the maintenance engineer cannot or is not confident to perform the task without the assistance of a service engineer
2	Without prior training the maintenance engineer can perform the task correctly with the assistance of a service manual
3	Maintenance engineer can perform the task correctly without prior training, assistance of a service engineer or reference to a service manual

Table A6.3   *Criticality ratings*

Criticality rating	Definition
1	Incorrect completion of the task results in a safety hazard or catastrophic failure of the equipment
2	Incorrect completion of the task results in the equipment functioning at an unacceptable level
3	Incorrect completion of the task affects the look of the product only

Another method of assessing the difficulty is to compare the time a freshly trained novice and a master performer take to complete the same task. The greater the difference, the more difficult the task.

The next step is to find a method of making a decision based on combinations of these criteria. One method would simply be to add up the frequency, difficulty and criticality ratings for each task. If a task's total falls below a cut-off point, we would eliminate the task from the course. The problem with this approach is that it gives equal weighting to all the criteria.

To overcome this you can give more weighting to the more important criteria, producing different ratings. However, getting the relative ratings correct starts to become somewhat of a mathematical nightmare.

The approach we decided to take was to list every possible combination of the criteria (111, 112, 113...). For each combination we used our experience to decide whether a task with that combination of ratings would normally be included in a course.

So, a task with a 111 combination of ratings (task encountered at least once every six months, very difficult to perform and a safety hazard) would definitely be included in the course. A task with a rating combination of 132 would not be trained. (The '3' difficulty rating signifies that the task can be performed correctly without any training.)

The decision matrix (Table A6.4) gives the 'train' or 'no-train' decisions for all these combinations of frequency, difficulty and criticality. You should only use this matrix as a guide. Give the training analysts the authority to make different decisions on the basis of their judgement and experience – provided that the reasons for those decisions are recorded.

Very experienced training analysts would probably not need to use the matrix in the normal course of their work, but it is an extremely powerful tool for communicating the rationale of training decisions to your clients. The matrix is also very useful for providing 'instant experience' to less experienced training analysts.

Notice that some of the ratings in the difficulty and criticality columns have been highlighted. These are to remind the analyst to make some checks before finally making a 'no-train' decision.

When the warning occurs in the criticality column the analysts should satisfy themselves that labels on the equipment and the service manual cover any safety hazard.

When the warning occurs in the difficulty column the analyst should be satisfied that field support is available or that there is detailed support in the service manual.

Table A6.4   *'Train–don't train' matrix*

Frequency	Difficulty	Criticality	Decision
1	1	1	Train
1	1	2	Train
1	1	3	Train
1	2	1	Train
1	2	2	Train
1	2	3	Borderline
1	3	1	Don't train
1	3	2	Don't train
1	3	3	Don't train
2	1	1	Train
2	1	2	Train
2	1	3	Train
2	2	1	Don't train
2	2	2	Don't train
2	2	3	Don't train
2	3	1	Don't train
2	3	2	Don't train
2	3	3	Don't train
3	1	1	Don't train
3	1	2	Don't train
3	1	3	Don't train
3	2	1	Don't train
3	2	2	Don't train
3	2	3	Don't train
3	3	1	Don't train
3	3	2	Don't train
3	3	3	Don't train

Appendix 7 Trainers' checklists

Trainer's kit and supplies for the session

- Bulldog clips
- Paper clips
- Drawing pins
- Packing tape
- Masking tape (25 mm width)
- Adhesive tape (Sellotape, Scotch tape)
- Blu-tack
- Flip-chart marker pens (water based)
- Overhead projector pens (water soluble and permanent)
- Spare overhead projector bulb
- Lens cleaner
- Cloths
- Overhead transparencies (blank)
- Pencils
- Erasers
- Rulers
- Ring binders
- Folders
- Note pads
- Name cards
- Flip-chart pads
- Post-it notes
- Self-adhesive labels
- Calculators
- Pencil sharpener(s)
- 2-, 3-, 4-hole punch
- Correcting fluid (Snopake, White-out)
- Stapler
- Staples
- Staple remover
- Scissors
- Glue stick
- Hammer
- Extension lead (with two sockets)
- Batteries
- Screwdriver
- Penknife/scalpel
- Videotapes
- Audiocassettes
- Audio and video leads and adaptors

Training location survey

- Size, shape and capacity
- Location
- Heating, lighting and ventilation
- Power sockets, light switches
- Toilets
- Doors, windows, emergency exits
- Parking

- Access for preparation
- Contact established
- Acoustics
- Wall space for flip-chart pages
- Meal and break arrangements
- Bedrooms

Pre-course checklist

- Obtain printed materials
- Review lesson plan
- Obtain audiovisual equipment and tapes
- Obtain stationery and other supplies
- Check course logistics
- Check room layout
- Check waste bins, glasses, water etc.
- Lay out participant materials, pencils, pads, name cards
- Check visibility of screens, charts etc.
- Test felt-tip and dry-wipe pens
- Check lighting, ventilation and heating
- Display direction signs
- Disconnect telephone
- Check process for handling messages and phone calls

Post-course checklist

- Collect and analyse course feedback forms
- Clear up room
- Transport equipment back
- Pay bills
- Return keys etc.
- Complete training records

Bibliography

Argyris, C and Schon, D A (1978) *Organizational Learning*, Wokingham: Addison-Wesley

BACIE/ITD (1996) *The Training Directory*, London: Kogan Page

Barrington, Harry and Reid, Margaret (1997) *Training Interventions: Managing Employee Development*, London: Institute of Personnel and Development

Bartram, Sharon and Gibson, Brenda (1997) *Training Needs Analysis*, 2nd edn, Aldershot: Gower

Bentley, Trevor (1990) *The Business of Training*, Maidenhead: McGraw-Hill

Boam, Rosemary and Sparrow, Paul (1993) *Designing and Achieving Competency*, Maidenhead: McGraw-Hill

Boyatzis, Richard E (1982) *The Competent Manager*, Chichester: John Wiley

Boydell, T H and Leary, M (1996) *The Identification of Training Needs*, London: BACIE

Bramley, Peter (1996) *Evaluating Training Effectiveness*, Maidenhead: McGraw-Hill

Bride, Mac (1996) *Teach Yourself html*, London: Hodder & Stoughton

Buzan, Tony (1989) *Use Your Head*, 3rd edn, London: BBC Publications

Crosby, Philip B (1993) *Quality Is Free*, London: Signet

Department of Employment (1971) *Glossary of Training Terms*, London: HMSO

Goldstein, Irwin (1992) *Training in Organizations: Needs assessment, development and evaluation*, 3rd edn, New York: Brooks-Cole

Imai, Masaaki (1989) *Kaizen*, Maidenhead: McGraw-Hill

Kamp, Di (1996) *The Excellent Trainer*, 2nd edn, Aldershot: Gower

Kelly, George A (1980) *Theory of Personality: psychology of personal constructs*, New York: VVW Norton

Kenney, John and Reid, Margaret A (1986) *Training Interventions*, London: Institute of Personnel Management

Kolb, D A (1985) *Experiential Learning*, Hemel Hempstead: Prentice-Hall

Mitrani, A, Dalziel, M and Fitt, D (1992) *Competency Based Human Resource Management*, London: Kogan Page

Newby, A C (1994) *Training Evaluation Handbook*, Aldershot: Gower

Orridge, Martin (1996) *75 Ways to Liven Up Your Training*, Aldershot: Gower

Pedler, Mike (ed.) (1997) *Action Learning in Practice*, 3rd edn, Aldershot: Gower

Pedler, Mike *et al.* (1991) *Learning Company: A Strategy for Sustainable Development*, Maidenhead: McGraw-Hill

Peters, T and Waterman Jr, R H (1984) *In Search of Excellence*, New York: Harper & Row

Pickles, Tim (1995) *Toolkit for Trainers*, Aldershot: Gower

Prior, John (ed.) (1994) *Gower Handbook of Training and Development*, 2nd edn, Aldershot: Gower

Rackham, Neil *et al.* (1971) *Developing Interactive Skills*, Northampton: Wellens

Rae, Leslie (1991) *The Skills of Training*, 2nd edn, Aldershot: Gower

Rae, Leslie (1995) *The Techniques of Training*, Aldershot: Gower

Rae, Leslie (1997) *How to Measure Training Effectiveness*, 3rd edn, Aldershot: Gower

Rae, Leslie (1997) *Planning and Designing Training Programmes*, Aldershot: Gower

Rose, Colin (1985) *Accelerated Learning*, Aylesbury: Accelerated Learning Systems

Senge, Peter M (1990) *The Fifth Discipline: The Art and Practice of the Learning Organization*, New York: Doubleday/London: Century Business

Spencer Jr, L M, McClelland, D C and Spencer, S M (1992) *Competency Assessment Methods: History and State of the Art*, London: Hay/McBer Research Press

Stewart, A and Stewart, V (1981) *Business Applications of Repertory Grids*, Maidenhead: McGraw-Hill

Thurbin, Patrick J (1994) *Implementing The Learning Organisation*, London: Pitman Publishing

Glossary

8 mm A videocassette format used in camcorders. The tape is 8 mm wide.

A4 A standard paper size (210 mm × 297 mm).

Alignment The process of ensuring that all parts of a company are pulling in the same direction.

Artificial intelligence Apparent computer intelligence that allows a computer to solve problems.

ASCII American Standard Code for Information Interchange. A code which uses numbers to represent digits, upper- and lower-case letters, punctuation and additional characters such as RETURN.

Assessment The process of determining the company's or organization's current situation.

AT Advanced Technology. IBM PCs or compatibles which are more advanced than the standard PC or XT.

Attitude A predisposition to behave in one way rather than another.

Authoring tool Software used to create instructional material delivered on a computer system.

Azimuth adjustment The process of adjusting the angle of the recording/playback head of a tape recorder with respect to the tape.

Behavioural event interviews A technique developed by McClelland and Dailey, used to identify competencies by getting detailed descriptions of a sample of individuals' performances. The sample includes both average and superior performers but the interviewers are unaware of the interviewees' performance records. The characteristics that emerge are coded, categorized and correlated to performance criteria.

Browser A computer program used for searching for and reading information on the Internet.

Camcorder A portable video camera with a built-in video recorder.

CBT Computer-based training. Uses a computer to present and control the sequence of instructional information.

CD-ROM A disk for storing computer data. The information is recorded and read by a laser.

CGA Colour graphics adaptor. A standard for a computer's display which has a definition of 640 × 200 dots (pixels) in monochrome and 320 × 200 in four colours from a choice of 16.

Check chart A chart used for collecting and organizing data.

Competence The ability to perform a particular task to the required standard.

Competency A personal characteristic that differentiates the superior performer from the average performer.

Control chart A chart that displays statistical process control data.

Cycle time The time it takes to go from the beginning to the end of a process.

Database A large store of information.

Disk A magnetic disk that a computer uses for storing information. There are two types of disk: a hard disk which is rigid and a floppy disk which is flexible.

Displays Devices that allow users to see the computer's output on a monitor. PC displays have developed over the years to yield greater definition and more colours. Starting with the least sophisticated, the standards are: MDA, Hercules, CGA, MCGA, EGA, VGA, SVGA and EVGA.

Double-loop learning A process by which an organization not only checks itself against standards but also reviews and challenges those standards.

Duplex Printing on both sides of a sheet of paper.

DVI Digital video interactive. Technology that allows real-time compression and decompression of graphics and animated displays.

EGA Extended graphics adaptor. A standard for a computer's display which has a definition of 640 × 350 dots (pixels) in 16 colours from a choice of 64.

E-mail Electronic mail where messages are sent via computer networks.

EPSS Electronic performance support system. Software that helps users perform their jobs more effectively while they work.

EVGA Extended VGA (see *VGA*).

Expert panel A group of knowledgeable human resource specialists, managers and superior performers who are used to identify competencies.

Expert system A computer system that stores expert knowledge in the form of rules. It is a tool that can be used by non-experts to make decisions.

Face-to-face ratio The percentage of a trainer's available time that is spent teaching in front of a class.

Floppy disk See *Disk*.

Focused interviews Used to assess competencies with the same techniques as behavioural event interviewing.

Formatting (1) The process of defining what a document will look like. For example margins, top and bottom spaces, page length, tabs and font types.

Formatting (2) The process of preparing a disk so that it can be used by a computer.

Gantt charts Used to schedule project tasks. They take the form of a horizontal bar chart with time on the horizontal axis and the tasks on the vertical axis. The ends of the bars represent the start and finish times of the tasks. Invented by Henry Gantt.

Goals Quantitative figures that are established by top management.

GOQs Genuine occupational qualifications. Qualifications which make it legal to select a person of a particular category while excluding people of other categories (e.g. gender or race).

GUI Graphical user interface. A screen design employing graphics and colour in a consistent manner so that menus and other system features are easy for users to understand and use.

Hard disk See *Disk*.

Hardware Computer equipment such as computers, printers and plotters.

Hercules A graphics standard for a monochrome computer display giving a definition of 720 × 348 dots (pixels).

Histogram A graph in which frequency distribution is shown by means of vertical bars.

HRD Human resource development. Used to be known as personnel.

HRDC Human resource development committee. A committee of peer managers who meet to make, review or approve decisions related to the organization and development of people in their areas.

HRM Human resource management or human resource manager. Previously known as personnel or personnel manager.

HTML HyperText Mark-up Language.

Hypertext Electronic information that is linked so that users can easily move from one topic to another.

In-tray exercise A simulation exercise in which participants work through a typical basket of items. This includes 'big picture' items as well as looking at more detailed issues. Items include memos, data analysis and problems which require urgent attention. It is a timed exercise and participants are expected to prioritize their responses.

Internet A global network of interconnected computer networks.

IPD Institute of Personnel and Development.

IPM Institute of Personnel Management. Now combined with the ITD to form the IPD.

ITD Institute of Training and Development. Now combined with the IPM to form the IPD.

IVD Interactive video disk. Video images stored on an optical disk so that a companion computer can control their presentation, based on user responses.

Job element analysis Identified by Boyatzis as a weighted list of characteristics that managers perceive as important in distinguishing superior from average performers.

Kaizen Japanese for 'continuous improvement'.

Kilobyte (Kb) A measure of a computer's memory. One kilobyte of memory will store approximately 1000 characters, about two-and-a-half pages of A4.

Knowledge Usable information that an individual has in a particular area. Examples: understanding the art and science of management; understanding what motivates employees.

Learning organization According to Pedler *et al.*, an organization which facilitates the learning of all its members and continuously transforms itself to achieve superior competitive performance.

Management by objectives (MBO) An objective-setting process which increases commitment by involving employees in setting their own objectives. Championed by Peter Drucker.

MCGA Multicolour graphics array. A standard for a computer's display which has a definition of up to 640 × 200 dots (pixels) in monochrome and 320 × 200 in 256 colours from a choice of 262 144.

MCI Management Charter Initiative. A coherent framework for management education in the UK, based on a nationally agreed qualification structure.

MDA Monochrome display adaptor. The original standard for a computer's display. It can only display text in 25 lines of 80 characters.

Mission A statement of what the company or organization exists to do.

Motive Reasons (e.g. achievement, affiliation and power) that drive, direct and select an individual's behaviour.

Mouse A hand-operated device for selecting text and objects on a computer screen. Moving the mouse over a flat surface causes a corresponding movement in a pointer (usually an arrow shape) on the computer screen. Pressing a button on the mouse selects the text or object to which the arrow is pointing.

MS-DOS Microsoft Disk Operating System. The standard, single-user, base operating system for IBM and IBM-compatible computers on which Windows may be loaded.

NTSC National Television System Committee. A US television standard.

NVQs National Vocational Qualifications.

OCR Optical character recognition. The ability of a scanner to scan a paper document and read the text into a computer's memory.

On-line reference Reference information presented on a computer screen. Often employs hypertext technology.

Operating system A piece of software that carries out a computer's basic functions. A computer has to have an operating system installed before it can run other programs.

PAL Phase alternation by line. A television standard used mainly in Europe.

Panning The side-to-side rotation of a film or video camera.

PC Personal computer.

Philosophy A statement of a company's values and beliefs.

Pixels Picture elements – the individual dots of a computer screen's image.

Policy A medium- to long-term course of action comprising a goal and a strategy.

Policy deployment The process for ensuring that a company's policies are understood from the highest to the lowest levels in the company.

Printer's dummy An example of a finished document so a printer can see exactly how the materials should be produced.

QCD Quality, cost and delivery.

RAM Random access memory. A computer's internal memory, measured in megabytes.

Read-only access A restriction on a computerized record system that allows a person to read the records but does not allow them to amend, add or remove a record.

Repertory grid A technique developed by Kelly that takes three individuals at a time from a sample that contains both average and superior performers. An expert panel is then asked in which way two of the individuals are similar to each other and different from the third. These similarities and differences form the basis of a set of competencies that are related to superior performance.

Role play A simulation exercise in which participants 'act out' a typical situation.

Scientific management Sets out to increase productivity by developing performance standards on the basis of systematic observation and experimentation. Frederick Taylor was known as the father of scientific management.

SECAM Séquential à mémoire, a French television standard. Also used in the former Soviet Union.

Simplex Printing on only one side of a sheet of paper.

Single-loop learning A process by which an organization checks itself against standards but does not review and challenge those standards.

Skill An individual's demonstration by behaviour of proficiency or expertise – the ability to do something well. Examples are: interviewing effectively; selecting the best job applicant; assigning work clearly and effectively.

SME Subject-matter expert. People who support training development by providing expertise on specific topics to be covered in the training.

Software Programs used by computers. Software is to a computer what a compact disc is to a compact disc player.

SPC See *Statistical process control*.

Stakeholder A person who has a vested interest in the outcome of an event. Stakeholders usually have the power to influence positively or negatively the outcome even though they may not take any direct part in the event.

Standard deviation A measure of variability – the larger the standard deviation, the greater the variability of the sample. In normally distributed data, approximately 68 per cent of the data will fall between plus and minus 1 standard deviation.

Statistical process control A method used to determine whether variation in a process is normal or abnormal. A decision can then be made on whether to adjust the process.

Stens A means of giving a 1 to 10 score for normally distributed data. One sten is equivalent to one half of a standard deviation.

Strategy The means of achieving a goal.

SVGA Super VGA (see *VGA*).

Tilting The up-and-down rotation of a film or video camera.

Trackball A ball-shaped device on a computer keyboard which acts in a similar way to a mouse (see *Mouse*).

Tracking Physically moving a film or video camera either parallel or at right angles to the subject.

Trainee-centred learning A form of training where a student's progress (and hence pace) through a course depends on the student's readiness to move on to the next learning stage. Usually involves a form of programmed instruction. Also called self-paced learning.

Training philosophy A statement of a company's or organization's attitude towards training.

Trait A relatively enduring characteristic of an individual's behaviour. Examples: being a good listener; having a sense of urgency.

Triad A group of three students working together on an exercise.

U-matic A semi-professional video format. It used to be the standard for training videos but it is now being replaced by VHS.

UNIX A computer operating system that supports multitasking and is ideally suited to multiuser applications.

Value Something that is held to be important by the individual. Examples: education; honesty; openness.

VDU Visual display unit. The 'box' that houses a computer's screen.

VGA Video graphics array. A standard for a computer's display which has a definition of 640 × 480 dots (pixels) in 16 colours and 320 × 200 in 256 colours from a choice of 262 144. SVGA and EVGA are extensions of VGA with definitions of up to 1024 × 768 pixels.

VHS Video home standard. A domestic video standard, now increasingly being used as the standard format for training videos. See also *U-matic*.

VHS-C A videocassette standard that is used in camcorders. It can be clipped into a carrier which allows it to be viewed on a domestic video recorder.

Virtual network A network whose members do not meet physically.

Vision An inspiring 'picture' of where the company or organization wants to be in the future.

Voice mail A process by which recorded messages can be left and retrieved by telephone.

XT Extended technology. A more sophisticated version of the original IBM PC.

Zooming Adjusting the lens of a film or video camera so that the subject appears to get larger or smaller.

Index

The Business Approach to Training

Teresa Williams and Adrian Green

The role of the trainer is changing rapidly. Internal trainers are increasingly having to justify their proposed solutions in business terms, while external trainers can sell their services only by helping customers to fulfil their business objectives. In both cases, they need a knowledge of 'business speak' that will enable them to deal with other managers on an equal footing.

At the same time trainers are themselves having to operate in a businesslike way: to recover their costs, to market their services proactively, and so on. This book explains the main ideas governing finance, strategy and marketing. By relating concepts like business planning, cash flow, breakeven analysis, pay back, SWOT analysis and the marketing mix to the training process it removes some of the mystery that surrounds them. The authors use a variety of methods to reinforce the learning, including exercises and activities.

This is a book that bridges the gap between the practice of training and the realities of business. For the trainer determined to survive and flourish in today's demanding climate, it will be invaluable.

Gower

Dictionary of HRD

Angus Reynolds, Sally Sambrook and Jim Stewart

Providing succinct definitions of over 3,000 terms *Dictionary of HRD* is the most comprehensive work of its kind.

Based on Angus Reynolds' successful American dictionary, this new version by Sally Sambrook and Jim Stewart has been extensively reworked   with a British and international readership in mind. The entries have been structured to meet the needs of the busy practitioner: definitions of theory are here, but the overall emphasis is on practice. Useful general business terms, which the professional would naturally encounter during the course of their work, are included too.

The *Dictionary* is organized as follows:

• Over 3,000 terms, arranged alphabetically. Definitions range from a succinct sentence, to a paragraph, depending on significance
• A list of '100 essential HRD terms'
• A list of acronyms and abbreviations
• A list of journals of interest to HRD specialists.

As well as being an invaluable source of reference and new ideas for training and HR professionals and academics, this will be welcomed by a much wider range of managers as an authoritative guide to HR issues, organizations and terminology.

Gower

Gower Handbook of Training and Development

Second Edition

Edited by John Prior, MBE

This *Gower Handbook*, published in association with the Institute of Training and Development, first appeared in 1991 and quickly established itself as a standard work. For this new edition the text has been completely revised to reflect recent developments and new chapters have been added on cultural diversity, learning styles and choosing resources. The *Handbook* now contains contributions from no fewer than forty-nine experienced professionals, each one an expert in his or her chosen subject.

For anyone involved in training and development, whether in business or the public sector, the *Handbook* represents an unrivalled resource.

Gower

A Handbook for Training Strategy

Martyn Sloman

The traditional approach to training in the organization is no longer effective. That is the central theme of Martyn Sloman's challenging book. A new model is required that will reflect the complexity of organizational life, changes in the HR function and the need to involve line management. This *Handbook* introduces such a model and describes the practical implications not only for human resource professionals and training managers but also for line managers.

Martyn Sloman writes as an experienced training manager and his book is concerned above all with implementation. Thus his text is supported by numerous questionnaires, survey instruments and specimen documents. It also contains the findings of an illuminating survey of best training practice carried out among UK National Training Award winners.

The book is destined to make a significant impact on the current debate about how to improve organizational performance. With its thought-provoking argument and practical guidance it will be welcomed by everyone with an interest in the business of training and development.

Gower

How to Set Up and Manage a Corporate Learning Centre

Samuel A Malone

The explosion in the type and availability of open, distance and flexible learning materials has created a revolution in the education and development of many employees. Through a corporate learning centre every employee can now have access to learning and development, when they want, where they want and how they want.

But setting up a cost-effective open learning centre in any organization and managing its continued development after the first flush of enthusiasm has worn off requires commitment from everyone, as well as careful research, planning and organization.

Sam Malone's book provides a concise and highly practical guide covering:

- the benefits, pitfalls and rationale behind corporate learning centres
- the mechanics of planning and setting up a new centre from scratch
- the launch and marketing of the new centre and its resources
- staffing, administration and support
- guidance on evaluating the usage of the centre and establishing the criteria for measuring success.

Also included is a 'learner's guide' to enable users to get the most out of their centre, and details of the experiences of Sun Life in setting up their learning centre.

Gower

The Techniques of Instruction

Roger James

What do effective instructors do that makes them effective? In this ground-breaking book, Dr James examines the whole process of instruction from the point of view of skill development to discover which are the best techniques and why. He shows:

- how to produce the best trainee performance possible in the shortest possible time
- how to structure practice sessions to maximize learning
- how to analyse the task involved so as to design the most appropriate exercise
- how to deal with the 'slow' trainee
- how to boost the trainee's confidence
- how to instruct 'at a distance'.

Although based on extensive research, the material in the book is presented in non-technical language and draws on a wide range of examples. The result is a comprehensive guide to the practice of instruction which will be of immense value to anyone involved in training, teaching or coaching.

Gower